PRACTICAL HOMEOWNER'S 1987
DO-IT-YOURSELF ANNUAL

Best Remodeling Options
for Today's Home

by the Editors of
Rodale's Practical Homeowner™ Reg.
Magazine

Rodale Press, Emmaus, Pennsylvania

Printed in the United States of America on recycled paper containing a high percentage of de-inked fiber.

Senior editor: Ray Wolf
Editor: Larry McClung
Copy editor: Linda Harris
Book designer: John Pepper
Book layout: Glen Burris
Illustrations: Frank Rohrbach (except where otherwise noted)

ISBN 0–87857–681–9   hardcover

2   4   6   8   10   9   7   5   3   1   hardcover

NOTICE

CONTENTS

INTRODUCTION

Owning your own home. That has always been an important part of the American Dream. For some of us, the house should ideally sit in the midst of a few acres of woodland and meadow. Others of us are content to make do with only a tiny patch of grass and a couple of beds of flowers as complements to our "castles." But we all seem to agree that, be it ever so humble, there is no place like home.

Interestingly enough, the recent period during which costs of land and building materials have rapidly escalated and mortgage interest rates have soared to record levels seems not to have seriously deterred most Americans from pursuing the home ownership dream. If anything, it seems to have heightened the pervasive feeling that buying a home is one of the best investments a person will ever make, and that owning a home provides an important form of security in a rapidly changing and uncertain world.

But Americans are not simply content with owning a home: they are constantly looking for ways to improve it—both for their own enjoyment and to improve its market value. In 1982, the Do-It-Yourself Research Institute, an organization managed by the National Retail Hardware Association and the Home Center Institute, released a report stating that of the approximately two-thirds of adult Americans who are homeowners, some 73.5 percent are involved in some form of home remodeling activity.

More recently, *Building Supply and Home Centers*, a trade magazine, conducted a home modernization study. The published results of this study indicate that home remodeling is an activity that has experienced dramatic growth over the past decade and shows no signs of tapering off in the near future. According to this study, nationwide during the year 1975, some $25.1 billion were spent on materials and labor for home improvement and modernization. In 1986, the amount more than tripled to $78.5 billion. *Building Supply and Home Centers* estimates that during the current year, 1987, Americans will spend a total of $91.4 billion on remodeling and maintaining their homes.

Rodale's Practical Homeowner (formerly *Rodale's New Shelter*) is a magazine whose aim is to serve the needs and interests of the dedicated home improver. We attempt to keep our readers informed about the latest tools and products that will help them accomplish their remodeling goals most effectively. We also share with our readers innovative design ideas gained from other readers, home designers, and building tradespeople with whom we maintain close contact.

Practical Homeowner's 1987 Do-It-Yourself Annual brings together some of the best articles published in our magazine over the past year. Since our own surveys indicate that most homeowners like to do a lot of their own remodeling and improving, we have placed special emphasis in this annual on step-by-step instructions that show you how to successfully complete many worthwhile home repair and improvement projects yourself. At the same time, we have included design ideas and cost-benefit analyses, as well as advice on finding and working with contractors, that will save you dollars and help you make wise decisions when undertaking remodeling projects for which you need professional assistance.

—the editors of ***Rodale's Practical Homeowner*** **magazine**

PRACTICAL HOMEOWNER'S 1987
DO-IT-YOURSELF ANNUAL

CHAPTER 1

VALUE-CONSCIOUS HOME REMODELING

Thinking of remodeling your home? If so, you are in good company. Thousands of others are doing the same. In fact, throughout North America to-day more existing homes are being renovated and remodeled than new homes being built. However, as you will learn in the pages that follow, not all remodeling projects result in an increase in a home's value. Indeed, certain types of alterations may actually result in a decrease in the salability of your home. And those that do increase its value may do so less than the amount you spend on completing them.

Of course, what makes your home valuable to you may differ from what will appeal to prospective buyers. Therefore, when you first begin to make your remodeling plans, give careful thought to exactly what you hope to accomplish. Are the changes you intend to make intended primarily for your own enjoyment, or are they aimed at enhancing the resale value of your home?

If you expect to remain in your present home for a long time, any changes you make in its interior or exterior should quite properly reflect your own needs and aesthetic tastes. However, if you are making improvements with an eye toward the possibility of selling your home within the next two or three years, it will pay you to make only those type of changes that are likely to make your home more marketable.

We asked writers Susan Weaver and Joseph Scrapits to conduct a survey of real estate professionals in order to determine how the most common home improvement projects compare in their ability to justify costs in terms of a home's increased resale value. As part of their effort, they put together an advisory panel made up of the following experts:

1

Photo by Mitch Mandel

- Edith Duncan, R.M., an independent real estate appraiser, Jupiter, Florida.

- Barry Gaw, a real estate broker with Century 21—R. M. Post Realty, Oak Lawn, Illinois.

- Felix Gonzaga, a real estate broker with Century 21—Able Realty, San Francisco, California.

- Thomas C. Jorgensen, R.M., a real estate appraiser with Sound Investments, Seattle, Washington.

- Elaine G. Kirsch, R.M., president of the Western Pennsylvania chapter of the American Institute of Real Estate Appraisers, Pittsburgh, Pennsylvania.

- William Metz, an appraiser and president of William Metz and Associates, Homewood, Illinois.

- Judy Nice, a real estate broker with Century 21—Flowers Realty, Kirkland, Washington.

- Pat Serkedakis, a real estate broker with Century 21—Southeastern Realty, Marietta, Georgia.

- Mary Jo Thomas, R.M., an appraiser with J. R. Kimball, Inc., Fort Worth, Texas.

All of the appraisers on our advisory panel are members of the American Institute of Real Estate Appraisers, which is headquartered in Chicago, Illinois.

The results of our remodeling survey are presented at the beginning of this chapter. The table, figures, and cost estimates used to illustrate the survey report (with the exception of the estimates for the major and minor energy upgrades and the landscaping package) are copyrighted by R. S. Means Company, Inc. They are reproduced with permission from the *Means Home Improvement Cost Guide* (Kingston, Mass.: R. S. Means Co., Inc., 1985).

Later in the chapter we will offer you suggestions on how to find and work with a contractor, along with advice on how to keep your remodeling costs within acceptable limits. You will also find in this chapter a discussion of the differences between "renovation" and "restoration" as well as some practical tips from a real estate pro on simple steps you can take to make your home more saleable.

Reading carefully through this chapter, you will notice that different authors use different sources of information and come up with slightly different cost estimates for basic remodeling projects. Keep in mind that costs of materials and contractors' fees will vary from place to place and at different periods of time. All estimates provided in this chapter are thus meant only to serve as general guidelines to help you as you begin making your own remodeling plans.—**the editors**

1986 COST VS. VALUE REMODELING SURVEY
A Guide to 20 Home Improvements

Near the seacoast town of Camden, Maine, a couple we'll call Chris and Annie fell in love with a 225-year-old Cape Cod farmhouse on five acres. They bought it for $80,000. "We thought we'd never move again," says Chris, so they jumped right into the renovation, gutting much of the house. They added a dormer, converted an upstairs half-bath into a full one, and doubled the amount of living space upstairs. Then, somewhere between opening up the downstairs living area and remodeling the kitchen, Chris got an out-of-state job offer too good to turn down.

Such situations often cost homeowners a pretty price. But in this case, a chain of smart decisions from the start and some last-minute design changes netted the couple a $32,000 profit when the house sold at $139,000—a phenomenal 218-percent recovery of their $27,000 remodeling investment.

The good news about home remodeling is that you can make a bundle. The bad news is that most people do not. It's so easy for homeowners, enthusiastic about the *potential* of their homes, to want the best of everything, falling into the trap of *over-improvement*.

Even a pro can do it. Consider the case of a Chicago real estate agent, Dave, who bought a $60,000 house in a "good area." He put $30,000 into a luxury remodeling job, complete with marble bathrooms. He expected to make a profit when he sold the house; but, as he now realizes, he "did too much for this size house and for this neighborhood." When he sold it five years after purchase, it brought only $86,500. He netted a $3,500 loss on his investment in the house, recovering 88 percent of the cost of his improvements.

Dave's consolation is that he "loved the house, really enjoyed living in it." Though the return on his remodeling investment was far lower than Chris and Annie's, even his 88-percent recovery isn't bad—considering that the first and best reason for remodeling is the convenience and enjoyment the owner gets out of the house while living in it.

Table 1-1—HOW THE TOP 20
HOME IMPROVEMENTS STACK UP

Rank	Project	Project Cost	Dollar Amount Recovered	Percent of Cost Recovered
1	Interior facelift	$4,500 ($2,025)	$4,800	106%
2	Attic conversion	$9,520 ($3,867)	$9,937	104%
3	Basement conversion	$6,580 ($2,354)	$6,437	97%*
4	Fireplace addition	$3,010 ($1,280)	$2,555	84%*
5	Deck	$3,320 ($1,003)	$2,727	82%
6	Minor energy upgrade	$1,255 ($440)	$966	77%
7	Major kitchen remodel	$11,140 ($6,005)	$8,277	74%
8	Garage	$9,280 ($3,900)	$6,866	73%
9	Standard bath remodel	$3,450 ($1,479)	$2,466	71%
10	Major room addition	$23,000 ($8,150)	$15,888	69%
11	Minor kitchen remodel	$6,830 ($3,728)	$4,655	68%
12	Major energy upgrade	$4,185 ($2,000)	$2,606	62%*

Still, after the labor, inconvenience, and expense of remodeling, it's natural for a homeowner to hope for a profit. But rarely is one guaranteed. Our tale of two houses indicates the importance of planning home improvements with both eyes open and at least one eye on possible resale.

How much will your planned improvement return on *your* investment compared with others that you might undertake? And how can you tip the scales in your favor? To find out, *Practical Homeowner* magazine surveyed nine real estate appraisers and sales experts from across the country. We asked them to take a hard look at 20 of the most common home-improvement projects, and to tell us how much they would pay back in increased market value.

Here's how we posed the problem to our panel of professionals: First, we described a hypothetical house—a 25-year-old ranch with three bedrooms and one and one-half baths, set on a quarter-acre lot

Rank	Project	Project Cost	Dollar Amount Recovered	Percent of Cost Recovered
13	New siding	$6,390 (cedar: $2,200) (vinyl: $1,924)	$3,925	61%*
14	Master bathroom remodel	$8,290 ($3,799)	$4,644	56%
15	Sunspace addition	$13,360 ($7,052)	$7,437	56%*
16	Landscaping	$4,800 ($2,850)	$2,511	52%
17	Roof window	$1,460 ($658)	$733	50%
18	Roof replacement	$8,640 ($2,970)	$4,000	46%
19	Swimming pool	$14,000 ($9,000)	$6,388	46%
20	Window and door replacement	$9,832 ($5,290)	$4,237	43%*

Note: The project costs outlined above represent the going rate on a national average for a complete service, including demolition, materials, cleanup, and contractor's fees. You can cut costs by shopping around for lower cost labor, by supplying the materials yourself if you can purchase them below retail, and by doing some or all of the work yourself. The dollar amounts in parentheses represent retail costs for materials only.

*This figure is based on the dollar amounts supplied only by the survey participants who live in regions where this home improvement was considered appropriate. For example, when calculating the cost-recovery percentage shown for the basement conversion, we did not factor in a figure for Florida, since basements are rare in that state (and finished basements even rarer).

in a suburban neighborhood. Valued at $80,000 before improvements, our sample house has a market value that represents the median in its neighborhood.

We then gave our experts an estimate of the cost for each of the 20 remodeling projects in our survey. We determined our cost estimates by referring to the *Means Home Improvement Cost Guide*— one of the books contractors often use to calculate their construction bids. (Descriptions of several projects are found in the figure captions, while table 1-1 summarizes all of the projects and how much they might cost.)

How much, we asked our panel, would each of the 20 home improvements add to our sample home's value at resale, several months after the improvements had been made? The answers ranged from investment recoveries of more than 100 percent for some projects to recoveries below 50 percent for others. Here, from the winners on down, are the results of this year's Cost vs. Value Remodeling Survey—along with tips on how to make the most of your remodeling dollars:

Interior Facelift: 106% Recovery

The interior facelift was our big winner. In most markets, money spent on painting, papering, and general freshening of the inside of your home will bring a 100-percent recovery or better at resale. Such an interior refurbishing will also lure buyers more surely than any other type of improvement, which is why every expert we interviewed recommends it to homeowners who are putting their houses on the market.

If you plan to redo your home's interior, it pays to keep abreast of current trends. "A 25-year-old tract house would probably have hardwood floors," said appraiser Mary Jo Thomas, of Fort Worth, Texas. "In the 1960s, people carpeted over the floors; now they're ripping out the carpeting and refinishing the wood. If the house doesn't have hardwood floors, I'd recommend just redoing the floors in the entranceway for a house in this price range [around $80,000]."

But don't be *too* trendy: "Think of appealing to the biggest market segment," our appraiser in Seattle, Thomas Jorgensen, added. "Go with neutral colors, small prints in wallpaper, and be fairly conservative on how much of an area you paper. Remember, it's easier to repaint than to repaper."

"If you want wild colors in your house, okay," noted appraiser William Metz, of Illinois. "But then do the redecorating package [in neutral colors] right before you sell."

Interior Facelift: *Complete repainting of all ceilings, walls, and interior trim; new wallpaper for dining room, one bedroom, and one bathroom; new carpet for living room and all bedrooms; new sheet flooring for kitchen and both bathrooms; new hardwood flooring for dining rooms; and contractor's fee. Total cost: $4,500 (materials $2,025).*

Attic Conversion: 104% Recovery

Turning your attic into usable living space may be one of the smartest home improvements you can make. Our experts rated it very high, with a recovery of at least 100 percent in most areas. (In some regions, like Florida, most homes don't have attics; these figures don't apply in such areas.)

Though the creation of additional living space doesn't automatically translate into higher market value, the chances are good that an attic conversion will be well worth the time and money invested. Most members of our panel felt that the price quoted in our example ($16.50 per square foot) would be "a good buy."

Photo 1-1. This attic in an old, Victorian house was remodeled to create the guest room shown in Photo 1-2. (Photo courtesy of Velux-America, Inc.)

Photo 1-2. The finished bedroom suite in this attic conversion is a money-maker for a growing bed-and-breakfast business. (Photo courtesy of Velux-America, Inc. Designer: Terry Sweet)

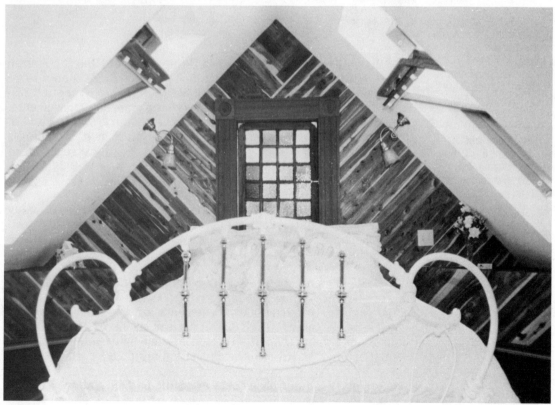

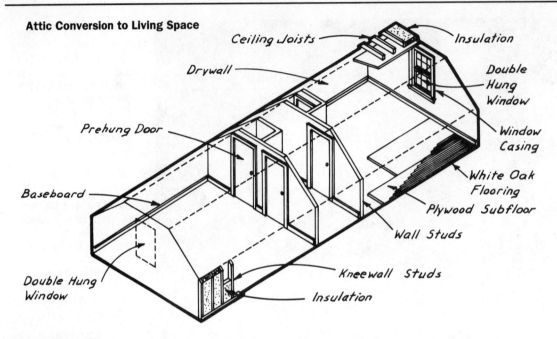

Attic Conversion to Living Space

Ceiling Joists — Insulation

Drywall

Double Hung Window

Prehung Door

Window Casing

White Oak Flooring

Baseboard

Plywood Subfloor

Wall Studs

Double Hung Window

Kneewall Studs

Insulation

Figure 1-1. Full attic (16′ × 36′): Two rooms and two closets with plywood subfloor, white oak flooring, wall insulation (R-11), ceiling insulation (R-19), drywall ceiling and walls, two double hung windows, four prehung doors, window trim, baseboard, painting, wiring (including light fixtures), and contractor's fee. Total cost: $9,520 (materials $3,867).

Elaine Kirsch, an appraiser in Pittsburgh, said she thought an attic conversion would enhance a home's value more than a basement conversion would. The reason: Attics don't have the subterranean gloom or the dampness problems that plague many basements.

Most experts assumed that the converted attic would be used for additional bedroom space. In that case, they said, including a full or half-bath in the project would ensure the fullest recovery of the remodeling investment.

Basement Conversion: 97% Recovery

Basement conversions are popular with homeowners in many parts of the country, and they're likely to make relatively good investments. According to a majority of our experts, a basement conversion usually returns nearly all of its cost and adds to a home's appeal at resale time.

Keep in mind, however, that regional differences and other factors will affect how much of your basement-finishing costs will come back to you at resale. "Basements are not common in new houses in our area," said our appraiser in Texas. "Some older houses have them, though, in which case we figure a finished basement has one-half to two-thirds the value of aboveground living space."

In Seattle, many basements are built partially above ground-

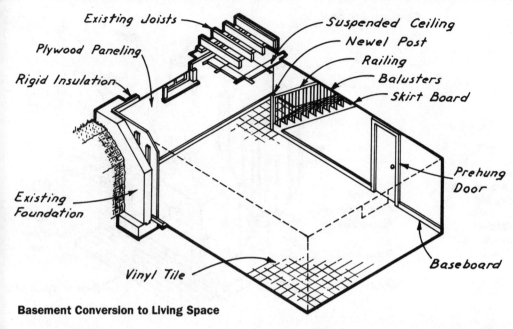

Existing Joists — Suspended Ceiling

Plywood Paneling — Newel Post

Rigid Insulation — Railing

Balusters

Skirt Board

Prehung Door

Existing Foundation

Baseboard

Vinyl Tile

Basement Conversion to Living Space

level, on sloping lots. Such "daylight" or "walk-in" basements are especially well suited for conversion to bedrooms with baths. Some homeowners in San Francisco (and in other areas where housing is expensive) have taken this a step further, creating self-contained rental apartments in their basements.

Kirsch offered a dissenting opinion on the value of the basement conversion. A finished basement that is completely underground, she said, will bring "minimal recovery—although it depends on how well it's finished, what functions it will serve, how it relates to the rest of the house. People feel that a social area should be a part of the normal flow of traffic patterns in the home."

Fireplace Addition: 84% Recovery

Our panel of housing-market experts generally had good things to say about fireplaces. A few noted that more and more homeowners are installing them in "great rooms" (combined living and dining areas), and even in bedrooms.

What's more, the appeal of a fireplace extends beyond the cold regions of the country, adding romance even in Texas and Florida—although a fireplace isn't likely to increase a home's value by as much in southern states. "We probably have more fireplaces here in Florida than you'd think," said appraiser Edith Duncan of Jupiter, Florida. "New houses of $100,000 and up often have a fireplace for

Figure 1-2. Standard basement (24′ × 20′): Vinyl flooring, insulation, paneling, suspended ceiling, staircase handrail, closet under stairs, light fixtures, trim (windows, doors, and baseboards), and contractor's fee. Total cost: $6,580 (materials $2,354).

Fireplace Addition

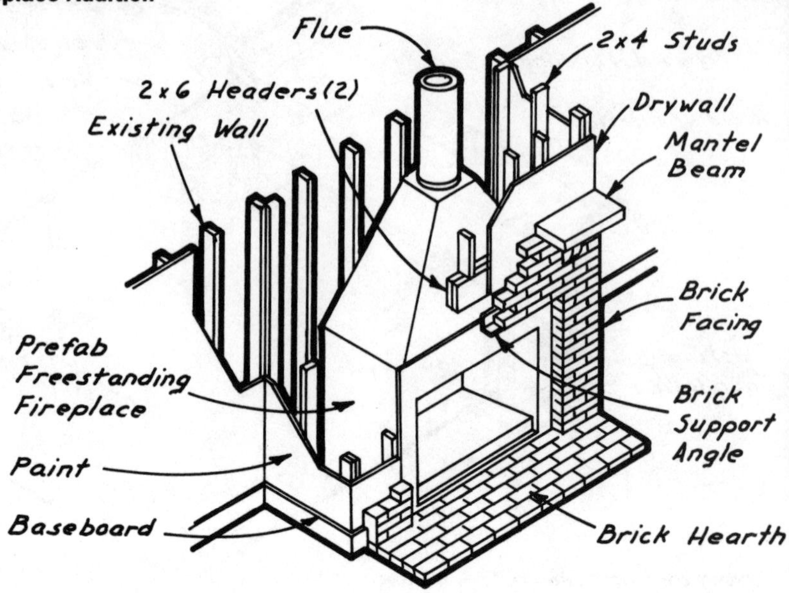

Flue

2x4 Studs

2x6 Headers (2)

Existing Wall

Drywall

Mantel Beam

Brick Facing

Prefab Freestanding Fireplace

Brick Support Angle

Paint

Baseboard

Brick Hearth

Figure 1-3. Built-in fireplace (5′ × 6′ × 13′): Flue installation, frame and fittings, fire-resistant drywall, facing, hearth, mantel beam, chimney top, prefab fireplace, cosmetic finishes, and contractor's fee. Total cost: $3,010 (materials $1,280).

the charm of it; builders offer them as an option. But not too many people in Florida go to the trouble to add one on."

A top-quality, built-in, prefab fireplace is likely to have better investment potential than a freestanding one. Our appraiser in Texas told us that a freestanding fireplace generally "isn't perceived as a quality product."

Deck Addition: 82% Recovery

Decks have become increasingly popular in all parts of the country in recent years, and for good reason. A handsome, well-constructed deck can enhance a home's exterior appearance and increase living space during warmer months. In places where the climate encourages year-round outdoor living, decks are almost mandatory.

Depending on where you live, a deck can return anywhere from 80 to 100 percent or more of its cost in added market value. And compared to most other building projects, the cost of a deck—not quite $15 per square foot in our example—is quite low.

Some experts we consulted thought the deck for our sample house might be an "overimprovement" in their areas. If recovering the lion's share of your investment is a top concern, plan to build a deck that is comparable in size and type to decks on other homes in your vicinity and price range.

Most owners like to personalize their decks by adding privacy walls, shading devices, even hot tubs and whirlpool spas. These features make attractive selling points. Though they may not add

Deck Addition

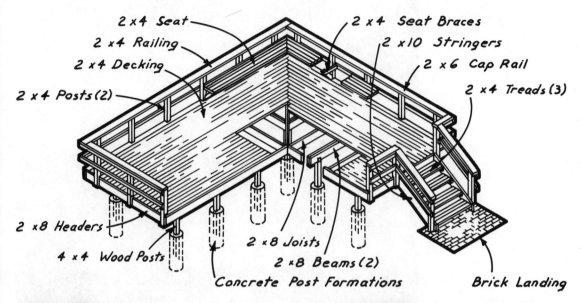

2 x 4 Seat
2 x 4 Railing
2 x 4 Decking
2 x 4 Posts (2)
2 x 4 Seat Braces
2 x 10 Stringers
2 x 6 Cap Rail
2 x 4 Treads (3)
2 x 8 Headers
4 x 4 Wood Posts
2 x 8 Joists
2 x 8 Beams (2)
Concrete Post Formations
Brick Landing

Figure 1-4. L-shaped elevated deck (8′ × 12′ and 8′ × 16′): Post-hole excavation, concrete, pressure-treated deck lumber, staircase with brick landing, hand railings, benches, and contractor's fee. Total cost: $3,320 (materials $1,003).

Photo 1-3. This barren New Orleans backyard was rarely used until its owners filled part of it with the deck shown in Photo 1-4. (Photo courtesy of California Redwood Association)

Photo 1-4. The hot, humid Louisiana climate causes most woods to rot, so the substructure of this deck is made of preservative-treated pine and the flooring is redwood. Cinderblock piers lift the deck above the marshy ground. (Photo by Maris/Semel, courtesy of California Redwood Association. Designer: Decks Unlimited)

much more to the market value of the house, they add considerably to their owners' enjoyment—which, after all, is what a deck is for.

Minor Energy Upgrade: 77% Recovery

An investment in your home's energy efficiency can yield cost-returns in two ways: Your fuel bills will be lower while you own the house, and the improvements *may* help you get a better price for the house when you sell it.

Even so, the consensus of our experts was that energy efficiency is rarely a home's most important selling feature. "People are getting more energy-conscious," real estate agent Barry Gaw in Chicago told us, "but energy efficiency isn't going to be a determining factor in selling a property. If buyers like the house for other reasons—location, layout, and so forth—they'll be willing to put up with higher utility bills."

According to some of our experts, added ceiling and roof insulation probably make the most difference to buyers. That may explain why, on average, our panel rated the cost-recovery of our minor energy upgrade higher than that of the major energy upgrade (which came in at 62 percent).

But opinions varied widely on the minor upgrade: Pat Serkedakis, our real estate agent in Marietta, Georgia, as well as our appraiser in Texas said that it would yield a full return of its cost, while three of our experts (in Chicago, Seattle, and Pittsburgh) thought the improvements described here would add nothing to the home's market value. If you're unsure about how much to invest in upgrading the energy efficiency of your home, it's probably best to compare your plans with other energy upgrades in your area. And remember that the primary value of energy improvements is in reducing operating costs, not in boosting resale value.

Minor Energy Upgrade: *Caulking and weatherstripping for two doors and 16 windows, setback thermostat for heating system, attic insulation (R-22), insulation jacket for water heater, and contractor's fee. Total cost: $1,255 (materials $440).*

Major Kitchen Remodel: 74% Recovery

Kitchen remodeling is one of the most commonly undertaken home-improvement projects in the country. The reason for this, said our experts, is that an inviting kitchen can increase a home's marketability, as well as its livability. But at a 74-percent recovery of investment, kitchen remodeling rates only fair-to-middling on the cost vs. value scale. You could increase that rate of cost-recovery, our experts said, by removing the old kitchen yourself, since demolition labor can account for one-third of the labor costs involved.

Understanding kitchen trends in your area (and knowing the average market value of homes in your immediate neighborhood)

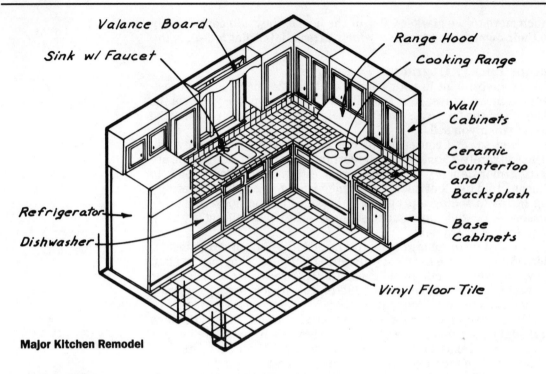

Valance Board

Sink w/ Faucet

Range Hood

Cooking Range

Wall Cabinets

Ceramic Countertop and Backsplash

Base Cabinets

Refrigerator

Dishwasher

Vinyl Floor Tile

Major Kitchen Remodel

Figure 1-5. Deluxe L-shaped kitchen (8′ × 12′): New, top-quality hardwood cabinetry, ceramic-tile countertops, appliances, complete decorating (vinyl floor tile, decorative trim, and painting), and contractor's fee. Total cost: $11,140 (materials $6,005).

can help you decide how much to spend on a kitchen remodel. Many families place a premium on time spent together, and the cook no longer wants to be isolated in the kitchen. As a result, the "great room"—a combined living and dining area with an open, informal atmosphere—is catching on in many parts of the country. (But if you're not comfortable with the concept, fearing that the dishwasher will be too noisy and the kitchen always cluttered, you'll probably be able to find a buyer who will share your preference, we were told.)

Kitchen renovation is also becoming more convenience-oriented as people have less time for cooking and cleaning up. As a result, the microwave is no longer just a wave of the future: Many cooks today consider it a necessity.

You may love the idea of a streamlined, contemporary kitchen, and so might many buyers. But they probably won't pay the additional cost if it pushes the home out of the price range of others in your area. If you're remodeling with resale in your future, a conservative approach is best: Refrain from knocking out walls or adding high-tech appliances that cost a great deal. Stick with good quality, but avoid luxury. And go with neutral colors in permanent items such as tile, built-in appliances, and fixtures. If you like, add dashes of color with curtains, accessories, paint, or wallpaper.

Photo 1-5. A new layout, an efficient lighting scheme, and floor-to-ceiling windows turned what was once a dark, dreary room into this sleek, spacious kitchen. (Photo by Gene Hennessey. Designer: LSK Design Associates, Ltd.)

Attached Garage Addition: 73% Recovery

Most homebuyers today are looking for a two-car garage. Ample garage space is especially important in cold climates where cars, like people, need more winter shelter. "If a house doesn't have a garage, adding one can return up to 100 percent of its cost," said our expert in Pittsburgh, "as long as the addition doesn't price the home above the value of other houses on the street."

Garages make good investments in the sunbelt, too. Basements are rare or nonexistent in the South, so garages are valued for providing extra storage space, as well as for protecting cars from constant exposure to the hot sun.

Attached Garage Addition (22′ × 22′): *Grading, concrete floor slab, wall and roof construction, aluminum siding, asphalt roofing, gutters and downspouts, two windows (2′ × 3′), one entrance door, one garage door (16′ × 7′), painting, and contractor's fee. Total cost: $9,280 (materials $3,900).*

Standard Bathroom Remodel: 71% Recovery

More bathrooms are remodeled each year than any other room in American houses. It's not hard to see why: A modernized bathroom not only adds comfort and convenience, but it can also be a big plus when it comes to selling older homes.

But a remodeled bath won't always add 100 percent of its cost to the home's resale value. That's because buyers tend to compare

Photo 1-6. Water damage loosened plastic tiles in the bathroom of this Mount Prospect, Illinois home, prompting the owner to make a complete remodel, shown in Photo 1-7. (Photo courtesy of Color Tile)

Photo 1-7. The old cabinets and fixtures were retained in this remodel, but the shower stall and floor were retiled, the walls papered, and the trim painted. (Photo courtesy of Color Tile. Designer: Color Tile)

Standard Bathroom Remodel

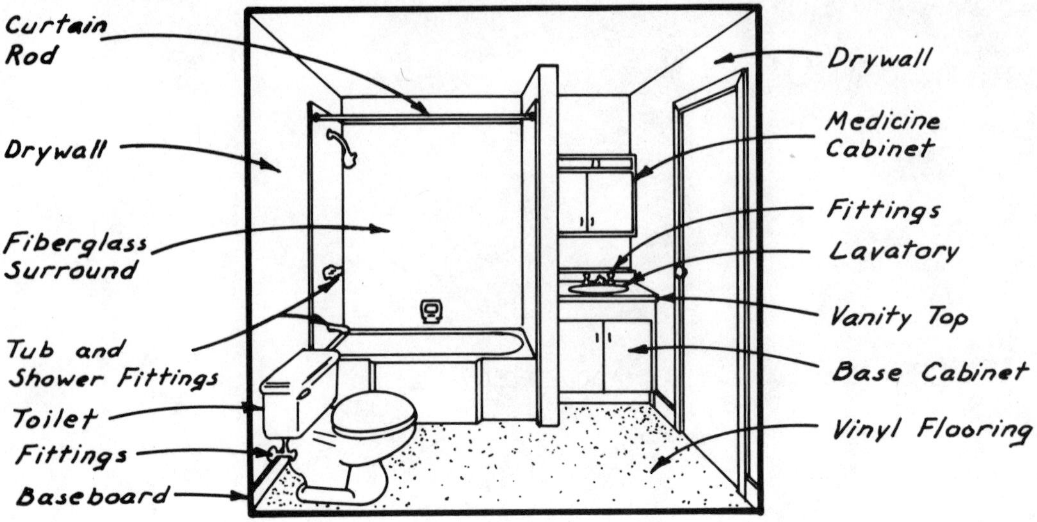

Curtain Rod

Drywall

Fiberglass Surround

Tub and Shower Fittings

Toilet

Fittings

Baseboard

Drywall

Medicine Cabinet

Fittings

Lavatory

Vanity Top

Base Cabinet

Vinyl Flooring

Figure 1-6. Standard full bath (7′ × 8′): New fixtures (tub, toilet, vanity, and fittings), medicine cabinet, partition walls, new flooring, wall covering, paint, baseboard, and contractor's fee. Total cost: $3,450 (materials $1,479).

the features in a remodeled bathroom with those in new homes. This puts remodelers at a disadvantage, since fully renovating a bathroom costs more per square foot than building a new one.

Much of the high cost of bathroom renovation comes from the labor involved in demolishing the existing fixtures. You can cut costs and boost your investment-recovery by doing that part of the work yourself. Tasteful decorating and a wise choice of fixtures will also add to the value of this project without costing you a fortune. The permanent components of the bathroom—the tub/shower, toilet, sink, and tile—should be neutral in color so they appeal to the greatest number of potential buyers. Less expensive (and more easily changed) elements, such as wallpaper, paint, and curtains, can be more colorful.

When selecting components, be sensitive to perceptions of quality in your area. "Fiberglass tub/showers are not well received in the upper price range, but are more typically used in rental properties," noted our appraiser in Texas. Just as you don't want to overimprove, you can lose dollars by underimproving for your neighborhood.

Major Room Addition: 69% Recovery

The value of a major room addition will depend on how well it is suited to the house and the neighborhood. With the trend in some parts of the country toward contemporary interiors, added space that is well integrated with other areas in the home could bring an investment-recovery as high as 100 percent.

Most experts rated our sample room addition considerably lower than that, saying that it would return an average of 69 per-

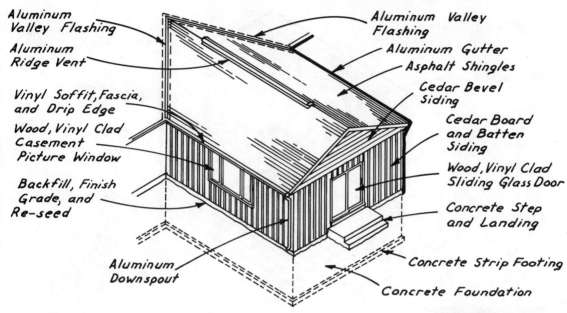

Aluminum Valley Flashing
Aluminum Ridge Vent
Vinyl Soffit, Fascia, and Drip Edge
Wood, Vinyl Clad Casement Picture Window
Backfill, Finish Grade, and Re-seed
Aluminum Downspout

Aluminum Valley Flashing
Aluminum Gutter
Asphalt Shingles
Cedar Bevel Siding
Cedar Board and Batten Siding
Wood, Vinyl Clad Sliding Glass Door
Concrete Step and Landing
Concrete Strip Footing
Concrete Foundation

Major Room Addition

Figure 1-7. Room addition (20′ × 24′): Frame roof, walls, floor, asphalt roofing, cedar siding, gutters, flashing, ceiling insulation (R-30), wall insulation (R-11), two casement windows, drywall, carpeting, paint, wiring, and contractor's fee. Total cost: $23,000 (materials $8,150).

cent of its cost. "This addition adds 480 square feet," said Seattle appraiser Jorgensen. "It's an overimprovement on a house of this size. An addition 50 to 75 percent as big would pay off just as well."

Our experts suggested that homeowners should look, above all, for the *utility* an addition can provide. "If it enhances function, fine," said our appraiser in Texas. "But too often, we see additions that actually *decrease* function—for example, a den added on to a kitchen that cuts off light because a window is removed."

And while a trend toward more space is apparent in some sections of the country, a few of our experts see an opposing trend in their areas: "Great rooms are very popular in newer homes," said Jorgensen, "especially if you have a fireplace included. People with young children like this. But some people in Seattle are going back to smaller rooms—formal living and dining rooms—particularly in less expensive homes and condominiums. They would rather have something small of good quality than something big of mediocre quality."

Minor Kitchen Remodel: 68% Recovery

As easy as it is to overimprove a kitchen, it's also possible to underimprove one. That's why the experts said our minor kitchen remodeling project would yield a somewhat lower investment recovery than the major kitchen renovation.

Our Chicago real estate agent explained it by saying that "packaging sells the product." In other words, if buyers perceive inferior

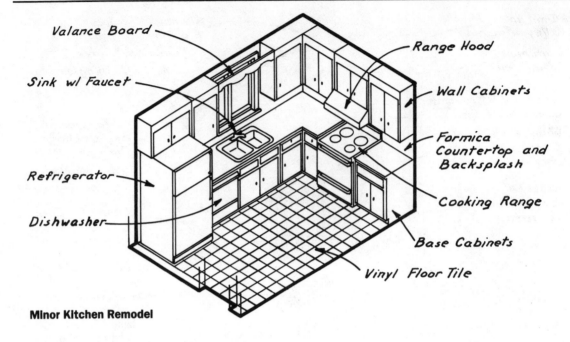

Valance Board

Sink w/ Faucet

Refrigerator

Dishwasher

Range Hood

Wall Cabinets

Formica Countertop and Backsplash

Cooking Range

Base Cabinets

Vinyl Floor Tile

Minor Kitchen Remodel

Figure 1-8. Standard L-shaped kitchen (8′ × 12′): Economy wood cabinets, standard (mid-priced) appliances, laminate countertops, painting, and contractor's fee. Total cost: $6,830 (materials $3,728).

materials, workmanship, or design, they'll penalize the seller by making a lower offer—or by making no offer at all.

Greater attention to surface details, such as countertops and cabinet doors, could increase the resale value of this project, as could things that add "pizzazz" and eye appeal, like better lighting and a tasteful, attractive color scheme. The trick is to make it look as good as you can without losing your shirt.

Major Energy Upgrade: 62% Recovery

The consensus of our experts was clear: The primary payback of a major energy upgrade comes from savings on your heating and cooling bills and from tax incentives. The longer you intend to remain in your home, the better your chances of recovering (and multiplying) your investment in this project.

Save your fuel bills if you're planning to make energy-related improvements in your home. That way you'll have "before and after" proof of energy savings when the time comes to sell. Said Kirsch, our appraiser in Pittsburgh: "How well this upgrade returns on investment depends on how a real estate agent sells it." So make sure your real estate agent talks up the benefits of your energy-efficient home.

Major Energy Upgrade: *Caulking and weatherstripping for two doors and 16 windows, setback thermostat for heating system, attic insulation (R-22), wall insulation (R-11), high-quality storm*

windows, insulation jacket for water heater, and contractor's fee.
Total cost: $4,185 (materials $2,000).

New Siding: 61% Recovery

Nice, new siding on a 25-year-old house can enhance its marketability and add to its resale value, provided that the siding it replaces was in bad shape. "You put on new siding to enhance the look of a house or to hide a problem," said Metz, our appraiser in Illinois. "If you're correcting an eyesore that really detracts from the house, you can probably count on getting a 100-percent recovery on the cost of new siding."

Buyers perceive vinyl and metal siding as being maintenance-free and energy-efficient. These are definite pluses, but are probably not enough by themselves to justify the cost of residing, especially if the exterior of your home is already in fairly good condition. And cedar siding, as our appraiser from Seattle noted, requires regular coats of preservative.

Photo 1-8. New siding can enhance the value of an old house if the old siding is in poor condition, but often it is more cost-effective to simply work to preserve the original siding. (Photo by Carl Doney)

Before residing your house, consider the perceived value of its original exterior. Preserving it, rather than siding over it, could pay off in the long run. This may be particularly true in light of the reported trend toward more traditional exteriors in many parts of the country.

New Siding: *1,500 sq. ft. of 6-inch beveled cedar siding over asphalt felt paper and contractor's fee. Or, vinyl clapboard siding over insulation board and asphalt felt paper, plus contractor's fee. Total cost: $6,390 (materials: cedar—$2,200, vinyl—$1,924).*

Master Bathroom Remodel: 56% Recovery

Our experts considered this project a good example of an overimprovement for a house in the price range of our $80,000, "typical" home. "True, we are seeing a trend toward more luxurious bathrooms in the upper price ranges," said Georgia real estate agent Pat Serkedakis. "Jacuzzis, sunken tubs—buyers like them, if they can afford them." But in a moderately priced home, the extra money put into such features would probably be lost when the house is sold. Consequently, real estate agents and appraisers rated the master bath remodel fairly low on the value scale, with an average cost-recovery of only 55 percent.

Our panel of experts also suggested ways to lower remodeling costs without seriously affecting the perceived value of the finished project: Use vinyl instead of ceramic tile on the floor, for example, or use the same kind of carpet that's in the master bedroom. Use wallpaper instead of tile wainscoting on the walls. "In our area, tile

Figure 1-9. Deluxe master bath (8′ × 10′): A new four-fixture package (shower stall, bathtub, toilet, vanity with double sink), mirrored medicine cabinet, ceramic tile walls and wainscoting, porcelain tile flooring, painting (ceiling, walls, and door), and contractor's fee. Total cost: $8,290 (materials $3,799).

Master Bathroom Remodel

Ceramic Tile Shower Stall

Paint

Medicine Cabinet

Tile Wainscot

Towel Bar

Towel Bar

Vanity Top

Ceramic Tile Wainscot

Vanity Base

Toilet

Bathtub

Porcelain Tile Flooring

wainscoting is considered outdated," reported Thomas in Texas. Choosing a white toilet and tub could save you 25 to 30 percent on the cost of these fixtures. You'll also save money by doing the demolition work yourself.

Sunspace Addition: 56% Recovery

Judged "a risky investment" by most of our panel, the sunspace is one project that should probably be evaluated more in terms of its worth to the current owner than for its potential resale value. "It's awfully expensive for living space that can't be used year-round," said our real estate agent from Chicago. "This is a 189-square-foot addition," noted our appraiser in Seattle. "At $70.69 per square foot, this is well above the usual cost for interior space [about $49 per square foot]." Others told us that many people don't think of sunspaces as significant energy-savers.

On the other hand, regional trends play a part in determining the desirability of sunspaces. Appraiser William Metz of Homewood, Illinois, said sunspaces are popular there. He suspects that a sunspace could offer a better investment-recovery than a conventional room addition, although he rated both at about 50 percent.

Another factor influencing the resale value of a sunspace is where it's located in relation to other rooms in the house. A sunspace off the kitchen, for example, can serve as an elegant dining area and is an attractive feature. Functional use of space and eye appeal will probably do more to sell a sunspace than abstract

Figure 1-10. Large sunroom-greenhouse (10′6″ × 18′): Foundation, kneewall, prefab greenhouse, excavation and site work, quarry tile floor, cedar siding, and contractor's fee. Total cost: $13,360 (materials $7,052).

Sunspace Addition

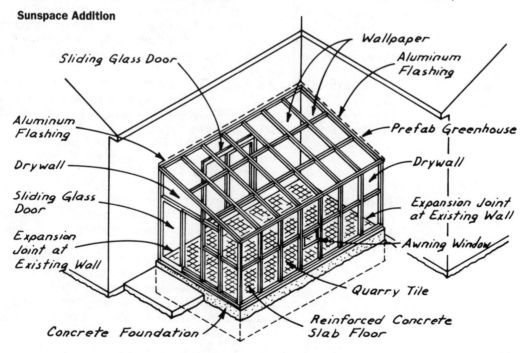

energy savings. "Energy efficiency is important," said Metz, "but it won't be a determining factor if people like the house for other reasons."

Landscaping Package: 52% Recovery

As might be expected, regional characteristics play a big role in determining the value of landscape improvements. In areas like the Southeast and parts of the West Coast, which have long, lush growing seasons, landscaping is popular with owners and buyers alike. Our experts in Atlanta and San Francisco told us homeowners in those cities could probably expect to reap a full recovery of a landscaping investment.

Appraisers and real estate agents in other regions were less enthusiastic about the value of an expensive landscaping package. "A lot of it depends on what was there before," said Metz in Illinois. "If the yard was really mediocre, you might expect to get an extra $500 on this improvement."

"People do want property that's nicely landscaped," said appraiser Kirsch in Pittsburgh. "They love the trees, but they don't want to pay for it." In Texas, landscaping can be as risky an adventure as farming. "Down here we see severe droughts and freezes," said appraiser Thomas—hinting that landscaping can be here today, gone tomorrow.

And, as our panel pointed out, a growing segment of the homebuying market is made up of people who are 65 and older; it pays to remember that many of these people might not relish yardwork. (Nor do some younger homeowners, for that matter.)

The general recommendation from our experts is that you should landscape primarily for enjoyment, not investment potential. If you anticipate resale in the short term, a few hundred dollars spent on pruning, edging, and general sprucing up is your best bet.

Landscaping Package: *Two new shade trees (18' to 20' tall), 12 new shrubs (40" tall) planted around foundation, 100 sq. ft. of new ground-cover beds added around existing trees, 20' of new flagstone (cut bluestone) walkway (4' wide) added from front door to driveway, one exterior lighting standard (including wiring), 120' of privacy fencing (6' tall), and landscaper's and electrician's fees. Total cost: $4,800 (materials $2,850).*

Roof Window Installation: 50% Recovery

Skylights and other types of roof windows are part of a growing trend toward interiors that have a "contemporary look"—open, airy, and light-filled. They're a definite hit with many homeowners, so if you're planning to install one, you're not alone. The logical place for a roof window is an area that gets little or no natural illumination, such as a bathroom without a regular window.

But there was no general agreement among our experts on whether or not skylights or roof windows add to a home's market

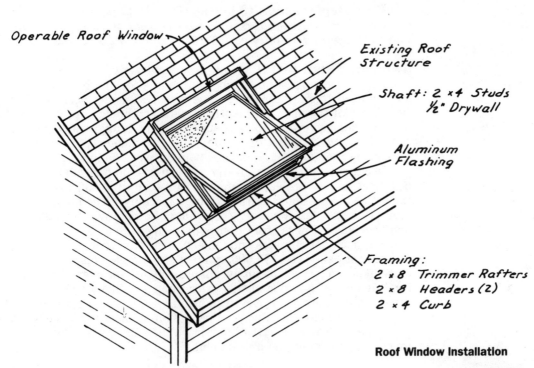

Operable Roof Window

Existing Roof Structure

Shaft: 2 x4 Studs ½" Drywall

Aluminum Flashing

Framing:
2 x 8 Trimmer Rafters
2 x 8 Headers (2)
2 x 4 Curb

Roof Window Installation

Figure 1-11. Operable roof window (52″ × 55″): Ceiling cutout, frame construction, operable thermopane skylight, flashing, shaft construction and painting, insulation, trim, and contractor's fee. Total cost: $1,460 (materials $658).

value. Roof windows can improve the salability of a home in areas where contemporary interiors are popular, but buyers in other regions remain wary of them. For all their advantages, skylights and roof windows still have a reputation for leaking water and allowing heat to escape.

Roof Replacement: 46% Recovery

There's nothing like a leaking roof to dampen buyers' interest in a home. "If you put your house on the market and it needs a new roof, the market will penalize you," said our appraiser in Texas.

On the other hand, a new roof is not likely to add much to a home's market value, our experts said—although it may make the house easier to sell. "It's hard to tell the difference between a new roof and one that's three years old," noted our appraiser in Seattle. Our other experts agreed: The cost of a new roof will not usually be recovered. In fact, in our survey it finished near the bottom of the cost vs. value scale.

Roof replacement generally becomes necessary after 20 years or so, and our sample home is about due. The decision to go ahead with the project should depend partly on whether the owner plans to sell the home in the near future. If a sale is imminent, and the roof isn't leaking, don't replace it.

Roof Replacement (3,000 sq. ft.): *Building paper, asphalt shingles, drip edges, gutters, downspouts, rake trim, soffit, fascia, and contractor's fee. Total cost: $8,640 (materials $2,970).*

Swimming Pool Installation: 46% Recovery

A private pool is one of those "dream" projects that more and more homeowners are making come true. Swimming pool installation is one of the most frequently undertaken home improvements nationwide, according to our survey, even though our experts ranked it low in terms of resale value. Obviously, people aren't measuring the value of a pool solely in terms of dollars.

In climates with long, hot summers, in-ground pools like the one described in our project summary can return up to 90 percent of their cost in additional market value, especially if the home is in a high price bracket. Generally, the value of a pool will be higher in neighborhoods where other homes have them.

But in colder climates and in neighborhoods where most homes fall near or below the $80,000 value of our sample house, pools are more likely to be seen as an overimprovement—or even as a liability. "Owners of a house in this price range are likely to have children and may not want the responsibility of a pool," said our appraiser in Pittsburgh. "I've seen people buy houses with pools and fill in the pool. With just the interest on the money you would have invested, you could join a swim club."

Swimming Pool Installation (16′ × 32′): *Excavation and site work, sidewall, pool, finish grade, seeding, and contractor's fee. Total cost: $14,000 (materials $9,000).*

Window and Door Replacement Package: 43% Recovery

Investing in new, energy-efficient windows and doors can make good sense in the long run, especially if yours is an older home in a region with long, cold winters. You'll save time and money on maintenance, since the vinyl-clad windows don't need repainting, and you'll cut energy costs. At the same time, you'll make the house more attractive to potential buyers, who are now more energy-conscious than ever.

In the short term, however, most of our experts consider window and door replacement a questionable investment, returning only about 43 percent of cost in added market value. "People don't go through this just to put their house up for sale," is how appraiser Jorgensen of Seattle put it. If you're planning to sell in three to five years, this project probably isn't a good idea, unless windows and doors are in such obviously poor condition that they detract from the house's appearance.

As with roofs and siding, buyers expect sound windows and doors; but they aren't likely to reward the owner by paying the full cost of replacement.

Window and Door Replacement Package: *16 double hung, plastic-clad wooden windows (3′ × 4′) with thermal glass, casing, trim, painting, and caulking; two pine, six-panel colonial doors (3′ × 6′ 8″), with frame, interior and exterior casings, sill, hinges, drip cap, weatherstripping, and painting; and contractor's fee. Total cost: $9,832 (materials $5,290).*—**the editors**

A RENOVATION PRIMER
What You Should Know Before Calling a Contractor

Many Americans live in homes built to suit the standards of a bygone era: dreary, dark rooms, insufficient electrical outlets, inadequate storage space, kitchens and baths that are too small.

Renovation—the updating of a structure to meet modern needs—is the solution to such problems. But before you get involved in what can be a time-consuming and costly process, ask yourself some questions. Do you like your neighborhood? If you don't, then buying another house, or building a new one in another location, is probably a better solution.

Ask yourself, too, whether you plan to move in a few years. If so, you'll have to find out how your renovation plans will affect the resale value of your home. Some renovations can help sell homes (an extra bath rarely hurts). Other projects, however, can actually decrease the value of your home. Adding a post-modern exterior to a home in a completely traditional and conservative neighborhood, for example, will restrict the number of potential buyers. A seasoned real estate agent can tell you how easily your renovated home would sell, and how much market value you would be adding or subtracting with your proposed project.

Also, examine your own and your family's needs, both currently and in the predictable future. At what times of the day are you at home? What do you do during that time? What spaces do you use? Do you entertain frequently? What spaces do you use for guests? Do you need more bedrooms for growing children or for new additions to the family? Who uses the kitchen? For what—just cooking, or other activities as well? Are you a private person? Your answers to questions like these will help you to understand your own needs and to set goals.

Once you have decided what you want to do, the next step is to work out a design that will meet your requirements. Consider your home a shell with partitions that create separate spaces inside. You may best achieve your goals by reorganizing spaces and partitions within that shell, or by adding onto the side or top of the structure.

Let's assume your kitchen is too small, and you've determined you need an informal place for the family to gather. Let's say you

Photo 1-9. These students at the Cornerstone owner-builder school are learning how to make a sunspace addition to an existing home. (Photo by Carl Doney)

have a huge hallway that is dead space, and a dining room you rarely use. Removing or moving partitions may provide you with an adequate kitchen and eating area, a sizable family room, a small hallway, and no dining room.

But before you knock walls down, you must consider the state of the existing structure. What if you live in an older home that can't accommodate repositioned wall partitions without a good deal of expense and inconvenience? In this situation, adding on might be more sensible.

If you can't easily see how your goals can become a reality, invest in the services of a competent design professional. You can hire an architect or renovator who provides consultation services on an hourly basis, or for a small fixed fee.

Home renovation is a specialized field, and you'll need to find professionals who know it well. To find the right professional, look for architects or renovators whose main line of work is renovation of single-family homes. An architect who is a friend, but who has worked only on large commercial projects, is not a good choice. Nor is a contractor who builds only new homes, or a carpenter who has never built the kind of addition you want.

You can find the right professional through ads and neighbors who have renovated, through magazines, through books about renovation, and through your local yellow pages. Two trade associations you could contact for the names of professional remodelers in your area are the National Remodelers Council (NRC) of the National Association of Home Builders, and the National Association of the Remodeling Industry (NARI). Members of NRC and NARI subscribe to codes of ethics, many of them have been in business for ten or more years, and regional chapters of these groups can intercede on the homeowner's behalf if there are complaints about work done by members.

The Home Owners Warranty Corporation offers HOW, a warranty program for its registered contractors. If there is no HOW office near you, contact the national office for names of local registered contractors.

Once you have a professional in mind, ask for client references and follow up on them by speaking to the clients and looking at the completed work. The type of work you see bears a resemblance to what you will get. Individual professionals have their own strengths, weaknesses, and styles. Learn what these are, and choose someone whose work is compatible with what you want. The professional you choose will discuss your ideas and needs with you, look at your existing home, and propose some design solutions with projected costs.

When you have a feel for the project, establish a budget: You don't want to end up with plans for something way beyond your financial reach. Your budget should include design and construction costs, legal fees for having a lawyer review any contract you enter into, any costs involved in obtaining local building permits, costs of any new appliances, decorating and refurnishing costs, contingency money for unforseeable problems that surface when walls are torn down (typically 10 to 25 percent of the overall construction costs), and financing costs if you are borrowing money. If you are planning to gut the entire house, you may need to rent storage space and temporary living space.

If the proposed design costs more than you want to spend, it can be amended to meet your budget. Another option is to break the project up into stages. Doing it this way may cost more in the long run than doing it all at once. But by establishing long-term renovation goals, you'll save more money and end up with better results than if you aimlessly renovate bits and pieces over the years.

Once you've agreed on a design, the project is ready to be contracted out. Legally, architects can act as general contractors, but for the most part they don't. More often, they'll recommend one or more general contractors they've worked with before. A general contractor schedules, coordinates, and supervises all of the trades involved in realizing your renovation goals. Plumbers, electricians, drywallers, and carpenters are seldom employed full-time by the contractor; instead, they usually work on a subcontract basis. Experienced contractors normally have a stable of tradespeople whose work they trust.

Next, ask for a written contract accompanied by detailed plans. A schedule of payments due at the completion of specified stages of the job should be part of this contract. With that settled, any needed building permits can be obtained and the physical work of renovation can begin. Your dream house is on the way.

Rules for Remodelers

The principles we have been discussing can be summarized and stated in the following set of rules:

- If you care about the investment value of your renovation dollars or expect to sell your home in the next few years, research the local real estate market before going ahead with the project.

- Take time to establish goals in line with your family's needs; knowing what you want is the key to a successful renovation project.

- Set a realistic budget; don't forget to factor in the cost of finishes, appliances, trim, and so on. In order to estimate costs realistically, you'll need a detailed set of plans.

- Plan thoroughly and stick with your decisions. Changes you make along the way can escalate costs dramatically.

- Don't start construction without having a written contract, detailed design and construction plans, and any applicable local building permits.

For Further Information

Home Owners Warranty
  Corporation
2000 L St., NW
Suite 400
Washington, DC 20036

National Association
  of Home Builders
National Remodelers Council
15th and M Sts., NW
Washington, DC 20005

National Association
  of the Remodeling Industry
1901 N. Moore St.
Suite 808
Arlington, VA 22209

—**Vera Tweed**

THE COST OF HOME IMPROVEMENTS
Price Guide for a Realistic Remodeling Budget

When you're ready to take action on a major home improvement, cost is often the key factor in deciding to go ahead with it, to scale it down, or to nix it altogether until a windfall comes along. Having a big new family room is a great idea, but learning that it will probably cost over $20,000 is bound to temper your enthusiasm.

Renovation can be surprisingly expensive. In the last two years alone, home improvement costs have gone up by as much as one-third. A typical new family room cost $21,000 in 1984, but last year the same addition went up to $27,000, according to *Remodeling World* magazine. That's the kind of surprise nobody needs.

To preempt the surprise and see if your dream remodeling project is on track with your real-life budget, consult the cost chart provided in table 1-2. Whether you're thinking of new flooring for your kitchen or a new garage addition, this chart can help you estimate what the job will cost. It lists average labor and materials prices for 18 common home improvements.

Though actual bids may vary widely from these figures depending on the scope of your project, the quality of the materials to be used, and where you live, these numbers will get you in the right ballpark. They will give you a starting point for finishing up your plans and dealing effectively with contractors.

An extensive, detailed listing of costs for these and other home improvements can be found in the *Means Home Improvement Cost Guide*, which was mentioned earlier in this chapter.

Now here are some tips that can help you secure the best deal when you're hiring for home improvements:

■ With costs going up the way they are, tip number one is: *Don't wait*. It's a booming time for renovation, which in some areas can make it a contractors' market.

■ Get prices from at least three contractors. This bit of advice is almost a cliché, but many homeowners don't make the effort. Some experts advise choosing the middle bid, but that isn't necessarily the best strategy for getting the best work.

■ The wisest first step in evaluating bids is to be certain of what each contractor is actually offering. Bids will be a lot easier to compare if you provide each contractor with the same detailed description of what you want done. Each contractor's proposal should specify the brand names and models of appliances, brands and grades of such materials as shingles and siding, lengths and

Table 1-2—WHAT PRICE RENOVATION?

Improvement/Average Cost	Description
1. Room addition $27,000	400-square-foot (15′ × 25′) addition with slab foundation, roofing, siding, gypsum-board interior, insulation in walls and ceiling, six insulated-glass windows, two skylights, patio door, electrical work, and decorating.
2. Swimming pool $17,000	16′ × 32′ in-ground pool with aluminum walls, vinyl liner, accessories, and 3-foot concrete surround.
3. Major kitchen remodeling $15,000	New cabinets, paint, and appliances (dishwasher, stove, range hood, and sink), vinyl flooring (12′ × 14′), ceramic tile for backsplash, and new laminate countertop and molding.
4. Windows and doors $9,500	Replace 16 exterior windows with new aluminum, wood, or vinyl windows with insulated glass, replace two wood entry doors with energy-efficient doors, and add two storm doors.
5. Solar greenhouse $9,200	8′ × 13′ solar greenhouse installed against house, with double-glazing, door, concrete foundation, and slab floor.
6. Add full bath $6,000	Tub and shower, vanity, sink, cabinets, tile for wall, and flooring for a 5′ × 7′ bath.
7. New siding with insulation board $5,500	New aluminum, vinyl, or steel siding for 1,600-square-foot house with ¼″ foam insulating board.
8. Minor kitchen remodeling $5,200	Refinish cabinets, new vinyl flooring (12′ × 14′), paint, sink, range, and new laminate countertops.
9. Remodel bath $4,400	Paint, new wall and floor tile, and complete new fixtures (sink, tub, and toilet) in a 5′ × 7′ bathroom.
10. Add wood deck $4,000	16′ × 20′ deck of cedar or preservative-treated wood with handrail and built-in bench, and concrete for posts.
11. Add fireplace $3,000	Energy-efficient, factory-built model with glass doors, floor-to-ceiling stone or brick face, 5′ × 5′ hearth, mantel (6′), flue, and fittings.

terms of warranties, and such often-overlooked details as whether or not debris will be cleaned up.

■ When you see what different parts of the project will cost, you may see some tasks that you can do yourself to save a few hundred dollars here and there. Labor, after all, is the most expensive variable, and you can save a lot by doing some of the "lowly" or easy tasks (such as demolition and removal or painting).

■ Don't hesitate to dicker. Contractors' bids aren't engraved in stone, and sometimes it's possible to close a deal by offering to sign if a discount is granted. Many home-improvement contractors aim for a gross profit of one-third of the total bid, so there is room for negotiation—especially if work is scarce, as it can be during the winter months. A rule of thumb is to ask for a 10 percent discount,

Improvement/Average Cost	Description
12. Two-car garage (shell, detached) $11,100	Frame construction on 20′ × 24′ concrete slab, fiberglass roof shingles, aluminum siding, two overhead doors, gutters, paint, window, and basic electrical service.
Two-car garage (shell, attached) $10,250	20′ × 24′, same as above.
13. Dormer (shell) $2,200	8′ × 10′ shell with shed roof, 7-foot ceiling, asphalt shingles, aluminum siding, and one window.
14. Re-roofing $1,370	260-lb. fiberglass shingles installed over old roof or cleared deck on roof of 24′ × 40′ house. Roof of average pitch.
15. Insulate attic floor $1,200	R-30 fiberglass or rock wool blown in between joists of 24′ × 40′ attic.
$770	R-30 fiberglass batts between joists of 24′ × 40′ attic.
16. Resilient flooring $1,130	Sheet vinyl (medium grade), with ¼″ underlayment and vinyl baseboard in 14′ × 20′ room.
17. Carpeting $980	Remove old carpeting. Interior carpeting priced at $12 per yard installed with padding in 14′ × 20′ room.
18. Skylight $510	Double-glazed skylight: 25″ × 49″ aluminum frame on wood curb installed in asphalt-shingled roof.

Sources: Cost figures 1 through 11 are average figures from a survey by *Remodeling World* magazine. Cost figures 12 through 18 are based on estimates for a typical metropolitan area in *Home-Tech Remodeling and Renovation Cost Estimator—1985*, compiled and edited by Henry Reynolds. All figures used by permission.

Note: Whether you're thinking of new flooring for your kitchen or a new garage addition, this chart can help you estimate what the job will cost. But keep in mind that labor and materials costs vary widely in different parts of the country, so the figures listed here are only ballpark estimates.

hope to get 5 percent, and settle for whatever the contractor will grant.

■ Pay as little as possible in advance. Some contractors want an advance of 50 percent or more of their total bid. But you should aim to pay no more than one-third up front, another third when the project is well underway, and the rest when the project is satisfactorily completed.

Good deals notwithstanding, before you finally decide on a contractor, you want to be sure you're hiring a reputable company that will do a thorough job. You've got to investigate. Here are some ways to go about it:

■ Deal only with established and experienced contractors. Since few states require licensing or examinations for would-be contractors, you can run into inexperienced or even unscrupulous operators. That makes references a must. Also, be sure to find out how long a contractor has been operating in your area. If it's less than five years, references become all the more important. Remember: Shoddy work isn't a bargain at any price.

■ There are currently two national organizations of remodeling contractors that have set standards for performance: the National Remodelers Council, of the National Association of Homebuilders, and the National Association of the Remodeling Industry. You can contact them for a listing of members in your area. Addresses for these organizations can be found in the "For Further Information" list a little earlier in this chapter.

■ If you remain unsure about a prospective contractor, you can investigate further by checking with a consumer group like the Better Business Bureau (listed in the yellow pages) to learn if there are any complaints on file. Also, find out what insurance the contractor carries to cover possible damage to your home and injury to workers, and to guarantee adequate performance.

■ Finally, keep careful records. Save copies of contracts, canceled checks, receipts, and any other relevant documents. Sometimes mistakes don't show up until well after a job is done and final payment has been made, so records are vital if you have a claim against a contractor.

Records can also be important for another reason: The cost of some improvements can mean important tax savings if your home is sold. Check with tax advisers about other possible tax savings, such as deductions for energy-related or medically required improvements and deductions for improvements made just prior to the sale of a home.—**Gene Austin**

HOME IMPROVEMENT OR BUST
Avoiding the Financial Pitfalls of Renovation

n a pleasant neighborhood, within commuting distance of a major city, a house is for sale. At first glance, it appears to be a nice place to live. Its yard is landscaped with old shade trees. Expensive new windows grace its facade. A large roof deck is a definite attraction. And inside the house, a magnificent stone fireplace, nearly 20 feet long, highlights the luxurious living room. Yet this house sits empty—and has for more than three years.

This "dream home" turned into a financial nightmare for its owners. A nice couple from all reports, they took flight to California, abandoning their investment in the house in the middle of renovation and leaving the mortgage company to recoup its losses when it repossessed the property. The problem is that $115,000 is owed on the house and, in its current, nearly gutted state, it's only worth a little over $72,000.

"It's just a mess," comments a nearby neighbor. "I talked to one couple who were thinking of buying it, and they figured it would take another $30,000 to make it livable. None of the real estate companies will even bother to list it anymore."

"It's not uncommon that a homeowner gets in over his head, runs out of money, and ends up with a gutted house," explains Barry Lebow, a professional renovator for many years and an editorial advisor to the trade publication *Real Estate Professional*. "The courts are full of cases where people have just walked away from their homes because they could not handle the financial burdens and could not raise the money needed to complete the work."

Such cases are frequent enough to show there are lessons to be learned—lessons that can help the homeowner avoid serious pitfalls and ensure that a planned renovation will be a wise investment and a financial practicality.

For major renovation projects, the first hurdle is usually finding the financing. The ideal way to finance large-scale home improvements is with a mortgage. You can pay back a mortgage over a much longer period of time than you pay back a home improvement loan; hence, the monthly payments are less. With low monthly payments, you may be able to borrow more money up front, fit all of the major renovations into your budget, and get them all done at one time—saving time, money, and inconvenience.

But, unless you've built up some equity in your house, you'll find it difficult in most states to refinance a mortgage along traditional lines based solely upon planned improvements. Where remodeling involves partly or fully gutting a house, the value of the property actually goes down during the construction period. While renovations may increase the value of the house once they're completed, you would be hard pressed to sell the home in the middle of the project without a discount. For this reason, most mortgage lenders regard the business of financing renovations as far more risky than new-home construction.

If you have built up enough equity in your home, a second mortgage based on this can usually be arranged to cover renovations. But if you plan major structural changes, even this may be hard to arrange in some areas.

Many professional renovators (people who buy houses to refurbish and then sell them) will often see their lawyer as a first step in looking for money. The private homeowner can do the same. Frequently a lawyer can put you in touch with a mortgage broker or mortgage banker able to arrange for a private mortgage to cover renovations. Failing this, you can directly approach a few registered mortgage brokers or mortgage bankers and ask for the deal you would like. It never hurts to ask.

Newspaper classifieds often advertise mortgages. Approach these with some caution. And never deal with any of these advertisers without getting a lawyer to represent your interests.

The most frequent avenue of credit for renovations by new homeowners is the home-improvement loan from a bank, finance company, or co-op. This type of loan is based on your established credit rating or other collateral rather than on the value of the proposed home improvements.

In going the traditional route—visiting your regular bank and seeing either your bank manager or loan officer—it is important to realize that the type of loan they are willing to give you is not necessarily the only deal in town. Attitudes toward renovation financing vary greatly from region to region, and even from branch to branch of the same bank. Shopping around, even by telephone, is well worth your time.

When banks are cautious or negative about providing a mortgage for renovations, they will sometimes suggest that the homeowner take out a short "bridging" loan. The idea is that you borrow against your personal credit to finance the work. Then, once renovations have been completed, you remortgage the house based on its increased value and use the extra money to pay off the loan. This is all very nice in theory, but the bug in this tactic is that the renovations you plan may not significantly increase the "appraised value" of your home. And it is the appraiser who determines what your home is worth for mortgage purposes.

Home appraisal involves many factors. But the bottom line is that your house is worth only what people are generally willing to pay for it. The most important things that determine this are location and neighborhood. If you have a $90,000 home surrounded by $90,000 homes, chances are that you will not increase its value to $110,000 by spending an additional $20,000 or even $30,000.

It is equally important to realize that poorly planned renovations can actually lower your home's value. Knocking out a wall to enlarge a bedroom, and turning a three-bedroom house into a two-bedroom house in the process, will almost always lower the selling price. People tend to think that two bedrooms, no matter what their size, should be cheaper than three.

Personal taste, that unfathomable aesthetic, can also count against you when it comes to getting a new enhanced appraisal. Changes that make a striking difference in the architectural character of your home can be devastating to resale value when, in the eyes of most beholders, they don't "fit into" the neighborhood.

On the other hand, visible improvements that enhance the comfort and convenience a home provides tend to add the most value. For example, improvements such as remodeling a kitchen or bathroom, adding an energy-efficient fireplace, building a deck, or building an extra room to augment the living area of a house will usually have the most impact on overall value.

So, before you take out a bridging loan, it's smart to go over any major renovation plans with either a professional appraiser or a veteran real estate agent familiar with your neighborhood. For $200, they'll be able to give you some idea of whether your planned improvements might be mortgaged, or whether they're strictly home-improvement loan material.

A house is the biggest investment most people ever make. Treating it as such when renovating just makes good sense.—**Ron Harris**

IMPROVING TO SELL
Value-Added Remodeling

Most homeowners think that preparing a home for sale means putting up a "For Sale" sign and contacting a real estate agent. But it takes more than that. If you want to sell your home as quickly as possible, and at the best possible price, you'll have to "dress your house for success," both inside and out.

Begin by taking a tour of your property, looking at it critically through the eyes of a prospective buyer. Make a list of repairs that need to be made. Also, look for opportunities to improve the *intangible* qualities of your house, such as its warmth and spaciousness.

If your home is in fairly good shape to begin with, making it look its best need not be costly or time-consuming. Here's a list of easy fix-up ideas that will cost you little and help you a lot when it's time to negotiate with a buyer.

Lawn and Garden

- Remove dead or ailing bushes; prune and water the rest to give them all a healthy look.

- Remove garden tools, hoses, toys, bicycles, garbage cans, pet excrement, and debris from the yard.

- Mow and rake your lawn regularly to give it a trim look.

- Remove distracting lawn objects, such as religious figurines, animal statues, and plastic flowers. (But leave the lawn chairs, picnic table, and grill—they'll help prospective buyers to imagine themselves relaxing and entertaining on your property.)

Siding

- Hose down dirty siding.

- Make sure that all painted surfaces are free of mold and mildew. Pay special attention to the southern exposure, under the eaves, and areas behind shrubs, which tend to weather and discolor faster than other areas.

- Repaint worn or peeling paint. Use light, neutral colors; they are the least likely to cause offense. If your house is small, painting it all a single color will make it look larger.

- Make sure your house number is clearly visible.

Windows

- Clean windows until they sparkle.

- Check that awnings and shutters are properly hung and that they have no holes, rips, or missing parts.

- Repair cracked panes and torn screens.

- For a neat appearance, keep window sashes, storms, and screens at the same position (preferably closed) especially in the front of the house.

- Window treatments should appear uniform from the exterior. The backs of shades or the linings of drapes look best when they are all the same color, such as white or off-white.

- In the evening, turn on at least one light in each front room.

- Brightly colored lamps, huge ornate statues, multicolored plastic flower arrangements, and bowling trophies are all distractions that may prevent prospective buyers from seeing your home as a whole. Remove them.

Interior Walls

- Paint walls and moldings a neutral color, such as white or beige. If you choose to use wallpaper, pick a solid color. Paper featuring mini-prints or small geometric patterns is your next-best bet.

- Tie adjacent rooms together visually by employing color-coordinated accessories.

- Remove all political and religious pictures, posters, and emblems from your walls.

- Clean surfaces of fingerprints and dirt, especially around front doorways and entranceways—daily.

Fireplaces

- Clean ashes from your fireplace when it is not in use.

- Check fireplace screens for holes and glass panes for cracks.

- During the cold winter months, set a crackling fire ablaze in your fireplace: Buyers will respond positively to the glow, the smell, and the sounds of the fire. Brighten up a non-working fireplace with decorative fans of paper or brass.

Bathrooms

- Inspect tiled walls for missing pieces and loose grout.

- Update your wall hardware.

- If your old shower curtain is moldy, buy a new one.

- Check caulking around the tubs and sinks to be sure it's tight.

- Repair dripping faucets.

- Check for proper flushing of toilets, and make sure handles and seats are securely fastened. Keep toilet seats closed on open-house days.

- Display at least one new fluffy bath towel, fingertip towel, and washcloth in white or beige.

Kitchen

- Ventilate the kitchen to get rid of any cooking odors.

- Unclutter your kitchen by storing small appliances such as blenders, food processors, electric mixers, and coffee grinders in a cabinet. (It's fine to leave the basics out, such as a toaster, coffee pot, and can opener.)

- Clean all appliances—especially the oven.

—**Valli Swerdlow**

RENOVATION VS. RESTORATION
When Is the Past Worth Preserving?

The terms "renovation" and "restoration" may sound alike, but in fact they stand for two different approaches to refurbishing homes. Renovation is the renewal of the interior or exterior of a building without regard to historical authenticity. Renovators commonly use modern building methods and such materials as aluminum siding, aluminum chimneys, and plastic skylights. Restoration, on the other hand, is an attempt to return a structure to its original appearance. Though restorers often use modern tools, they attempt to use authentic materials and original craftsmanship whenever possible.

Renovation is usually the cheapest and easiest way to fix up a building, but it does have drawbacks. Removing such architectural treasures as dormers, stained glass windows, and gables can reduce the value of a home. On the other hand, restoration usually increases a house's market value by preserving (or reintroducing) the building's original details. It enhances the community, too, by preserving the historical fabric of the neighborhood.

What sort of house is a good candidate for restoration? Many people assume that any old house can—and perhaps should—be restored, as long as the house is truly old (that is, built a century or more ago). But such an assumption is misleading; in fact, not every old house can be restored, and some "modern" houses actually may be good candidates for restoration.

A house that has historical significance is a prime candidate for restoration. But what, exactly, is "historical significance"? A house that is representative of an important architectural style or development is clearly worthy of preservation. Many homes built in the 18th and 19th centuries fall into this category; but so do many later homes—for example, homes that represent the "art deco" style of

Photo 1-10. Restoring the grandeur of this Victorian house in all its original detail significantly increased the home's fair market value. (Photo by J. Michael Kanouff)

the 1920s. Even homes built in the 1950s may be worthy of restoring if they represent an important aesthetic style of that decade.

A building that is located in a neighborhood that played an important part in the history of a community or city may be significant, too, even if the neighborhood isn't especially remarkable for its architecture. A house that once sheltered a famous person is probably worth restoring, as well. To find out whether your house has unusual architectural features or played an important part in community history, check with your local historical society, or consult a local architect.

If you don't already own a house and are shopping around for one to restore, these same guidelines apply, but with two additional cautions: First, make sure the house is structurally sound. Second, avoid houses that are victims of well-meant but truly tasteless "remuddling." Otherwise, you could spend thousands of extra dollars getting the house to a point where you can seriously begin a restoration.

Once you conclude that your house is worthy of restoration, the next step is to come up with a feasible plan. During the planning stage, it is important to keep in mind that your object is to restore the house as nearly as possible to its original appearance; don't go overboard in giving the house features it never had (don't, for example, put frilly Victorian woodwork on a simple building).

It's a good idea to consult a good restoration specialist, even if you plan to do the work yourself. Only an experienced eye can tell you, for example, whether the bricks are so soft or discolored that they should be protected with paint, or whether they are just soiled and need to be cleaned—or whether they aren't dirty at all, but merely have acquired patina (a picturesque surface quality that develops with age).

A professional restorer can also help you avoid costly mistakes. Not long ago, for example, sandblasting equipment became a familiar sight in some neighborhoods. The dangers of sandblasting are only now being publicized. "A brick is like a baked potato," explains John Bridges, a restoration specialist based in Toronto. "If you put it in the oven at 350°F for 45 minutes, it will be hard on the outside and soft on the inside. If you remove the hard skin, the soft inside is subject to deterioration. A brick is the same." Sandblasting can *decrease* the value of your brick home by $10,000 or more, he adds. (The best way to clean bricks is with a water or chemical wash, a time-consuming process that you may prefer to contract out.)

Using the wrong kind of paint on a masonry home is another trap that inexperienced homeowners should try to avoid. Oil-based paints, for example, seal moisture inside walls. Moisture freezes during cold weather, then thaws during warm periods. The "freeze-thaw-freeze" cycle causes erosion of the brickwork. A paint that "breathes" is a better choice.

Another common mistake is removing the original windows of a house, or covering them with plastic glazing on the outside in the name of energy conservation. (Plastic on the outside of windows can damage leaded stained glass.) It's possible to upgrade old windows without changing their character. Interior storm windows will do the trick without ruining the appearance of your house.

Look at other examples of restoration in your area and ask the owners about their projects and the professionals they hired. With a proper sense of history and some expert help behind you, you'll discover the pleasures of living in an older house with features and craftsmanship that are seldom, if ever, produced in houses built today.—**Jane Widerman**

CHAPTER 2

DESIGN IDEAS AND RESOURCE OPTIONS

The decade of the 1980s might well be known as the decade of home remodelers. It's not that no new homes are being constructed or that the dream of owning a new home has lost its allure. The continuing power of that dream is evidenced by the flurry of housing starts that occurs every time mortgage interest rates experience a small decline. Still, the rapid inflation in the cost of real estate and steady rise in interest rates that have occurred over the past 10 to 15 years have lead many Americans to see the economic advantage to improving their existing homes instead of moving to new ones.

But Americans in the mid-1980s are not interested solely, or even primarily, in cutting costs and saving money on their homes. What they are looking for is quality as well as economy, efficiency as well as affordability. Thus, in unprecedented numbers, homeowners are choosing to commit their resources to upgrading their existing homes, often doing much of the work themselves. Manufacturers have responded to this trend with a wealth of new products, many of which are marketed with the do-it-yourself home remodeler in mind.

There is certainly no shortage of attractive, high-quality products available to today's home remodeler. Many resourceful remodelers have also discovered the charm of using materials salvaged from older, demolished structures. In this chapter you will learn where to look for such materials. We will also present you with many smart design ideas and examples of successful remodels from which you can draw inspiration for making your own remodeling plans.—**the editors**

Photo by Carl Doney

FRESH APPROACHES
How to Create a Grand Entrance

Curb appeal. Does your house have it? The answer probably has a lot to do with the area around your front door. A pleasant front porch, a well-landscaped walk, good lighting that makes nighttime coming and going safe and appealing—such amenities make visitors feel welcome.

A well-appointed entrance should have some sort of overhang to keep visitors dry (if only temporarily) and to prevent rain or snow from dripping on the stoop and steps and creating a hazard. The overhang should be at least as wide as the stoop it's protecting. You might choose to build an overhang that contributes something architectural to your home, or you could go with something as simple as an inverted V of metal or plastic embedded in roofing material. A gutter should be incorporated into the design to help carry away rain and melting snow.

It would be nice if your entrance also offered protection against the wind, although this is trickier to achieve. A vertical screen of wood louvers, metal, or glass built on the windward side of the entrance may block the breeze, but could also create an eddy that makes doors slam. In northern climates, the screen may act as a snow fence, encouraging snow to drift across the stoop. Before you install a permanent screen, erect a temporary one (a cheap, plywood mock-up will do), and observe what effects it has.

A storm door can reduce heat loss from your entrance area, but will probably be an aesthetic compromise. If you do install a storm door, it should open against the prevailing wind and, if possible, should be hinged on the same jamb as the main door.

A slippery stoop or step can cause accidents; make sure these surfaces are properly sloped (⅛ inch per foot is adequate). Walks of concrete or mortared masonry must also slope slightly to one side for drainage. To ensure firm footing for walks of loose bricks, flagstones, fine gravel, or tanbark, dig 4 to 6 inches below the surface, leaving a mound of earth in the center ½ to 1 inch high.

Fill the space on either side of this center ridge with sand. Set the bricks or stones in, then fill around them up to ground level with gravel or tanbark. The slope of the base and the sand fill allows water to drain and helps keep surfaces dry.

It's also important to make sure the surfaces of stoops and steps offer good traction. Rough-finish concrete or stained wood are two materials that provide enough surface texture to make walking safe. If you want a painted finish, use a deck paint mixed with clean sand; brushing the mixture on will be hard work, but the sandy surface will be nonskid and surprisingly easy to wash clean. If your steps are made of bricks or stone, make sure the mortared joints are filled level so that rain won't puddle.

Photo 2-1. This entryway is well lit, has a slip-free surface in front of it, and a place for visitors to sit while waiting. (Photo by Mitch Mandel)

Any flight of steps with more than two risers should have a handrail on at least one side. There should be a baluster for each step and the stoop. A wood rail looks good with wood steps, but a narrower wrought-iron rail is easier to grip and secure.

All too often, lighting at entrances defeats its purpose. Over-bright bulbs can blind visitors while leaving steps in dark shadow.

To illuminate steps safely, light should be directed from one or both sides at a low angle, thrown mostly on the step treads, but some also hitting the vertical risers. Good lighting is especially important when you're walking down the steps; the edge of each tread should be clearly outlined against the tread of the step below.

Photo 2-2. This inviting entryway is sheltered from the weather and thoughtfully equipped with handrails for safe movement up and down the steps. (Photo by Carl Doney)

If you have only a short flight of steps, you can achieve the same effect by placing lights beside the middle step.

Ideally, lights along an entry walk should also be low—no more than 2 feet above grade—with caps to shield light from the eyes of walkers. One light every 15 to 20 feet is adequate.

For your own safety, you'll want some light to fall on the faces of visitors. A pair of lights flanking the entrance should suffice.

Photo 2-3. This entryway features a custom-made door along with overhead and ground-level lighting. (Photo by Carl Doney)

Shields on these fixtures can help direct rays downward onto the stoop and perhaps upward and to the sides for attractive effect but will keep light from shining directly into the eyes of visitors. A round peephole, installed at eye level in the front door, will enable you to see who's there before you unlock the door. Translucent glass—fluted or otherwise distorted—installed in the door or sidelights will admit light but blur any view into the house.

If your main entrance is located on the street side of your house, you might consider screening the entrance from view with a wall, fence, or landscaping. If properly planned, the screened- or fenced-off area can create an enclosed courtyard, making attractive use of what is typically wasted space.

A fence or wall can be made from a variety of materials, depending on your needs and budget and the style of your home. A solid wall gives the most privacy but slows air circulation. Decorative openings let more air through but reduce privacy. Any wall must rest on a footing, which adds to the cost.

Less expensive is a wood fence employing vertical panels. Sink treated 4 × 4 posts 18 inches into the ground, spacing them 6 to 8 feet apart. Attach treated 2 × 2s across the posts—one 6 inches off the ground, another 6 inches below the top, and one midway between. Attach 1 × 6s vertically that extend 2 inches above and below the 2 × 2 frame, spacing them 2 inches apart. On the back side, center another set of 1 × 6s on the openings. This type of fence provides complete privacy yet lets breezes through.

A hedge forms the best living screen, although it may not do so for several years. Choose a type compatible with your climate. Dense, easily shaped hedges, such as boxwood, are best. Before you erect either a wall or a fence, or plant a tall hedge, check local building codes. Many have restrictions on heights and locations.

As a final touch, you might want to consider some sort of landscaping to delineate your walkway. Shrubbery requires the most care, because you must constantly trim it to the right height and thickness. A flower bed is better, adding color much of the year; but a flower bed also needs care and can be a mud collector. Lawn extended right to the walk has the fewest drawbacks and requires the least care.—**Mortimer P. Reed**

THE LURE OF THE OLD
Finding, Buying, and Using Architectural Salvage

Ron and Alice Mason run a kind of home for aged and orphaned pieces of buildings. The handsome stained glass window in the couple's den, for example, came from a 100-year-old Baptist Church, torn down in the 1950s. Their wrought-iron spiral staircase is from a demolished apartment building. The tile-and-walnut fireplace in their bedroom once graced a Civil War-era mansion. And the slate on their dining room floor was originally the roof of another old church.

The couple takes great pleasure in their salvaged treasures, if for slightly different reasons. Alice feels "they give the house more character." Her husband likes the solid workmanship of bygone days. "Old structures were built to last," he says, "so this salvage is sturdy and well made." And he's pleased that most of the pieces were so inexpensive (the spiral stairs cost $35; the fireplace, $100).

The Masons, who live in Des Moines, Iowa, began collecting salvaged pieces in the 1950s. They were pioneers of what has grown into a full-scale trend. Hundreds of thousands of Americans are now scouring the countryside in search of lost craftsmanship, the elegant look of old paneling, the rough texture of hand-carved stonework, or the delicacy of finely worked gingerbread.

While enhancing their homes, these people are also helping to preserve little pieces of history that would otherwise be lost to the

Photo 2-4. Ron and Alice Mason bought these massive oak doors more than 20 years ago for $3.50 each, including hardware! (Photo by Sid Spelts)

wrecking ball. "You're saving works of art, objects with some heart and soul in them," says William Wagner, a restoration architect and the salvager who helped the Masons design their home. "It's also smart, because you're recycling quality."

Although many people began their salvage collections by prowling through buildings slated for demolition, it's no longer necessary to wield the sledgehammer yourself. The demand for antique building elements has spawned a whole new kind of business: the architectural salvage depot. So far, salvage emporiums have popped up in about 50 American cities.

Visitors to these showrooms find a chaotic assortment of materials and fixtures—doors stacked in rows, gargoyles grinning from crowded corners, stained glass by the square yard, and a myriad of moldings, lamp posts, plumbing fixtures, heat grates, odd bits of hardware, and cornices—none of it arranged in any particular order. Treasures abound for those patient enough to sift through the dust and clutter.

Some dealers even have more specialized and unusual items like church pews, choir lofts, bank cages, carousel horses, entire bars from old saloons, art deco elevators, and barbershop poles. Others limit their wares to more functional materials, like floorboards and ceiling beams. A few even stock entire rooms, all but intact. For example, United House Wrecking in Stamford, Connecticut—one of the largest and oldest emporiums in the country—recently had a 1930s barbershop in stock, complete with cabinets, mirrors, and barber pole. Architectural Antiques in Oklahoma City once offered an entire English walnut-paneled library. (The asking price: $27,500.)

What you probably won't find in one of these specialty stores is a bargain. Sure, there's the occasional buried treasure, but demand has sent prices soaring. A panel of stained glass that 15 years ago sold for $5 will bring $175 or more today.

If you're looking for that underpriced diamond-in-the-rough or a very special item, there are other salvage sources to consider:

Wrecking Companies: Many demolition firms maintain salvage yards where they stockpile reusable materials. Such yards are a virtual Salvation Army of architectural hand-me-downs, with heaps of battered bricks, stacks of nondescript windows, and grim-looking bathroom fixtures scattered here and there. Prices tend to be low because these companies don't bother with display, and they rarely refinish materials. To find a demolition salvage yard in your area, check the yellow pages under "Demolition Contractors" and "Salvage." It's best to call before you visit.

City Salvage Yards: Some cities, such as Baltimore and New York, have established nonprofit salvage warehouses for the benefit of residents who are restoring older homes. Most require proof of residence before admitting shoppers, but some open their doors to

Photo 2-5. Among the most sought-after types of architectural salvage are windows and doors made of stained or etched glass. (Photo by John Hamel)

anyone for special sales once or twice a year. Check the yellow pages under "City Government" to see if there's a city-run salvage depot in your area.

Specialty Stores: If you're looking for a specific item, check out salvage stores that specialize in a single architectural style or material. Period Pine in Atlanta, for example, stocks only Southern yellow-heart pine floorboards, paneling, and millwork. Such specialists carry large inventories and usually have many contacts. Specialists often work by mail, and will send Polaroid photos of items they have in stock. To find a salvage specialist, talk to antique dealers in your area, check with your local landmarks preservation organization, or consult the *Old House Journal Catalog*, an annual buyer's guide published by the editors of the *Old House Journal*.

If you've looked in vain for a specific item, try placing a classified ad in your local paper describing what you need. Also, put the word out along the salvage grapevine by talking to wrecking contractors, restoration architects, and collectors.

That's how architect Wagner found his unusual fireplace mantel, which was originally a pediment over the window of a courtroom built in the 1870s. Word of mouth is also how he came across most of the marble that covers the floors in his hallway and baths, along with a pressed-tin ceiling from an old livery stable.

The key to successful scavenging, Wagner says, is flexibility. "Most of my architecturals were serendipitous finds—things I just couldn't pass up," he notes. "I'd haul them home one by one, where they'd sit around for a few months until I could find an ingenious use for them. That's the fun for me."

To help you through the maze of products and prices, we will focus the remainder of our discussion on the most sought-after salvageables.

Staircases offer a rich assortment of architectural elements. Only in rare instances is the entire stairway taken apart and reassembled. More often, dealers salvage the railing, balusters, and newel posts. Staircase elements can be used in a restoration, or you can take them out of context—assembling them as the backboard for a bed, or as legs for a table.

Mantels are the most ornate, and the most popular, of all salvaged architecturals. They're easy to remove, and just as easy to install in a new location. Some people who don't even have working chimneys use recycled fireplaces as decorative pieces.

Demand is always high for *stained and beveled glass*. Prices, too, are high. Small, simple windows from Victorian homes cost at least $100 today. More elaborate versions start at about $200.

Cast iron pieces have developed an enthusiastic following in recent years. Grates, gates, and fences can be used for their intended purposes. They also lend themselves to imaginative reuse as coffee tables, magazine racks, or simply as decorations that evoke the past.

Keystones, fence-top "pineapples," gargoyles, griffins, and other *carved stone* sculptures look great mounted on living room walls or just leaned in a corner. In today's market, prices begin at about $250 for a simple keystone.

Most large salvage outlets have a wide selection of *hardware and lighting*. For the price, you can't beat the quality of old brass hinges and doorknobs. You may be able to buy originals for less than the cost of reproductions. Old gas/electric lighting fixtures are a lucky find. They were manufactured briefly at the turn of the century, when electricity was still a new phenomenon, but can easily be adapted to today's wiring.

Old *plumbing fixtures* are often of higher quality than new ones. Claw-foot tubs, pull-chain toilets, and pedestal sinks are making a comeback, yet can still be found at reasonable prices.

Boards and lumber from houses built before World War II came from old-growth timber stands and were dried in lumberyards for as long as two or three years before being sold. If you can find salvaged lumber, it may be cheaper, less prone to warping, and more attractive than new wood.

Finding good salvage takes time, an inquisitive spirit, and maybe a little chutzpah. First, drive around looking for buildings that are abandoned, burned, or boarded up; then check the city or county tax records to identify the owner. Or ask the contractor in charge of demolition whether materials can be removed before the wrecking crew arrives. Some contractors discourage scavenging for insurance reasons. Others do their own salvaging. A few will let you help yourself, provided that you supply the transportation to haul away your finds.

Salvaging can be hard and dirty work, but it's rewarding. Remove items carefully and inspect them thoroughly before reuse.

Photo 2-6. Bricks removed from a pre-Civil War fort in Iowa, set in herringbone pattern, add character to Ron and Alice Mason's kitchen floor. (Photo by Sid Spelts)

Check anything made of wood for termites, carpenter ants, or powder post beetles. If interior wood has been exposed to weather, look for signs of rot.

Old bricks are often easily salvageable, and some have interesting histories. The brick the Masons used on their kitchen floor came from the officer's quarters of a pioneer fort and cost them next to nothing.

But before reusing old bricks, you'll need to determine their hardness. Those made before 1900 are often softer and more porous than those used today. Immerse one of the salvaged bricks in a bucket of water. If it bubbles, it's too porous for patios, landscaping, or in any structure that comes in contact with the earth (the pressures of freezing and thawing will cause the bricks to disintegrate).

The market for architectural salvage in 1987 is bigger than ever. Not only are more people interested in restoration and preservation, but salvaged pieces are finding their way into plenty of new buildings.

With such a demand for old building parts, and with fewer old buildings being torn down today, is it possible that the best sources of salvage will dry up? Not any time soon: Experts estimate that less than 60 percent of the available material is currently being saved from destruction.

And though demand is increasing, it's subject to the vicissitudes of taste and trends. "Uses for architecturals are changing all the time," says Reynold Lowe, owner of Materials Unlimited in Ypsilanti, Michigan. "A few years ago, Victorian items were all the rage. As they got scarce, art deco became the 'in' thing to have. American ingenuity is a marvelous thing. It's always creating a demand for something."—**Linda M. Hunter**

THE YOU-FINISH OPTION
Lower New-Home Costs through "Sweat Equity"

One smart way to beat the high cost of new home construction is the you-finish option: Have a contractor build the basic structure of your house and rough in the plumbing and electricity, then do some or all of the finishing yourself. Your labor—your "sweat equity"—can cut the cost of a new home (or major remodeling project), resulting in lower mortgage payments and, later on, a higher profit if you sell.

Along with the savings, taking the you-finish route puts you more in control of the way your new house will be painted, trimmed, and otherwise appointed. You can tailor the finishing touches to suit your personal tastes, needs, and whims. You can also translate your savings into "more house"; you might be able to install components of better quality and equipped with features, like that spa or sauna you didn't think you could afford.

According to Pennsylvania architect Mic Curd, who has supervised the construction of several owner-finished homes, you save not only on the cost of professional labor but also on the contractor's add-ons for overhead costs, profit margins, and markups for materials.

Successful owner-finishing starts with early planning and a realistic assessment of your abilities and your availability. With your architect or contractor, you can work out design features and budget strategies that maximize savings and minimize the potential for problems.

You should also devise an appropriate building schedule that doesn't make the tasks of professional crews dependent on your progress. Interruptions in their work can undo your you-finish savings. "What we like to do," says Curd, "is to have our crews take a house through a certain stage of construction, then turn it all over to the owner-finisher."

Owner-finishing also affects financing. In most cases, a construction loan for a new house is allocated as a series of payments upon completion of specified tasks. Your chances of getting a construction loan are greater if you plan your sweat-equity work late in the overall construction schedule, after the bulk of the house has been completed by professionals.

In order to get a handle on just what kinds of savings are possible, we looked at a house on which Curd's architectural firm did a complete construction bid. We created a list of specific tasks that would typically be part of a you-finish plan, tasks that come after the basic shell is completed, and compared the you-finish costs for each with the contracted cost. Table 2-1 shows the results of our comparison. For this example, we considered the basic house shell to include all structural elements, exterior sheathing and siding, roofing, rough wiring and plumbing, and a central heating system. (The shell of the 2,000-square-foot house taken as our example cost about $85,000.)

The figures in this table reflect actual contracted costs for an existing single-family, passive-solar heated home with a finished square-footage of 2,048 square feet (3,168 square feet including unfinished basement and garage) built in eastern Pennsylvania and completed in 1985. The you-finish costs reflect prices for materials alone. The difference between the two accounts for contractor's *labor*, *premium*, *overhead*, and *profit*. The cost per finished square foot of the house, which was built entirely by contract labor, was $57.50 per square foot. Were it to have been owner/finished, the cost per finished square foot would have been $47.39.

As you can see from this example, if you did all the finishing work on your home, you'd certainly reap the greatest savings. But instead of jumping in all the way, you should strike a balance between saving yourself money and saving yourself headaches. Use the skill-level column in the table to assess your own ability to do the various tasks.

Table 2-1—YOU FINISH, YOU SAVE

Job	Skill Level	Contracted Cost	You-Finish Cost
Insulation (fiberglass)	1	$2,150	$1,035
Drywall	1	4,300	1,425
Drywall finishing	2	575	
Baseboard and trim	2-3	1,303	690
Interior doors (prehung)	2 (prehung)	1,945	1,220
Interior wall finish	1 (painting) 2 (papering)	2,139	600
Cabinetry	2 (prefab) 3 (custom work)	7,865	5,900
Shelving	1	617	200
Appliances	1-2	1,223	900
Plumbing fixtures	1-2	4,011	1,921
Plumbing extras (spa)	3 (some warranties void unless appliance installed by authorized service)	3,872	3,200
Water heater	2	518	350
Bath accessories	1	443	250
Finish flooring: oak tongue-and-groove	2 (3 for sanding/ finishing)	3,481	2,083*
vinyl sheet or tile, ceramic and masonry tile	2	634	525
carpet	3	1,694	1,320
Electrical fixtures	3	4,242	2,720
Gutters and downspouts	2	615	275
Totals		$41,627	$24,614

Note: Skill levels: 1 = no prior experience necessary; read up on the topic and practice; 2 = thorough understanding of job and general ability with tools required; some experience helpful; 3 = previous and extensive experience necessary.
*Add $700 if you subcontract floor finishing

A strong point in favor of having work done for you is that good contractors are reliable: They'll do the job and do it right, usually with some sort of guarantee. Consider the effects of having your self-assigned tasks go undone for too long, or the inconvenience of living in an unfinished house. (You should also check residential occupancy requirements in your area. In some places, you may not legally move into your house until it is "completed" in the eyes of the law.) You can use our table to compare you-finish costs and skill levels with typical contractor prices. But first, read more about what's involved with each task.

Insulation: In most cases, installing insulation is a simple job that even a not-too-skilled homeowner could handle. You must be meticulous in filling gaps and sealing vapor barriers, but the actual techniques aren't difficult. Special insulation methods, such as sprayed foam, should be left to professionals.

Drywall: Hanging drywall is not something for the uninitiated, although the hanging can be done without much prior experience if you've studied how-to literature and obtained some professional advice. A good strategy to consider is hanging the drywall on your own (you'll definitely need the help of an extra person or two) and then hiring professionals to do the finishing with tape and joint compound.

Baseboard and Trim: Trim work is traditionally done by skilled finish carpenters; you should bring a fair amount of experience into this job. But you can take your time with trim; it's one of the last finishing chores, coming after even wall painting or papering. Practice cutting and fitting with scraps, and bring all your patience with you on trim day.

Photo 2-7. John Mehltretter, an electrical engineer, got more house for his money by doing much of the finish work himself. (Photo by Mitch Mandel)

Interior Doors: Prehung doors are usually simple to install, but nonetheless require precision in lining everything up. (Instructions for installing a prehung door can be found in chapter 4.) Fitting and hanging doors into your own jambs is somewhat more difficult. You must know how to use a level and be proficient in finish nailing.

Interior Wall Finish: Painting interior walls is the most common finishing step performed by homeowners. With care, anyone can do a creditable painting job. There is plenty of how-to literature on the basic techniques, which require just a little practice.

Wallpapering, however, is another matter. If you've never done it before, try it—perhaps by signing up for a wallpapering class—before attempting it for real.

Cabinetry: Finish cabinetry work includes installation of kitchen cabinets, bathroom vanities, countertops, and any other built-ins. Naturally, the difficulty of the work depends on the scope of the project, but seasoned do-it-yourselfers without prior cabinetry experience can install prefabricated cabinets, vanities, and countertops.

Shelving: Shelving includes fitting out utility rooms and pantries, as well as installing shelves and hanging rods in clothes and linen closets. The techniques are not difficult, and even if the job doesn't come out quite right, it's more or less invisible, an excellent project for beginners.

Appliances: Installing your own dishwasher, clothes washer, and dryer will save money if the cost of installation isn't already included in the appliance's purchase price. If the rough plumbing and electrical connections have been done properly by your shell builder, installation shouldn't be complicated, and most appliances come supplied with the necessary instructions. Of course, these appliances are big, heavy, and can be hard to move around.

Plumbing Fixtures: It's not as difficult as you might think to install your own toilets, basins, bathtubs, showers, and sinks. You should do it if you consider yourself skilled with tools and have some plumbing experience. Read about each process first; you'll probably need help putting the heavy, awkward items in place.

Plumbing Extras: Spas, whirlpools, hot tubs, and the like are far more complicated to install than basic fixtures. Unless you have considerable experience with plumbing, electrical, and carpentry work, it's best to leave this job to pros.

Water Heater: You can read up on how to make all the right connections for a gas or electric water heater. Installing a gas unit is more complicated than installing an electric unit because of gas line and fuel connections.

Bath Accessories: All bath accessories—shower doors, mirrors, towel racks, paper holders, toothbrush receptacles, and other simple fixtures—are easy to install, even for the inexperienced.

Finish Flooring: Many owner-finishers elect to do finish flooring, and the savings can be quite rewarding. The job is not for novices, however.

The easiest floors to lay are plastic tile and staple-down roll flooring. Laying masonry or ceramic tile that you have to glue to the subfloor is more difficult; grouting between the tiles is especially tricky. With hardwood floors, a smart way to proceed is to lay the strips yourself and have the sanding and finishing done by professionals. Wall-to-wall carpet should be installed by pros, since there's little room for error, and mistakes can be disastrous.

Electrical Fixtures: Serious do-it-yourselfers may elect to install their own ceiling lights, receptacles, wall switches, and electric baseboard heaters. The work isn't technically difficult, but you should be thoroughly knowledgeable and practiced in this kind of electrical work to preclude possible dangerous errors. Some local codes don't allow an unlicensed person to do the work; others may not even require an inspection.

Gutters and Downspouts: A job ready-made for do-it-yourselfers with intermediate skills is installation of gutters and downspouts. Of course, you have to be ready to work in high places, and it's definitely a two-person job.

Table 2-1 shows that for the house in question, you could save about $16,000 if you handled all the finishing jobs yourself. The cost of the totally contractor-built version ($126,000) would be reduced by about 13 percent (although in talking with architect Curd and other owner-finishers we heard reports of savings as high as 20 percent).

Try to observe as much of the shell construction as you can. Since you're taking over where professional crews leave off, it's important to know what they've been up to. If the people working on the shell know that you'll be doing some finish work, they might pave the way to make it easier, by numbering rough wiring, for example, or by labeling frame members that may be irregularly spaced. Watch out for the opposite reaction: A builder's attention to detail may lapse when the blueprints say "to be finished by owner."

Finally, get involved only in work that will lead to significant savings. Don't nickel-and-dime the operation by signing on for tasks such as cleanup work or merely assisting with general labor. Remember, you are finishing your house, not building it.—**John Warde**

ROOMS THAT WORK
Great Ways to Spice Up Dreary Spaces

You may love your house dearly, but no doubt there are things you'd change if you could. Take that room that's too dark, for example. Wouldn't it be wonderful if there were some way you could lighten it up? And that room that's too wide—is there some way to better manage that space without spending a fortune?

Basically, there are three ways to deal with less-than-perfect space: Try to camouflage faults through the use of fabric, color, and strategic decorating; create a more efficient space-within-a-space by installing new partitions or partially altering existing ones; or tear down and rebuild the interior from scratch. This last option is the most expensive; if you can, it's smart to avoid making any large structural changes.

Often, making just one major change—installing a skylight, for instance, or creating an archway between two rooms—can make a room feel like a whole new place. The key is to come up with an approach that responds to the prime needs of the individuals who will be using the room.

Too-small rooms are a common problem today, especially since more and more of today's houses are smaller. But living in a giant Victorian isn't necessarily the answer; while older houses have plenty of space in theory, much of it is often chopped up into boxy, small rooms suited for the social customs and structures of another age. And in any house, bad proportions, lack of light, low ceilings, and inconveniently placed windows and doors can make even a good-sized room feel tiny.

Choosing the right furniture is one solution. Space-saving furniture, built-ins, and wall units all have their place in a small-scale design. You can often make a room seem larger simply by rearranging your furniture.

But furniture placement is only the beginning. To make a small room seem larger, try these tricks:

- Extend the flooring from an adjacent room into your too-small room to make it look larger. Stick to a plain style: Patterned flooring can make a small room look too busy.

- Paint the small room's ceiling a lighter color than its walls. This technique will make the ceiling appear to recede.

- Keep detailing simple. Don't overload a small room with ornate moldings or heavy hardware. Clean, simple lines are your best bet.

Photo 2-8. In this kitchen, decorative quarter-rounds atop a standard over-the-sink window help direct the eye outdoors. (Photo by J. Michael Kanouff. Designer: Sid Del Mar Leach, AIA)

- Go with a neutral or pastel color scheme. The lighter the colors, the larger the space will look. Strong colors appear to come toward you, paler ones to recede.

- When wallpapering, look for smaller-figured patterns. A dark figure on a light background gives the viewer a sense of space extending beyond. Another possibility is a pattern with a strong direction—vertical stripes, for instance, will lead the eye up or out.

- Long windows with low sills can limit space available for furniture placement in small rooms. To give yourself more options, consider raising the sill by installing a shorter window so that you can put furniture underneath.

- Light is a great room expander. Adding small, fixed, decorative windows can open up a room without contributing significantly to your fuel bills or costing you a lot of money. A skylight is a wonderful way to bring light to a dark room. You could also install overhead lighting: Track or recessed lighting provides light without taking up precious floor space.

- To give a room a spacious feel, do it with mirrors. Run mirrors into corners or from floor to ceiling, or simply hang a mirror in a frame to make the most of your natural light source and expand your impression of space.

- Finally, open up a small room literally by combining it with an adjacent room. If that's too drastic a change, consider installing an archway, glass doors, or a half-partition between it and an adjoining hallway or room. (But don't cut into any wall unless you're sure it's not load-bearing. If it is, you'll have to figure out another way for the load to be carried.)

Too-large rooms are even easier to deal with than small ones. You can divide up a large room or a series of rooms that flow into one another to gain privacy, quiet, or definition by carefully grouping furniture to create zoned areas. There are a lot of other possible solutions as well:

- Lower the ceiling over one part of a large room to help define a special place, like a dining alcove.

- Take advantage of color. Paint a too-high ceiling a color slightly darker than that of the walls; it will look lower. Paint the end of a long passageway a bright color, and it will appear to be shorter. Apply a strip of molding or a stripe of color around the entire room to draw it in.

- Patterned flooring can also help define areas. You might outline specific zones in a great room, for example, with either a tile or a carpet border.

- Use lights to define an area or to emphasize the separation between areas.

- Partition off part of a large room. Folding screens or movable partitions might do the trick, or you could build something more permanent (remember, though, the heavier the weight, the more support it'll need below).

- How about a platform? The change in floor height will make a large room seem like a whole new space.

- Lofts are another possibility, as is dividing one room into two. But make sure you check with your local building code before you make any major alterations. In most cases, new, permanent rooms will have to have access to a hall or an entrance, light, and access to the outside (usually through a window) for reasons of fire safety.

Long, narrow, rectangular rooms are not only psychologically uncomfortable to be in but are also practically worthless for any kind of activity other than bowling or shuffleboard.

- Visual elements, like wide stripes of light and dark floor tiles or beams running horizontally, can help make such a room seem wider. But to make the space truly useful, you'll have to take more drastic measures.

- If one of the narrow ends of the room is free of doorways, you might consider running a window seat, alcove, bookcase, or closet across its length. You'll shorten the room visually and put at least part of it to a worthwhile use.

- Look beyond the wall of a narrow room. If it's an exterior wall, could you install a bay window or a greenhouse bumpout? It doesn't have to be large. Often only a few feet of extra space will be sufficient to relieve the "tunnel-vision syndrome."

- On an interior wall, consider borrowing space from the next room; just 3 feet will make a niche deep enough to hold a small couch.

Dark, dreary rooms, such as those on the north side of the house or in the center, can be lightened up with a south-facing clerestory.

- Installing glazed panels or internal windows in wall partitions is another option, if the adjoining room is a sunny one. You'll increase the space visually while maintaining privacy. For more light but less noise, try glass block.

- Artificial lighting is another possibility, but it's more than likely that a single hung fixture won't do. To create a light-hearted ambience, consider painting the walls a light color, then washing them with light from tube lighting hidden under ceiling-high soffits. It won't be so obvious, then, that you had to resort to artificial rather than natural light.

- If the problem room is a seldom-used hall, consider getting rid of it entirely and incorporating it into an adjacent room, where the extra space will be put to better use.

Photo 2-9. The installation of a skylight is a great way to open up a small or dreary space. (Photo by Mitch Mandel)

Too-cold rooms could mean you need more insulation. Make sure your windows are caulked and weatherstripped and that their frames are tight.

- Install wallcoverings, carpeting, and flooring to help warm up a cold room; use textured materials and bright colors to heat it up psychologically.

- As a last resort, consider installing double-pane insulating windows if you don't have them already, or a window with one of the low-emissivity coatings (chemical coatings for glazing that reflect body heat back into the room). Or cover your windows with an insulated shutter or shade.

Rooms that are too noisy can be quieted with the installation of sound-absorbent materials, such as cork and rubber tile or carpeting. Insulating a floor will help reduce noise further.

- Noise that penetrates a partition wall is sometimes the most difficult type of sound problem to handle. About all you can do is try to build up mass in the wall. A double-thick layer of drywall can be helpful.

- If the noise is coming from outside, you have a number of options. Double-pane insulating glass, in addition to being energy-efficient, also reduces sound. Also, some manufacturers make a glazing specifically for noise-control.

- As a retrofit option, consider heavy drapes or some other form of movable insulation. Landscaping with earth berms or fences can help block noise coming from a nearby road or highway.

Traffic-control problems might be solved easily by changing the direction in which a door opens. A room that has too many doors and allows too much in-and-out traffic can be improved simply by closing up one or more of the doors, or by grouping the openings together.

Before you do anything, make a "dry run" of your proposed changes. Cut out your proposed new window from paper, and tack it up on the wall; mark where your new partition or divider is going to be with another strip of paper or a piece of string. Try living with your proposed plan for a week or so. Does it do what you hoped it would? If not, try something else. If it doesn't look good on paper, chances are it won't work when it's built.—**Marguerite Smolen**

MAKE ROOM FOR THE BATH
Finding Space for an Extra Bathroom

The trend today in new homes and renovations is toward large, luxurious bathrooms; yet many households still struggle with baths that are Spartan at best. In some homes, the master bath is a closet-sized room with a tiny stall shower, no counter space or electrical outlets, and a cramped toilet area. Other homes have no master bath at all—only a

Photo 2-10. A cramped, poorly planned master bath was transformed into this inviting retreat by building a 36-inch addition to the house. To minimize the cost, the bumpout was planned so that it would fit beneath the existing roof overhang. (Photo by J. Michael Kanouff)

single small bathroom that must serve the whole family and guests as well.

But there is hope for the underplumbed. In most cases, more bathroom space can be carved out of a home's existing floor plan—without the expense of a room addition. All it takes is some creative rearranging.

Your first task is to determine the main problem with your home's existing bathroom situation. Rarely can every inconvenience be remedied, so try to identify a single realistic remodeling goal. Writing out your priorities as the plan develops will help you make the trade-offs that are always part of a renovation project.

Take, for example, a home with a children's bath that suits the youngsters fine, but is a continual source of embarrassment when friends drop by. In this case, a powder room (reserved for guests) should be the top priority.

If, to take another example, the family bath is a center of traffic tie-ups and tension in the mornings, the goal should be to break the existing space into compartments—or divide it into two smaller baths—so that more than one person at a time can get ready for the day's activities.

Or perhaps the adults in the household are fed up with sharing a bathroom with the kids. It may be time to add a master bath—or to expand the old one into the minispa of your dreams.

Photo 2-11. A towel-warming rack, double vanity sinks, and roomy shower with hand-held faucet make this newly expanded bathroom a great place to begin and end any day. The enlargement was made possible by borrowing space from an adjacent bedroom. (Photo by J. Michael Kanouff)

If a guest bath is what you need, you can keep it simple; powder rooms normally require only a toilet and lavatory. Very little storage is necessary: just a decorative towel bar and an attractive soap dish. An efficient, quiet ventilation system and good lighting are also key elements. And since the surface areas involved are tiny, elegant coverings for floors, walls, and ceilings may be an affordable luxury.

Powder Rooms

Powder rooms do not have to take up a large amount of space—as little as 36 × 72 or 48 × 54 inches should suffice. The smallest space recommended for a toilet is a yard wide, with a minimum of 24 inches in front of the bowl.

The lavatory is usually either a small pedestal fixture or a sink on top of a cabinet. Most bathroom vanities are 21 inches deep and 24 inches wide, although they are also available in 18 × 24-inch sizes. The extra 3 inches of floor space gained by using the smaller fixture sometimes make all the difference.

Space for such a tiny bath can be carved out of an existing floor plan in several ways. Could the powder room go under a stairway? Maybe the entryway coat closet could be reassigned, or a bedroom closet could be shortened, to make way for the guest bath. Or consider replacing a side-by-side washer-dryer combination with a stacked unit, thereby freeing space for a half-bath adjacent to the utility room. (Vertical laundry units are no longer down-sized, stripped-down models; at least two major manufacturers—Maytag and Speed Queen—have recently introduced full-sized appliances that can be stacked, one on top of the other.)

When considering any of these possibilities, make sure that the entrance to the powder room is at least somewhat shielded from areas where guests are apt to assemble. Comings and goings to the "privy" shouldn't be in full view of the dinner party.

Family Baths

If your family is plagued by morning gridlock in the bathroom, keep in mind that having a toilet, lavatory, and tub in one room means that a single occupant monopolizes all three fixtures. As a solution, you could divide the existing family bath into two separate rooms. But it's doubtful you'll find space enough for two full baths. You'll need to determine which fixture is most in demand.

If the lavatory is the most sought-after spot, you could create additional grooming centers outside of the main bath. A child's bedroom or a sectioned-off part of a bedroom closet is a good potential site. Another possibility is to make the utility room sink do double duty as a spot for morning and bedtime routines, as well as for the usual laundry chores. All any sink needs in order to become a grooming station is a drawer or two, a recessed medicine cabinet, at least one duplex electrical outlet, and good lighting.

It's equally possible that the toilet or shower is responsible for the traffic jam. In that case, consider borrowing some space from an adjacent bedroom or closet for an additional shower and toilet. If you arrange the space so that both pairs of fixtures are accessible from a common lavatory area, you will have created the feeling of two bathrooms in the floor space of one and a half.

To make the most of the available floor space, consider exchanging a 60 × 32-inch tub for a 48 × 32-inch stall shower. The shower will be safer and more pleasant to use than a tub-and-shower combination, and it frees 12 precious inches to be used in other ways. Narrow vanity cabinets (those that are 18 inches deep rather than 21 inches) can add 3 inches to the walkway space. Also, avoid swinging doors in the bathroom entrance. Pocket doors, which slide into the wall, are great space savers.

Master Baths

Adding a new master bath—or expanding an existing one—means that something has to get smaller. Can you eliminate a linen closet? Relocate your clothes closet? Transfer clothing storage from a closet to some additional furniture pieces, such as an armoire and a chest of drawers?

Another option is to make the bedroom itself smaller so that an adjoining hall bath can be widened. Then squeeze a new bathroom behind the existing reshaped facility, as in the third case study described below.

A good way to fit a big tub into a small space is to select a fixture that is shorter but deeper. Kohler, for example, offers a tub called "The Greek," which is only 48 inches long. Its 22-inch depth and 32-inch width, however, make it comfortable for most average-sized adults.

Space may be at such a premium that none of these options offers enough space for that big, luxurious bathtub you've been hankering after. You may need a small room addition. If the roof overhang outside your bedroom is at least 24 inches long, perhaps you can "bump out" the wall enough to create an inviting bathing retreat.

But the chances are good that you'll find the needed inches for more (and more functional) bathroom space within the boundaries of your current home. Make a scale drawing of your floor plan, and cut out some templates of basic fixtures and furniture. Then ask yourself, "What if?"

One Designer's Solution

As a practicing bathroom designer, I've faced the challenge of squeezing more bathroom space into a wide variety of homes. Here are a few case studies that illustrate workable solutions to some common problems:

An inviting place for guests. The hall bath was adequate for the two children in this family—but the space wasn't special enough for visitors. The solution: a powder room reserved for guests (see figure 2-1).

72

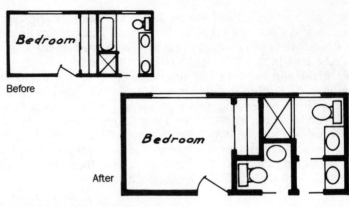

Before

After

An Inviting Place for Guests

Figure 2-1. To add a small powder room reserved for visitors, the homeowners borrowed space from the existing family bath and an adjacent bathroom closet. By adding a second pole for hanging garments, storage space in the closet was not reduced.

To create two bathrooms where there had been only one, the owners replaced the old tub with a spacious stall shower. They split the vanity into two grooming areas separated by a sliding door. Borrowing some space from the old bathroom, plus a few feet from an adjoining bedroom closet, they added a mirrored powder room with a pedestal lavatory. The closet didn't even suffer: By raising the existing pole and adding another one at waist height, they were able to hang the same amount of clothing in the smaller space.

Rush-hour relief. A busy family of six had one hall bath to serve four children—two girls and two boys. Morning bathroom time was a disaster. By rearranging the floor plan, they created two separate bathing facilities and three grooming stations (see figure 2-2).

To do it, they moved the closet in the girls' bedroom to the opposite wall. The old tub and toilet remained where they were, but became part of a "new" bathroom, accessible only from the girls' bedroom. The boys' new bathroom, complete with new toilet, single vanity, and stall shower, doubles as a powder room for guests.

Masterful minibath. This small home had only one bath for five family members. The owners had long wanted a master bathroom but didn't know where to put it.

Figure 2-2. To meet the needs of four busy children, this hall bath was divided into two. The boys use the reshaped hall bath; the girls use two new grooming stations, now accessible from a bedroom. The displaced closet was moved to another wall.

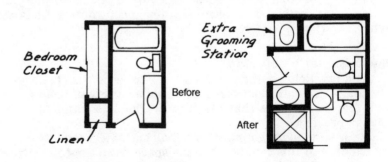

Rush-Hour Relief

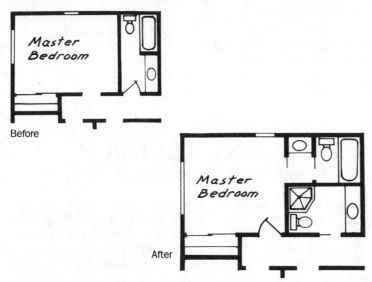

Before

After

Masterful Minibath

Figure 2-3. This original hall bath once served an entire family of five. By reshaping the old bath and borrowing floor space from the adjacent bedroom, the owners made room for a small master bath—making life more pleasant for the whole family.

The answer is shown in figure 2-3. It involved making the bedroom slightly smaller, changing the proportions of the hall bath, and using the existing toilet and tub for the newly created master bath. The small vanity installed for the new bath can be closed off from the other fixtures by a sliding door. In the hall bath, the old vanity stayed where it was, complemented by a new toilet and stall shower.

Bathroom bumpout. The master bath in this house was cramped and poorly designed. Whoever used the vanity couldn't help obstructing the passage leading to both the closet and the claustrophobic room housing the toilet and small stall shower (see figure 2-4).

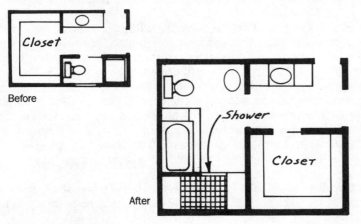

Before

After

Bathroom Bumpout

Figure 2-4. Wanting to keep their large walk-in closet while expanding the cramped master bath, these homeowners made room by adding a small bumpout under the existing roof overhang.

The only way to maintain the generous proportions of the walk-in closet was to build a 36-inch-deep addition to the house. To minimize the cost, the bumpout was planned so that it would fit beneath the existing roof overhang. The closet was moved, opening up a large area for a new tub, shower, and pedestal lavatory.—**Ellen Cheever**

REPLACEMENT BY DESIGN
Creating a New Look with Windows

You know all of the practical reasons why you want to replace your old windows: You want something more efficient, something easier to operate and maintain. But before you buy, there's one more thing you should think about. How will your new windows look on your old house?

Window openings create distinctive architectural patterns and rhythms on facades and give a house character. As a general rule, new openings should be similar in proportion to those that already exist, especially for houses that are symmetrical in appearance, or nearly so.

Of course, if you don't like the present appearance of your home, you could consider replacing your old windows with new ones that look totally different. To give your home a more contemporary look, consider replacing old-fashioned, divided-pane, double hung units with full-pane casement windows.

Units that are divided vertically in the center—along the lines of a traditional French door—can help a squat house seem taller and better proportioned. Horizontal divisions—of the kind, for example, you would create if you positioned a contemporary awning window directly below a fixed pane—tend to make a house look longer and lower.

You might also want to consider adding a window where none now exists, or enlarging existing openings. These alternatives involve more work and expense than mere replacement but can add appreciably to the livability and appearance of your home.

Whatever the effect you decide to go after, be sure to assess the impact of any new windows on the usability and safety of adjacent areas both inside and outside the house. Awning and casement windows swing open beyond the plane of the wall and may impede traffic flow or furniture placement. The best way to study such functional matters is with the aid of a simple floor plan of your house.

It's also a good idea to use drawings to help you study the visual effects of various potential window configurations before you make a replacement decision. Some window-replacement contractors and suppliers may be willing to supply sketches, or you could hire an architect. But even for someone who's never drawn, it's not hard to produce a useful sketch of a house elevation by measuring and transposing actual dimensions to paper with a scale, T-square, and triangle. If drawing is out of the question, take photographs, and work from those.

Once you've decided what look you want, it's time to shop around. Finding replacement windows that meet your aesthetic needs may not always be easy. If you're seeking to keep the flavor of your original facade, you may discover that windows billed as "reproduction" don't exactly match the older windows that you are replacing.

Modern manufacturing methods are often the culprit. Frames and mullions on today's windows are likely to be thinner than those of older windows. And if you're buying double-glazed or other kinds of insulating glass, you may have a very hard time finding "true divided lights," that is, windows whose surfaces are divided into several smaller panes.

Contemporary materials also make a difference. Aluminum and vinyl frames look quite different from wooden ones, even when the plastic or metal has been color-impregnated or painted.

The look of your new windows will also depend on how well they fit. If you install a new stock window in an existing opening that's too big for the window, you may end up with the thick and ungainly edge where the new window unit meets the wall.

Ensuring the aesthetic appeal of your replacement windows is a process that can take time and serious thought. But with all of the choices available—and the unhappy, costly consequences of choosing something you don't really like—you'll find it pays to put your efforts up front.—**Thomas Vonier**

THE CONVENIENT KITCHEN
Designed by and for People Who Love to Cook

There's a lot going on in today's kitchen. You may go there to eat, to socialize with family and friends, to pay your bills. But no matter how many extra purposes this room serves, its original function is still its most important. It is the place where you make your meals—preparing food, cooking it, and cleaning up afterward.

All too often, a kitchen's design works against the people who use it. That was certainly the case in the kitchen of David and Nikki Goldbeck, the authors of *Nikki and David Goldbeck's American Wholefoods Cuisine* (New York: New American Library, 1983) and

Photo 2-12. David and Nikki Goldbeck salvaged this classic diner booth to create an "old-timey" look in their Convenient Kitchen. (Photo by Christopher Barone)

several other natural-foods cookbooks. Though the kitchen is the center of both their lives and their livelihoods, until recently the Goldbeck kitchen was a drab, cramped, outdated place.

But that's all changed since the Goldbecks accepted our challenge to transform that tired old space into the kitchen of their dreams. Here are some of the very good ideas they incorporated into what they've named the "Convenient Kitchen." (Figure 2-5 provides a sketch of the original tiny kitchen, while figure 2-6 describes the expanded new kitchen.)

A Growing Space: For their natural foods cuisine, David and Nikki longed for easy year-round access to fresh herbs and greens. A small kitchen garden would be just the thing, but their existing kitchen was a dark and dreary place that received almost no natural

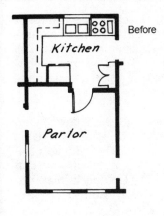

Before

Figure 2-5. The original Goldbeck kitchen was a cramped, 7′ × 11′ space lit only by one small window over the sink. (Illustration by John Kline)

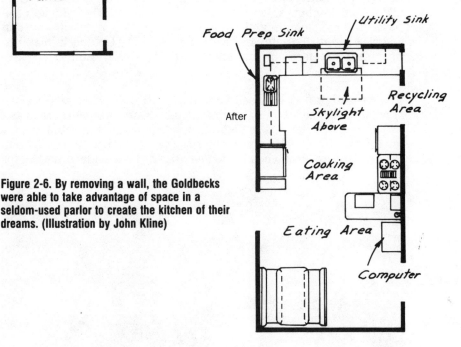

After

Figure 2-6. By removing a wall, the Goldbecks were able to take advantage of space in a seldom-used parlor to create the kitchen of their dreams. (Illustration by John Kline)

light. The Goldbecks added a skylight, then installed Plexiglas shelves in its shaft to give the indoor garden a place in the sun.

The Goldbecks use full-spectrum fluorescent lights throughout the kitchen. Full-spectrum lights imitate daylight; installed under upper cabinets, the lights shine down on countertop pots of herbs and vegetables.

To ensure a steady supply of sprouts, David built a sliding sprouting tray that tucks in under the sink.

Fresh Storage: The fresher the food, the more nutrients it retains. In order to preserve root vegetables and other staples of the natural-foods cook, the Goldbecks designed a modern-day root cellar. It's a metal box hidden away in the naturally cool crawlspace beneath the kitchen floor. The "cellar" is accessible via a trap door.

Another versatile storage space in this kitchen is a Goldbeck invention. It can serve as a regular kitchen cabinet, but contains movable shelves and racks and an electric heater with a blower. The Goldbecks can use the cabinet as a drying rack for washed dishes and utensils, or for dehydrating food, incubating yogurt, or proofing bread.

Help from a Computer: A personal computer is a key component of the Convenient Kitchen. With the help of some of today's affordable kitchen software, the Goldbecks use their home computer to plan menus and to analyze recipes for nutritional and caloric content. Through its internal modem, the Goldbeck computer plugs into an electronic bulletin board, the Health Education Electronic Forum.

An Adjustable Counter: With tall and short cooks often sharing the same kitchen, a counter that can adapt to the person and to the task at hand is a definite convenience. At the touch of a button, one Goldbeck counter can rise from a 27-inch desk height all the way up to 41 inches, 5 inches above the standard height for

Photo 2-13. One of David Goldbeck's smartest inventions is an adjustable counter that can accommodate cooks of any height and of any dimension. (Photo by Christopher Barone)

kitchen counters. To ensure reliable operation, the system rides on industrial bearings and uses a commercial-grade electric motor.

A Second Sink: David Goldbeck cites several practical reasons for the luxury of having two sinks. "A second sink makes it much easier for two cooks to work together," he says. "It's also more hygienic to clean food in a sink separate from the one where you wash dirty dishes."

Cooking Versatility: Many experienced cooks prefer to cook over a gas burner but to bake in an electric oven. With no such dual-option stoves on the market, the Goldbecks designed their own. Its stainless-steel frame houses an electric oven and a gas cooktop, as well as drawers, shelves, and slots to store pots, pans, and utensils. The cooktop's pilotless ignition minimizes combustion gases from the stove, which are drawn off by a low-hanging range hood. The fan for the exhaust system is mounted outside the house to minimize noise pollution in the kitchen.

Like a second sink, an extra cooktop can enhance any kitchen. Nestled into a counter peninsula in the Goldbeck kitchen is a portable induction cooktop. Induction "burners" heat by inducing a current in a metal pot, pan, or skillet. Because only the pan heats up, induction cooktops are extremely safe, efficient, and nonpolluting.

Sit-down Dishwashing: When it comes to cleaning up in the kitchen, sitting down on the job can be a blessing. In the Convenient Kitchen, cabinet doors open to reveal a knee-space under the sink. An adjustable ergonomic chair, there to serve footsore dishwashers, is used other times for working at the computer desk or the multi-height counter.

Recycling: To dispose of food scraps, the Goldbecks simply slide back a small countertop lid and drop in the garbage. The garbage is stored in a plastic pail that's sealed off—odors and all—from the kitchen. The Goldbecks remove the garbage can from outside the house for easy dumping in their compost bin. Bottles and paper have their own separate recycling bins in the Convenient Kitchen.

A Quieter Space: Because kitchens can be very noisy, the Goldbecks installed an acoustical ceiling. It consists of painted, tempered Peg-Board with a layer of sound-absorbing fiberglass above. In between Peg-Board and fiberglass, there's a layer of cloth that keeps fiberglass fibers out of the kitchen.

Safety: More house fires start in the kitchen than in any other room. With safety in mind, the Goldbecks surrounded their cooking unit with noncombustible materials; they keep a fire extinguisher nearby. To prevent "ganging up" plugs in too few outlets—a common cause of fire—they installed strips of outlets, called Plugmold,

Photo 2-14. The Goldbeck Convenient Kitchen is packed with handy innovations for people who enjoy cooking. A small step stool, which is stored safely under drawers when not in use, puts tall kitchen cabinets within easy reach. Bins to the right of the kitchen sink make recycling cans and bottles practically effortless. (Photo by Christopher Barone)

throughout. Childproof locks on cabinets and special hinges that let cabinet doors disappear into side pockets are other safety features.

Clean Air and Water: To supplement the range hood, the Goldbecks found a portable, nonducted air cleaner that can purify the emissions from the gas stove. They mounted the device on the wall, above the cooktop-oven unit.

To improve the taste and quality of the kitchen tapwater, the Goldbecks plugged an activated-carbon filter into the supply line.

Construction work on the Convenient Kitchen was done by Stephen Robin Associates of Woodstock, New York. David Goldbeck did the design work and is currently completing a book about his kitchen, entitled *The Total Kitchen*. You can order a copy by sending $12.95 plus $2 postage and handling to Ceres Press, P.O. Box 87, Woodstock, NY 12498.

Manufacturers

The following products found in the Convenient Kitchen were chosen by David and Nikki Goldbeck because of their superior design and quality of materials.

*Air de-pollution unit
    #200LMF*
Air Conditioning Engineers
P.O. Box 616
Decatur, IL 62525

*Belaform 18/10 stainless
    steel sink*
Luwa Corporation
4404 Chesapeake Dr.
P.O. Box 16348
Charlotte, NC 28216

Chrome plating
ChandlerRoyce
185 E. 122 St.
New York, NY 10035

*Classic Line faucet #31.735
    with hose*
Grohe America, Inc.
2677 Coyle Ave.
Elk Grove Village, IL 60007

Clear red oak flooring
Missouri Hardwood Flooring
    Company
Birch Tree, MO 65438

Clear red oak flooring
National Oak Flooring
    Manufacturers' Association
804 Sterick Building
Memphis, TN 38103

*Cooktop with ComboGrille
    GT483*
Modern Maid
P.O. Box 1111
Chattanooga, TN 37401

*Digital refrigerator
    thermometer, Energy Teller,
    faucet water miser,
    oven thermometer, silicone
    spray, under-cabinet
    jar opener*
Brookstone
565 Vose Farm Rd.
Peterborough, NH 03458

*Dimmers and fan speed
    control*
Lutron Electronics Company,
    Inc.
Coopersburg, PA 18036

DLC7 Superpro food processor
Cuisinarts, Inc.
P.O. Box 353
Greenwich, CT 06830

*DuroLite plant light,
    VitaLite tubes,*
DuroTest Corporation
Nort Bergen, NJ 07047

*Dustbuster #9330
Toast-R-Oven #T93B*
Black & Decker
20 Distribution Blvd.
Edison, NJ 08817

Gilitsa Swedish floor finish
Gilitsa American
327 S. Kenyon
Seattle, WA 98109

*Health Education computer
    bulletin board*
Health Education Electronic
    Forum
Box 546
Ames, IA 50010

*Kaypro 4 computer and
    software*
Kaypro Corporation
P.O. Box N
Del Mar, CA 92014

Lacquer, tung oil
Mohawk Finishing Products,
    Inc.
Amsterdam, NY 12010

*Refrigerator/freezer,
    model #BC-20E*
Amana Refrigeration, Inc.
Amana, IA 52204

Stainless steel panels
Ken St. John
9 Reynolds La.
Woodstock, NY 12498

Water's Edge clock,
  style C4802
Bulova Clocks
Bulova Park
Flushing, NY 11370

Water treatment system
Amway Corporation
7575 E. Fulton Rd.
Ada, MI 49355

—**Marguerite Smolen**

RULES OF THUMB
Handy Tips to Help You Make Estimates on Home Projects

"**O**ne ostrich egg will serve 24 people for brunch" is one rule of thumb that may not be of much use to most of us. But there are hundreds of other gems of advice that almost anyone can put to work as helpful "guesstimators" in a wide variety of home projects.

Rules of thumb are homemade recipes for making rough estimates, such as "a used hand or power tool should never cost more than 50 percent of the price of a new one." It's an easy-to-remember nugget of information that falls somewhere between a scientific formula and a shot in the dark. A good rule provides a guideline that lets you guess and get away with it. For instance:

Framing Layout: When using a carpenter's square to lay out a frame wall or partition, sharpen your pencil after every five or six marks. Using a dull pencil can add as much as an inch to the overall dimensions after about 20 feet, throwing the whole structure out of whack and making it difficult to fit wallboard, sheathing, and other modular materials. (Dick Demske, Ventura, California)

Working Concrete: If you can flow concrete into place, it contains too much water. Excess water weakens concrete, making it less durable. (Richard Day, Palomar Mountain, California)

Building to Sell: If you're making something for sale, the cost of materials shouldn't be more than 20 percent of the selling price. (Robert Brightman, Great Neck, New York)

Doweled Joints: The diameter of dowels in dowel joints should be one-half the thickness of the boards being joined. For example, ¾-inch stock should have ⅜-inch-diameter dowels; ⅞-inch stock should have 7/16-inch dowels. And the length inserted should be three times the thickness of the dowel. Thus a ⅜-inch dowel

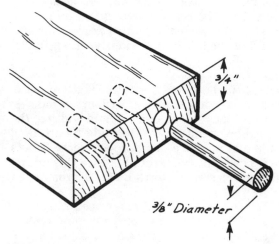

Figure 2-7. The diameter of dowels in dowel joints should be one-half the thickness of the boards being joined.

3/4 "

3/8" Diameter

Doweled Joints

should be about 2¼ inches long to penetrate 1⅛ inches into each member. (David Warren, Crystal Lake, Illinois)

Buying Fasteners: When buying quantities of standard fasteners (such as screws, bolts, etc.), if you need almost half a box or more, buy a full box. The second half is virtually free compared to the higher per-piece costs. For example, 45 individual screws will cost about the same as a box of 100. (Bill Rooney, Portland, Oregon)

Used Wood: Recycling used lumber from standing buildings is only worthwhile if you can get it for nothing. (Leroy Nistler, McGregor, Minnesota)

The Remodeling Factor: Working from scratch may be as much as 100 percent easier than remodeling, so always allow some extra time for the unexpected when, for example, you uncover a wall. (R.J. DeCristoforo, Los Altos Hills, California)

Plywood Weight: An easy way to estimate how much a sheet of plywood weighs is to figure about 25 pounds per ¼ inch of thickness. A 4 × 8-foot sheet of ¼-inch plywood will weigh approximately 25 pounds, ½-inch about 50, and ¾-inch about 75 pounds. (Bill Rooney, Portland, Oregon)

Project Time: Unless you have considerable experience, when estimating time needed to complete a project, make a guess, then double it. If the project involves techniques you haven't used before, a lot of small parts to be bought, or factors beyond your control (such as the weather), triple or quadruple your first guess. (Ron Bruzek, Eagan, Minnesota)

Buying Faucets: A higher-priced faucet may last as much as three times longer than a cheap faucet. By buying better faucets, you not only save the cost of the second and third faucet, but also the trouble or cost of having them installed. (Marlyn Rodi, Inglewood, California)

Estimating Framing: To determine the total length of material needed for any framing job with miter joints (doors, windows, picture frames, etc.), multiply the combined height and width of the inside dimensions of the frame opening by 2, then add the molding width multiplied by 8 and add an extra inch for saw kerfs. That's how much material you'll need, but cut carefully, since this allows only ½ inch for error. (Kenn Oberrecht, North Bend, Oregon)

Corroded Pipes: To see if your water pipes need replacing, fully open the laundry tub faucet, then turn on your most remote fixture. If you don't get a stream at least the size of a pencil at the remote fixture, your supply pipes are corroded to the point where they should be replaced. (Milford Roubik, St. Paul, Minnesota)

Handyman Specials: To check floors for level when looking at a "handyman special" house, set down a marble at various intervals along the walls. It will roll to the low spots. How fast it rolls will indicate how level the floor is. Fast marbles mean don't buy! (Charles R. Self, Goode, Virginia)

Estimating Framing

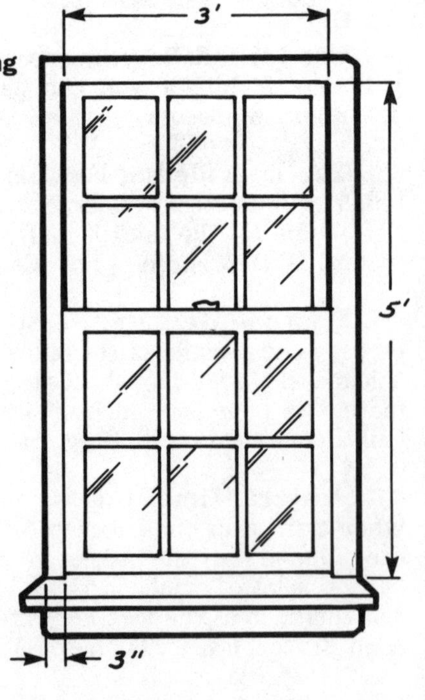

Figure 2-8. To estimate the amount of lumber you would need to frame this window, multiply the combined width and length of the inside dimensions by 2 (you get 16 feet), then add the molding width multiplied by 8 (you get 24 inches) and add an extra inch for saw kerfs. The total lumber needed in this case is 18 feet, 1 inch.

Buying Concrete: If you need more than a couple of cubic yards, get ready-mix. If you can't dump it on the site, hire a concrete pumping contractor to get it where you want it. (Richard Day, Palomar Mountain, California)

Sizing a Round Table: When making a round dining table, you can figure the maximum number of people it will seat will be twice the table's diameter in feet. For example, a 5½-foot-wide table would seat 11 people. The circumference is 207 inches, allowing 18¼ inches per place setting. (Kay Keating, Bethesda, Maryland)

Wiring Problems: If your home is 20 or more years old, you can expect to find as many as three "generations" of wiring and up to a dozen minor infractions of the National Electrical Code. (David Chapeau, St. Paul, Minnesota)

Trips to Store: Most plumbing projects won't be complete until you've gone to the store three times for parts and materials. (Don Geary, Salt Lake City, Utah)

Painting Rooms: When painting a room where the walls are in good shape, plan on spending about half as much time on preparation and cleanup as on the actual painting. Where walls are in poor condition, the nonpainting time will increase accordingly and may even take longer than the paint application. (Dick Demske, Ventura, California)

Drilling: The larger the bit or the harder the material, the slower the rotation should be. (Rosario Capotosto, Greenlawn, New York)

Checking Foundations: If you find more than one foundation crack that's at least 1 inch wide by 3 inches long in the foundation of a house you are looking at, either keep looking or plan on jacking up the house and putting in a new foundation. (Charles R. Self, Goode, Virginia)

Rules of thumb can come to your rescue in almost every aspect of life. In fact, writer Tom Parker recently compiled a collection of nearly 900 rules on a variety of subjects in his book *Rules of Thumb*. If you'd like a copy, send $6.95 (that includes postage and handling) to Houghton-Mifflin Co., Customer Service, Wayside Rd., Burlington, MA 01803.—**Gene Schnaser**

CHAPTER 3

HOME MAINTENANCE AND REPAIR

Along with the joys of home ownership come the responsibilities of maintaining the home in good condition and repairing things that break or deteriorate. For residents of older homes, this can sometimes seem like a never-ending job. You have hardly finished stripping and repainting all the exterior trim, when you discover that half the windows need reglazing. By the time you get around to completing that task, you have spotted a half dozen other minor repairs that need your attention.

After spending a few years struggling to keep up with the needed repairs, it is not surprising that many owners of older homes begin to consider the virtues of aluminum siding and vinyl-clad windows. To be sure, in some situations, clothing your home in new, low-maintenance siding and equipping it with a new set of windows and doors may be the best way to give it new life while reducing your home-repair burden.

At best, though, the ideal of a "maintenance-free" home is an illusion—a dream that is not likely to ever be completely realized. What is possible is to reduce the burden of home maintenance by approaching it in a thoughtful and intelligent way. First and foremost, that means placing your emphasis on *prevention*—preventing minor problems from turning into major ones and in general trying to take care of your home in such a way that few serious problems ever arise.

In this chapter you will be reminded of such simple matters as the need to occasionally treat the exterior of your home to a good bath. The dust and grime found in the air around our homes not only dulls their appearance, it can also gradually eat away at their skins.

87

Photo by Carl Doney

A good washing now and then will improve the looks and extend the life of a home's exterior.

Also discussed in this chapter are ways to avoid those perennial disturbers of homeowner peace, frozen pipes and faulty wiring. You will find practical advice on how to spot potential problems of both types and learn ways to deal with them.

But, of course, the modern home consists of more than roof and walls, windows and doors, plumbing and wiring. There are also the numerous electrical appliances we depend upon to make our lives more comfortable. Thus, you will find included in this chapter some step-by-step instructions for troubleshooting dishwasher problems and maintaining air conditioners in good condition.—**the editors**

A SPRING CLEANING
Giving Your House a Fresh Look

Exposed constantly to dust, dirt, grime, and the elements, houses get dirty. Usually, the homeowner's first response is to apply a new exterior skin in the form of paint or new siding.

But how many of us repaint our cars after they've been driven through a few mud puddles? When cars get dirty, a good washing will do a world of good. It's the same with houses.

The appearance of many types of building exteriors, including brick, wood, aluminum, and vinyl, can be transformed by a simple washing. Even in extreme cases—say, where a brick facade has become a chronic maintenance problem due to layers of peeling paint—a special chemical washing can be a less costly solution than residing. At the same time, washing preserves the original exterior of the building, leaving its character intact.

And on exteriors that must be scraped, sanded, and repainted, a good bath is a crucial but often overlooked step in the renovation process. The best paint, applied carefully by the best painter, won't adhere well to a surface that is coated with a fine layer of grime.

Cleaning Materials
The most common prescriptions for exterior house cleaning are simple: They call for warm water, a nonabrasive household detergent, and a soft brush. Mix ⅓ cup of liquid detergent with 1 gallon of water.

Bleach can be added to the mix to combat mold and mildew. Although proportions can vary, a solution of up to 25 percent household bleach (1 part bleach to 3 parts water) should be strong enough for even heavy accumulations of mildew. But don't mix bleach with a cleaner that contains ammonia. Mixed together, bleach and ammonia produce chloramines, whose fumes are, at best, highly irritating and, at worst, deadly. If you are unsure about the contents of a liquid detergent (many contain some ammonia), read the label. If left in doubt, do not combine the cleaning agents.

Be careful, too, with lye solutions. Lye, whose main component is potassium, is water soluble and biodegradable. It does not usually harm surrounding soil and vegetation. However, too strong a solution may wash from the walls paint or other materials that may not

Photo 3-1. With an extension washer like this one by Oscrow, you can reach high overhead to clean windows, walls, and woodwork. The handle contains soap, and the head sports both a spinning brush and a squeegee. (Photo by Mitch Mandel)

be so benign. To be safe, test the solution on a patch of wall before washing the entire exterior, wear protective clothing, and use drop cloths to protect surrounding plants and soil.

House washing can be a family affair if you recruit the kids, round up extra buckets, hoses, and soft scrub brushes, and do the job by hand. Given the carnival atmosphere that often prevails at family house washings, someone is likely to turn a hose on you as well as on the house, which makes this project a good choice for a warm day.

If you don't have any willing conscripts at hand, special house-cleaning equipment is available to help you do the job yourself. The Gardena Clean System (suggested retail price: $69.95) is a typical outfit. It includes a 4-foot handle, a 3-foot knee-joint extension, a brush attachment, and nine "shampoo" tablets, which the company describes as a very mild, nonabrasive cleaner. (Stronger tablets, extra brushes, and another handle extension are optional.)

Another kind of system consists of a canister with a nozzle. You pour the desired cleaning mixture into the canister, then connect a garden hose to the handle. Cleaning solution and water combine in the canister and spray through the nozzle when you depress the trigger. (Such units are often used, with different solutions, for spraying insecticides or washing cars.)

Gilmour makes an all-purpose hose-end sprayer (model 362D, suggested retail price: $15.49), which has a 1-quart canister and an adjusting dial that regulates the ratio of detergent to water. The company says that, given normal water pressure, this unit puts out a 25-foot stream of water. Even with the strongest sprayer, you'll still need to scrub stubborn patches of dirt, heavy mold, tree sap, nail head rust, and other blemishes by hand. Also, washing is not a substitute for thorough preparation before repainting or restaining siding. Peeling paint not dislodged by the water stream must still be scraped off, edges must be sanded down, and bare wood must be primed.

Cleaning by Professionals

Another option is to have a professional cleaning company do the job. This may be a necessity for older houses where years of accumulated grit and grime, or several layers of deteriorated paint, must be removed. Such projects generally require large volumes of cleaning chemicals that are more potent than those generally available for household use.

Brick buildings often benefit most from a professional, heavy-duty cleaning. Getting down to bare brick simplifies ongoing maintenance; it also restores the distinctive character of most old brick, which has gradations of hue and texture comparable to the rich patina on fine wood furniture.

There are two ways to remove layers of surface material from old brick and woodwork: sandblasting and chemical cleaning. Each has advantages and disadvantages. Chemical treatment is easier to control, while sandblasting is more of an all-or-nothing affair that can have a devastating effect on some brick and woodwork surfaces.

On brick homes built before 1900, chemical treatment or sandblasting will probably have to be followed by repointing. The mortar commonly used until the turn of the century was lime-based, which made it softer and more porous than later mixes that include portland cement along with hydrated lime and sand.

Like early mortars, old brick is softer and more porous than modern brick. That makes it more easily damaged by freeze-thaw cycles, gradual chemical attack (most commonly from sulfur), deterioration from organic substances like mildew and moss, or from vigorous cleaning. Sandblasting at pressures of 10,000 pounds per square inch (psi) or more would seriously erode or even shatter 19th-century brick, which may not tolerate more than 100 psi.

Even if sandblasting leaves the brick structurally sound, it can still produce unwanted results. In the sandblasting process, sand hits the brick at a uniform rate and pressure—but old brick is anything but uniform. This mismatch can lead to pitting and channeling, producing a ragged, cratered surface. So if an old brick building has made it through this much of the 20th century intact, be very cautious about turning high-powered technology loose against its walls.

Working with Chemicals

Chemical cleansers are gentler on the house, but are dangerous to use without taking proper precautions. Professional firms normally test the chemical process on a sample section of wall before cleaning the whole house. John Tadych, president of American Building Restoration Chemicals, Inc., reports that employees of his firm begin by scraping off a paint chip to determine how many layers must be removed. Then they mix a batch of stripper to the appropriate strength and test it on the wall.

Tadych stresses the difference between professional-grade, full-strength chemical strippers (a very potent 80-percent lye solution), and the 2-percent lye solution with alcohol that the firm sells to do-it-yourselfers. Professional-strength cleaners, Tadych says, are simply too hazardous to sell to consumers since they cause severe irritation and burning on contact with skin.

Commercial-grade strippers also contain some detergent and an emulsifier, which thickens the mix and helps it adhere to the wall. On a typical job, one or two coats of the stripper are applied and rinsed off. Then the lye's chemical action is "stopped" with an application of a mild acidic solution. When this coating is rinsed off, the brick's acidity is neutralized.

Another prominent firm in the field, Diedrich Chemicals, uses chemical strippers on wood siding as well as on brick. They spray an alkaline solution onto the woodwork, allow it to soak into the wood for 14 hours, then remove it with pressurized water. After the walls are neutralized, they're allowed to dry for at least 10 days. Finally, the woodwork is tested for dryness. Any raised grain is sanded down before the entire surface is repainted or stained. You'll pay for this kind of exterior rehabilitation, but you'll be rewarded in years to come with easier maintenance, *plus* the assurance that your home's good looks go more than skin deep.

Manufacturers

American Building
   Restoration Chemicals, Inc.
9720 S. 60th St.
Franklin, WI 53132

Diedrich Chemicals
   Restoration Technologies, Inc.
300A East Oak St.
Oak Creek, WI 53154

Gardena Inc.
6031 Culligan Way
Minnetonka, MN 55345

Gilmour Manufacturing Co.
P.O.Box 838
Somerset, PA 15501-0838

—Mike McClintock

WARMER WALLS
Insulate to Save Heat and Money

You've blown insulation into your attic. You've tackled air leaks with a caulking gun, weatherstripped your doors, and double-glazed some windows. Your house is fit to fend off the high cost of winter heat—but it could be even fitter if it's a candidate for "warmer walls."

"Warmer walls" is shorthand for "adding insulation to exterior walls." Rising energy costs and improved insulation retrofit methods have moved warmer walls into the category of cost-effective energy improvements for many an existing house. And like attic insulation and weatherstripping, the warmer walls option makes a home more comfortable while it reduces the heating bill.

To find out just how valuable adding insulation to an existing wall can be, we calculated cost vs. savings data for different types of walls in two different climates. The model for our calculations was a medium-sized, two-story house with 1,920 square feet of exterior wall area and 20 exterior windows. Use the information in table 3-1 to see if energy savings would offset the cost of adding insulation to your walls in a reasonable number of years.

Using the Table

The first step toward using table 3-1 is to find out what your walls are made of and whether or not they already contain some insulation. Most homes have walls made either of studs or some kind of masonry. If the wall type is concealed by layers of siding, you'll have to do some closer inspection. But correctly identifying

Table 3-1—THE COSTS AND SAVINGS OF WARMER WALLS

Wall Type	Retrofit Option	R-Value Increase	$/ Sq. Ft.	Cost for Model House	Payback Period (Years) for Model House					
					Albany, NY			Albuquerque, NM		
					Elec.	Oil	Gas	Elec.	Oil	Gas
Stud wall	Blow in fiberglass.	R-4 to R-12	$0.61	$1,000	0.8	1.4	1.9	1.5	2.5	3.4
Stud wall	Add studs to exterior wall, 6″ batts, new siding.	R-12 to R-30	$3.71	$6,060	17.0	29.0	38.0	33.0	54.0	72.0
Stud wall	Add 2″ foam to exterior wall, furring strips, new siding.	R-12 to R-24	$3.95	$6,450	21.0	35.0	46.0	39.0	65.0	87.0
Stud wall	Add 2″ foam to interior wall, furring strips, new wall finish.	R-12 to R-30	$3.58	$5,850	17.0	28.0	37.0	32.0	52.0	70.0
Brick, stone, or concrete block	Add 2″ foam to exterior, furring strips, new siding.	R-2 to R-13	$3.95	$6,450	2.1	3.5	4.7	3.7	6.0	8.1
Brick, stone, or concrete block	Add studs to interior, 6″ batts, new wall finish.	R-2 to R-21	$3.71	$6,060	1.8	3.0	4.1	3.2	5.2	7.0
Post-and-beam	Add studs to exterior, 6″ batts, new siding.	R-5 to R-24	$3.71	$6,060	4.0	6.7	8.9	7.4	12.0	16.0
Post-and-beam	Add 2″ foam to exterior, furring strips, new siding.	R-5 to R-17	$3.95	$6,450	4.8	7.9	11.0	8.5	14.0	19.0
Post-and-beam	Add 2″ foam to interior, furring strips, new wall finish.	R-5 to R-21	$3.58	$5,850	4.1	6.7	9.0	7.3	12.0	16.0
Log	Add studs to interior, 6″ batts, new wall finish.	R-12 to R-30	$3.68	$6,000	17.0	28.0	38.0	33.0	54.0	72.0

Note: In this table, we've calculated the payback period of various insulation retrofit options for a model house in two climates: Albany, New York (6,900 heating degree days) and Albuquerque, New Mexico (4,300 heating degree days). The model house has 1,632 square feet of solid wall area and 288 square feet of double-glazed windows.

If your climate is similar to either Albany's or Albuquerque's, then the table will provide a fairly close estimate of the payback periods for your house, even if your home has more or less wall and window area than our model. (But keep in mind that labor and materials costs vary widely from place to place. Higher unit costs will lengthen payback periods.)

If you live in a place that's colder than Albany, your insulation payback periods will be shorter than those listed in the "Albany" column; if your climate is warmer than Albuquerque's, payback periods will be longer than those in the "Albuquerque" column.

Another factor that can greatly affect payback is energy cost. The periods given in the table were based on electricity at $.07 per kilowatt-hour, oil at $1.10 per gallon, and natural gas at $.65 per therm. If your energy costs are higher, you could realize a faster payback.

the materials in your walls is important, since your findings will determine your insulation options.

There are a few clues that can make the search easier. If an exterior wall is about 8 inches thick, it may be made of concrete block; but you should probe through any surface finishes to find out for sure. If the exterior side is brick and the interior side is drywall or plaster, the wall is either a stud wall with brick veneer or a solid brick wall. A wall with exterior siding is likely to be a stud wall, though the siding may conceal masonry. If you get a hollow sound when you thump on it, you've probably got some kind of frame construction.

You can also get an idea of how your walls were built by looking at them from the attic. A 2 × 4 top plate typically caps a stud wall, while a heavy 8 × 8 or larger beam often indicates post-and-beam construction. The tops of masonry walls, too, are often exposed in the attic. If you live in an older home, you may find a few different kinds of walls because of rooms that have been added on over the years.

In the search for your wall type, you may also have found out whether the walls contain any insulation, and if so, how much. You may have to pry something loose to find out. Then look at our graph, "How Much Insulation Is Enough?"(figure 3-1). It compares various wall R-values with the energy savings they produce. As the graph shows, improving a wall from, say, R-3 to R-11 yields a big energy savings. But going further—say from R-12 to R-20—doesn't produce anywhere near the savings. So if your walls already have some insulation, they may be "warm" enough.

Where to Add Insulation

Depending on your wall construction, there are as many as three places where you can add insulation. You can add a layer on the inside, on the outside, or in the cavities found in stud framing and some types of masonry construction.

Figure 3-1. As this graph shows, the heating needs of a house go down as the R-value of the home's exterior walls goes up, no matter where the house is located. The graph also shows that doubling the R-value of exterior walls will not double energy savings. The greatest reduction in heat loss occurs when insulation levels are increased from R-2 to about R-12. Adding insulation beyond the R-12 level is cost-effective only in very cold climates.

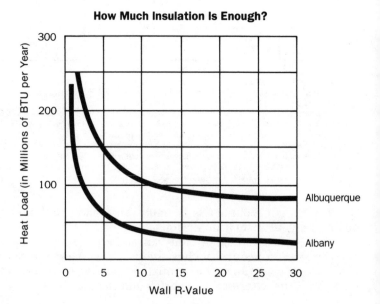

How Much Insulation Is Enough?

Filling existing wall cavities is usually the most economical option. Blown-in cellulose, fiberglass, or mineral wool are the materials most commonly used to insulate stud walls. All three have good R-values (R-3 to R-4 per inch). Fiberglass and mineral wool have better fire resistance, but do not seal out the wind as well as cellulose (which is still fire-resistant enough to be code approved).

All three materials can be blown in by a professional installer or by a knowledgeable do-it-yourselfer. Care must be taken to make sure that blown insulation fills the total cavity, leaving no uninsulated voids where heat can escape. Preventing voids is mostly a matter of careful work—especially around places where the flow of blown insulation can be blocked, such as cavities below windows, fireblocking, bracing in cavities, and small cavities in corners.

Settling can occur after installation, usually causing voids at the top of a cavity. The best way to prevent settling is to use adequate pressure when blowing in the insulation. But it's a good idea to leave a place where you can check to see if settling has occurred, because even a 3- or 4-inch gap at the top of the wall can reduce the overall R-value. Some professional installers check their work with temperature-sensing scanners to make sure they've left no voids. Some will provide a guarantee against settling and voids.

You'll help preserve the full R-value of blown-in insulation if you paint the interior wall surface with vapor barrier paint and seal openings (such as those for electrical switches and sockets) that could be a path for moisture into the stud wall. Bathrooms and laundries should be equipped with fans to vent excess moisture.

Cavities in masonry walls can be filled with vermiculite or perlite *poured* insulation. These materials are rated at R-2 to R-3 per inch and have a very high resistance to fire, rot, and moisture. When they're poured, they behave almost like a liquid, filling in most nooks and crannies. Neither material settles very much, but you have to be careful to seal any holes where they might leak out of the walls.

A new material that can be used in both stud wall and masonry cavities is *cementitious foam* insulation. Unlike other "wet" foam applications, this product doesn't expand as it cures, so it can be used to fill an enclosed cavity with no concern for a "blowout." Being cementitious, or cement-based, the foam has very good fire resistance.

Insulating Solid Walls

If you have walls with no cavities (such as poured concrete, filled concrete block, brick or stone, log walls, or a stud wall that is already filled), then you can add a layer of insulation to the interior or exterior of the wall.

To add interior insulation, first put up furring strips or studs (depending on how deep a cavity you want to create) along the walls to be insulated. The cavities formed by furring out the wall can then be filled with rigid foam or fiberglass batts.

A good choice for rigid foam for interior use is foil-faced isocyanurate or the new phenolic foam made by the Koppers Company, Inc., both of which have high R-values (R-7 to R-8 per inch). If you tape the seams between sheets of foil-faced foam, the insulation will also serve as a vapor barrier.

Adding a layer of interior insulation means, of course, that you'll have to add a new wall finish (such as paneling or drywall), extend window and door jambs and trim, and reinstall electrical outlets and switches. It's also a good idea to insulate the rim joist between floors to reduce both heat loss and the risk of condensation between floors. This isn't an easy job by anyone's standards, since it often involves removing part of the ceiling. You should also consider the loss of floor space and the general remodeling ruckus that this approach causes.

Exterior insulation can be added in a few different ways. Furring strips or full studs can be fastened to the outside of the wall to create new cavities for foam or fiberglass insulation. As on the inside, this approach will require adding a new finish and extending door and window frames, sills, and trim. Expanded or extruded polystyrene foam make good choices for exterior-wall insulation, since they don't tend to trap as much condensation inside the wall as foil-faced foams.

You can also use a system in which sheets of rigid foam are actually bonded to the exterior, then covered with two layers of an acrylic- or cement-based stucco. This strategy makes sense with solid masonry walls, since it overcomes the difficulty of using mechanical fasteners.

If you're adding insulation to a frame building, you can reduce air infiltration a good deal by wrapping the house with polyethylene film before installing the insulation. Just be sure that at least two-thirds of the R-value of the wall insulation is on the *outside* of the vapor barrier, in order to eliminate potential condensation problems.

If you're considering an interior renovation that requires gutting some walls, or if you're removing exterior siding for replacement, it may make sense to make "warmer walls" part of the project. Such major renovations create opportunities to insulate without furring out or studding out the wall. And you can add such important elements as a vapor barrier (interior) or air infiltration barrier (exterior) in the process.

Conclusion

Our cost-payback table can, at best, give you a ballpark idea of how much an insulation retrofit could cost, and of how quickly that cost would be "repaid" by energy savings. Many variables (such as local climate, materials and labor costs, and the idiosyncracies of specific houses) enter into the payback equation, so the table is best used only as a general *indicator* of feasibility.

The savings figures listed in table 3-1 are based purely on reducing *conductive* heat loss—but an insulated wall also blocks cold

Photo 3-2. One good way to create warmer walls is to install sheets of rigid foam insulation on the exterior of your house, seal the joints between the panels, then cover them with new siding. (Photo by Carl Doney)

air infiltration, which could increase the savings figures, especially in the case of frame walls.

It's up to you to decide if a possible 7-, 10-, or 15-year payback is an acceptable rate of return. But remember that even a 10-year payback represents a 10 percent annual rate of return, tax free. In our current period of low inflation and low interest rates, that kind of return could make "warmer walls" one of the most satisfying investments around.

For Further Information

The Exterior Insulation
  Manufacturers Association
1133 15th St., NW
Washington, DC 20005

Koppers Company, Inc.
436 7th Ave.
Pittsburgh, PA 15219

—**Terry Brennan and Chuck Silver**

ENERGY LOOPHOLES
Costly Heat Leaks You May Have Missed

Recent studies have revealed some surprising places where your house may be leaking heat. These "energy loopholes" lose heat in two ways: by air leakage (infiltration or exfiltration) and by conduction (heat passing through a solid material). Hidden heat leaks may well account for up to 70 percent of the infiltration losses and 45 percent of the conductive losses in houses that have been conventionally insulated, caulked, and weatherstripped. By plugging these energy gaps, you can shave off *over* one-third of your present heating bill.

A prime place to start looking for energy loopholes is in your basement. In an uninsulated house, foundations and basement floors account for a fairly small proportion of heat loss—less than 20 percent of the total. But as other parts of the house are thermally improved, the basement's share of heat loss can amount to as much or more than 35 percent of the total.

A brick, fieldstone, or masonry block foundation often has gaps and loose mortar, both inside the basement and out. Because the blocks are partially hollow, air that leaks through a below-grade hole on the inside can escape through an above-grade hole on the outside, creating a convective loop that cools the basement (see figure 3-2).

It's amazing how many older homes are afflicted by this phenomenon. The remedy is to stuff all interior and exterior holes with compressed fiberglass and apply polyurethane foam sealant. Caulk hairline cracks with butyl rubber caulking. As additional insurance against future leaks, cover all repairs with mortar.

Convective loops that begin in the basement don't necessarily stop there; some can rob a house of heat all the way to the attic. The cool basement and attic areas are connected to many hollow interior wall cavities. If cool air gets into these wall cavities, it cools the surfaces of interior partition walls, robbing warmth from rooms by conduction.

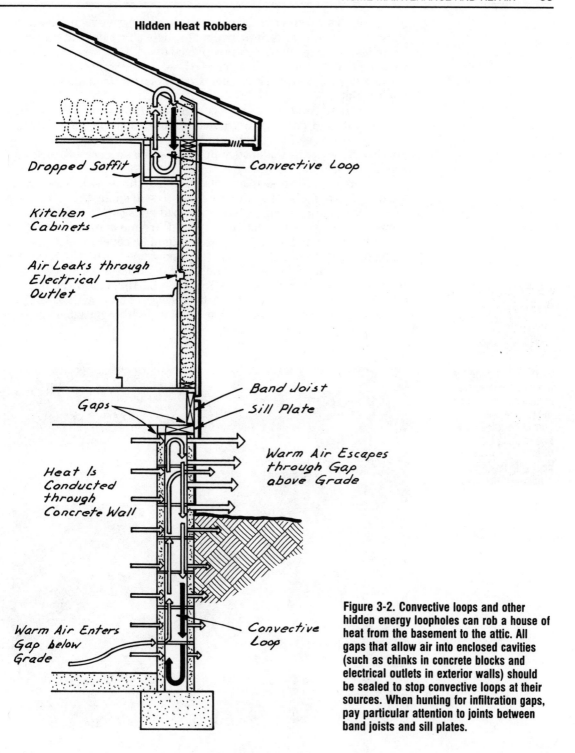

Hidden Heat Robbers

Dropped Soffit — Convective Loop

Kitchen Cabinets

Air Leaks through Electrical Outlet

Gaps

Band Joist

Sill Plate

Heat Is Conducted through Concrete Wall

Warm Air Escapes through Gap above Grade

Warm Air Enters Gap below Grade

Convective Loop

Figure 3-2. Convective loops and other hidden energy loopholes can rob a house of heat from the basement to the attic. All gaps that allow air into enclosed cavities (such as chinks in concrete blocks and electrical outlets in exterior walls) should be sealed to stop convective loops at their sources. When hunting for infiltration gaps, pay particular attention to joints between band joists and sill plates.

Cool air in wall cavities also causes convective heat losses: As heated room air leaks into walls through electrical outlets, wall switches, and gaps in trim, it is replaced by cold air from the attic or basement. A telltale indication of these air currents is the black residue left by airborne dust and dirt on plaster, framing members, and insulation.

To seal off these convective currents at their source, you'll need several tubes of good quality silicone caulk, a staple gun, polyethylene plastic sheeting (6 mils thick), duct tape, fiberglass batting, polyurethane foam sealant (which comes in an aerosol can), and acoustical sealant.

Before trying to seal any gaps, clean them with a brush or vacuum cleaner. Use the silicone caulk to seal small gaps (those up to ¼ inch), and foam to fill medium-sized gaps (up to 1 inch wide). Larger openings—such as those found around wiring, plumbing, heating ducts, and laundry chutes—should be covered with plastic, stapled well around the perimeter, and sealed around the edges with acoustical sealant. As a final touch, reduce conductive losses through these gaps by securing fiberglass batting below the plastic. (Contrary to popular belief, stuffing larger holes with fiberglass alone will not remedy infiltration problems. Fiberglass batting is a conductive barrier, not an air barrier.)

Photo 3-3. Among the most common energy loopholes found in older homes are cracks between walls and door and window frames. Caulk is a good way to deal with this problem. (Photo by Carl Doney)

Outdoor air often leaks into the basement in the area where the sill plate meets the band joists (see figure 3-2). To solve this common leakage problem, first sweep or vacuum the sill to remove dust, then lay a generous bead of foam sealant along the joint where the sill plate and band joists meet. While doing this, also fill any gaps you see *over* the sill plate, another common problem area. Next, cut pieces of extruded polystyrene insulation (or of 6-inch fiberglass batt) and fit them tightly between the floor joists.

Other common causes of basement air leaks include window frames, bulkhead doors, dryer vents, and washing machine or floor drains. If you haven't done so already, caulk and weatherstrip all doors and windows, filling the larger gaps with polyurethane foam sealant. Check the operation of your dryer's vent flapper and cover floor drains when they're not in use (uncovered drains have been known to admit enough of a draft to blow out a match). Also, seal all joints in the ductwork with quality duct tape.

After you've given your basement walls, floor, and ceiling a good overhaul, you're ready to examine another basement air thief—your oil- or gas-fired space heating system and domestic water heater. The same units that heat your house also swallow some of the air they've warmed and send it up the chimney.

The worst offenders in this regard are leaky wood-burning units, older gas furnaces without forced-draft fans, and old oil-burners. All of these heating systems require large amounts of warm indoor air for combustion and encourage the infiltration of cold outdoor air.

One way to remedy these losses is to install an insulated duct that will bring in outside air to the heater's burner for combustion. You could also put in an automatic flue damper that will reduce draft losses when the furnace or boiler isn't on. Another option is to purchase a new energy-efficient heating system with built-in features to eliminate the need for add-ons.

Now go to the attic and finish the job begun in the basement, sealing off all points where air may be penetrating into partition walls and living spaces. Wearing work gloves and a face mask, move the existing insulation around in order to locate the tops of partition walls. Seal the cavities with plastic and acoustical sealant, then reinsulate.

Attic hatches are notorious sources of both conductive and convective heat loss. To stop air leakage, make sure that the hatch fits snugly in its frame (weatherstripping and sash clamps are a help). Then, from the attic side, caulk around the frame. Finally, insulate the hatch door with fiberglass or foam-board insulation to cut down on conductive losses.

Recessed light fixtures and metal chimneys also deserve special attention. Make sure that some clearance remains between them and the attic insulation. A plastic air/vapor barrier should *not* be installed within 3 inches of a flue pipe or light fixture. Instead, place a metal cylinder around the stack or fixture at the point where it

Sealing a Chimney

Figure 3-3. Chimney flues are prime sites for air leaks, but it's important to seal them in a manner that will not create a fire hazard. A metal cylinder that provides a 3-inch clearance around the flue pipe keeps insulation from coming into contact with the chimney. At the base of the cylinder, a sheet metal firestop provides a surface to which the air/vapor barrier can be sealed.

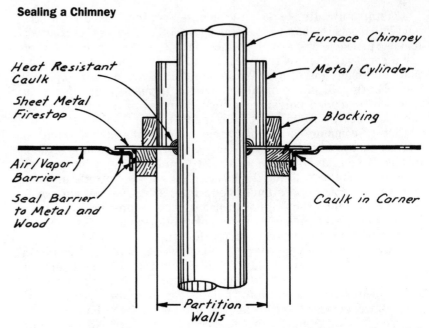

penetrates the attic. Then install a sheet-metal "firestop" at the bottom of the cylinder and seal the cylinder to the firestop with a heat resistant caulk (see figure 3-3). Ceiling mounted exhaust fans should include a built-in damper to slow heat loss.

Many sources of heat leakage can be dealt with from within the living space. Here's a list of measures you can take to fix several of the most common:

- Caulk all suspect door thresholds and baseboard with clear silicone caulk.

- Seal the collars around pipes leading to radiators, kitchen fixtures, and bathroom fixtures with foam sealant or silicone caulk. Also, seal any openings that may exist around a built-in bathtub.

- If you have forced-air heating, remove all floor registers and caulk around each duct to ensure a tight fit.

- Check above any removable drop ceiling tiles for any holes that need sealing.

- Dismantle pocket door trim, remove doors and seal the cavity off from convective channels.

- Investigate the possibility of opening up, sealing, and insulating soffit cavities found at the top of some kitchen cabinets (see figure 3-2).

- Remove the cover plates from all electrical outlets and switches on both interior and exterior walls, and install a foam gasket to seal the openings. (Or, use plastic box enclosures that enable you to seal a standard electrical box to a plastic vapor barrier.)

- If you have a fireplace, seal the joints between the wall and the fireplace surround, as well as the mantel, with caulk. Check the damper for a tight fit, and replace it if necessary. If the fireplace is not used, insert a piece of foil-faced fiberglass snugly against the damper.

After completing these forays into your home's far corners, you can expect a pleasant surprise when your next heating bill arrives. You'll even reap some side benefits, including fewer rodent problems and reduced chances of frozen pipes.

But if you've searched high and low for heat losses and *still* have a nagging draft or hefty heating bill, try calling in an expert. "House doctors" now offer their services in some parts of the country; they're equipped with blower doors, smoke guns, and infrared scanners that are sure to pinpoint your home's hidden energy loopholes.

For Further Information

Tremco
10701 Shaker Blvd.
Cleveland, OH 44104   **—Roger Harris**

FREEZEPROOF YOUR HOUSE
Winterize Now and Beat the Big Chill

Most of us wouldn't think of letting cold weather arrive without checking the antifreeze in our cars. It's a simple enough job, almost a rite of fall: Pour in a few quarts of that bright green liquid, and the radiator is ready for winter. But when it's time to protect an entire house from winter's fury, there is no single liquid and no simple fill-up that'll do the job.

Winterizing a house is decidedly more involved than adding antifreeze. But when you consider the risks of not making the effort—troublesome and costly events like a burst water pipe, a leaky roof, or serious water damage—freezeproofing begins to look like a pretty important part of keeping your home from getting under the weather.

The best way to avoid (or at least limit) the problems caused by ice, snow, and freezing temperatures is a little preventive maintenance, backed up by an early-warning system to alert you to trouble. It also helps to be prepared for making emergency repairs in case all else fails.

The most vulnerable part of a house in winter is the plumbing system. Water-supply pipes sitting unused overnight can freeze into long, tubular ice cubes. Winter weather, particularly cycles of cold, sunny days followed by frigid nights, also attacks roof shingles, wood siding, stucco, driveways, and patios.

Start your prevention program during construction or renovation. Make sure that exposed water pipes are *inside* the house's insulation, not outside against a cold exterior wall. When installing plastic pipe, leave some slack. Several firms recommend allowing about 6 inches of expansion room for every 50 feet of pipe. The extra flexibility will make plastic pipes less likely to rupture if they freeze.

You may still have lingering cold spots that freeze even after you've caulked, insulated, and bumped up the thermostat. The best solution for these trouble spots is a thermostatically controlled heat tape. Looking like flattened extension cords, these wires can be spiraled around the freeze-prone pipe (the tighter the spiral, the greater the protection) and plugged into an outlet. When the temperature drops, a built-in thermostat turns on enough heat to keep the pipe from freezing.

Outside, the idea is to keep everything moving. Be sure gutters slope toward the downspout. (Test them with a hose before winter.) Otherwise, water can collect and freeze, causing ice dams that pry up shingles and create all sorts of chaos.

Check your roof flashing, too, especially where the shingles meet the chimney. On reroofing jobs, too many contractors simply press new aluminum flashing into a bed of roof cement. This treatment keeps water out for a season or two, but, eventually, expansion and contraction break the seal, and the flashing becomes a funnel, channeling rain and snow under the shingles and into the house. To prevent this effect, the upper edge of flashing must be folded into the seam between chimney bricks, then mortar must be added to seal the seam and secure the flashing.

Exterior faucets are another place to check. First, drain and detach all garden hoses. Ideally, each outside faucet should have a cutoff valve inside the house. When cold weather approaches, turn off the supply at the indoor cutoff, then open the outside faucet to drain any remaining water.

If you're likely to forget such things, consider installing a freezeproof valve. It's an outside faucet with a long stem that reaches inside the house to the shutoff valve. A freezeproof valve operates just like an ordinary faucet, only when you turn the outside handle, you're actually shutting down the water supply inside.

Devices that warn of impending disasters are almost as important as measures that prevent them, since it's impossible to predict freak storms and power outages. The Brookstone Thermo Cube (about $10) can be plugged into any grounded outlet and responds to falling temperatures by activating a warning light, alarm, autodial phone, or heater you've plugged into it. The Thermo Cube uses a built-in, temperature-sensitive switch that can activate outlets at 0°, 20°, or 35°F.

The Eveready Freeze-Up Signal Light (about $30) turns on a flashing red light when the temperature at its remote sensor drops to 45°F. Installed near freeze-prone pipes, it can give you or your neighbors ample warning of an impending freeze.

Sump pumps are supposed to spring into action when water seeping into the sump pit raises the float to switch on the motor. Of course, if a pipe bursts while the power is out (which often happens, since no power usually means no heat), the float will rise—but the pump won't turn on. The Brookstone Sensitive Water Alarm ($17) is a battery-powered device that sounds a warning when there's as little as $\frac{1}{100}$ inch of water on the floor.

One of the most versatile early-warning devices is Gulf & Western Electronic's Sensaphone (about $200). Connected to the house wiring and phone lines, it monitors temperature, noise level, and power-supply status. Accessories can tie the system into burglar alarms, remote fire detectors, and other devices. The phone part of the system can be programmed to dial four telephone numbers in sequence until one is answered. Then a computer-synthesized voice reports the problem.

No preventive measures can stop a winter storm from dumping mounds of snow on your roof. Before the heavy covering damages your roof, shovel off as much snow as you can. Clear the snow early in the day, so the sun can melt any ice remaining on the shingles. If the gutter or downspout is frozen solid, flush it with hot water.

Looking ahead to the next snowstorm, think about installing heat tapes in a zigzag pattern over the shingles. They'll produce enough heat to prevent ice dams and protect the roof and gutter system.

How to Cope with a Broken Pipe

Despite the best commonsense preventive measures and the latest high-tech warning devices, pipes still manage to burst. How to cope with the middle-of-the-night-broken-pipe emergency is a perennial question with any number of answers.

If the leak is literally a pinprick spouting a small but steady stream of water, try plugging the hole with a thin piece of copper wire or a sharp lead pencil. For larger leaks, where frozen water has split apart a straight section of pipe, wrap the area with a heavy piece of flexible rubber and secure it with hose clamps.

Locating the frozen section can sometimes be a problem. Chances are, it will be in an out-of-the-way spot, such as an underinsulated wall behind a sink. Try drilling a series of small holes in the wallboard under the sink to let warm air into the cavity. (You can speed the thawing process with a hair dryer.)

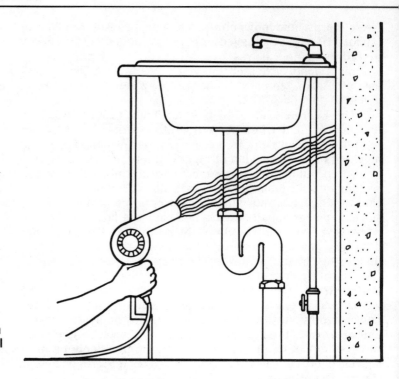

Figure 3-4. If you find yourself with frozen pipes, a small hair dryer will help you thaw them.

Most residential plumbing is either copper or plastic. Both kinds are easy to repair on the spot. Plastic can be recut, cleaned, and recemented with solvent. In some areas where polybutylene is used, fittings are joined with a crimp connector that requires a special tool.

To resolder a copper joint, first drain the line. Instead of reusing old fittings, which have to be cleaned of any remaining solder, keep a few short lengths of pipe and some L- and T-fittings on hand, along with a coil of solder, flux, a torch, and a rotary pipe cutter.

Use the pipe cutter to remove the split section. If the pipe is tight against a wall, try a hacksaw. Push down on the pipes a bit to drain any remaining water. Scuff up the ends of the copper pipe with sandpaper or steel wool, then apply a liberal layer of flux. Scuff the inside edges of any fittings required, join the sections, then apply heat, moving the torch around the joint. When the flux bubbles, and the joint is hot enough to make solder flow, remove the torch and apply the solder all around the joint.

A few safety reminders: In tight quarters, be careful not to ignite surrounding materials. Be sure that both you and the pipe joint are in a secure and stable position during the soldering. And let the pipe cool for a few minutes before turning the water back on. Of course, a good professional plumber will use just the right amount of flux, heat, and solder, then wipe the joint to leave a neat, silvery ring. But who cares if your emergency repair is a little messy—as long as it's watertight.—**Mike McClintock**

COMING CLEAN
Keep Your Dishwasher Running Smoothly

I f your dishwasher isn't getting the dishes as clean as you'd like, don't automatically blame it on the detergent. The machine itself may be the cause. A malfunctioning dishwasher can make all the appropriate sounds when you turn it on, while behind the closed door a mechanical glitch is interfering with the cleaning.

Many dishwasher repairs are simple. So before you call in a professional, do a little troubleshooting to see if you can fix the problem yourself.

Start with the obvious. Look for objects that might be obstructing the operation of moving parts. Small items like measuring spoons can fall under the racks and block the sprayer or the water flow to the pump. Sometimes silverware slips through the basket and stops the sprayer arm. The dishwasher will run when moving parts are blocked, but it won't do its job very well.

Open up your dishwasher's access panel (see steps 1 and 2 below) and look around inside for signs of trouble. Check hoses for cracks, kinks, or worn spots. Look for corrosion or stains that might indicate a leak in the seal around the shaft that passes through the bottom of the washing compartment.

If your dishwasher runs but doesn't fill with water, the water inlet valve is probably the culprit. What follows are step-by-step instructions that will help you diagnose and replace a faulty inlet valve.

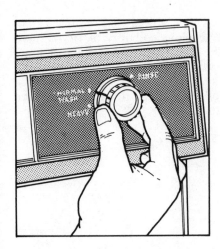

Step 1: Disconnect the dishwasher from the power supply. If you have a plug-in model, simply unplug it. But if the unit is permanently wired, turn the circuit off at the main distribution panel. To facilitate later testing, be sure the timer switch is in the "Off" position.

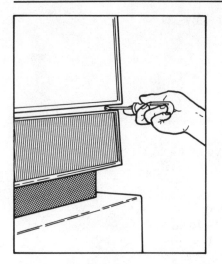

Step 2: Remove the access panel. On most brands it's below the door on the front of the machine. Locate the water supply pipe that leads to the inlet valve. The electrically-operated valve will be fastened to the chassis of the machine. You'll usually find a plastic-covered two-conductor plug snapped onto terminals on the valve.

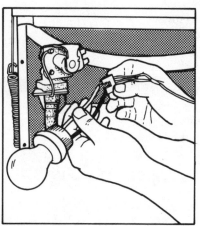

Step 3: With the electricity off, connect a circuit tester to the hot and neutral leads of the solenoid. Turn on the power and set the indicator knob to the wash cycle. The circuit tester should light. If it doesn't, there's no power getting to the valve. But don't change the valve yet.

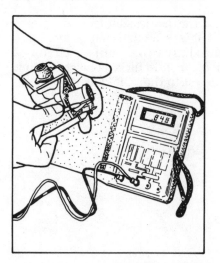

Step 4: The inlet valve is operated by an electromagnet, which looks like a long coil of wire. If you have an ohmmeter, check the coil for damage. Touch the meter leads to the valve terminals. If the needle shows no resistance, the coil is shorted. An infinite resistance reading means the coil is broken. In either case, the valve must be replaced.

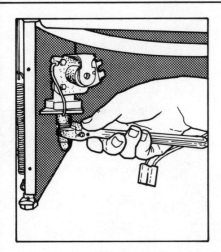

Step 5: To replace the valve, shut down the power and water supplies and disconnect the plumbing. Even with the water off, a small amount may drip out of the pipes when you open them. Work over a shallow pan, or keep a rag handy.

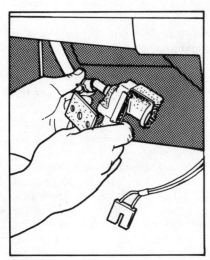

Step 6: Remove the old inlet valve. In most cases several bolts or screws hold the valve to the chassis of the machine. Keep track of these fasteners, since you'll probably need them to install the new valve. Take the broken valve, and the make and model of the machine, to your service center to get a replacement. If they don't have the exact part, you may be able to substitute one from a similar model.

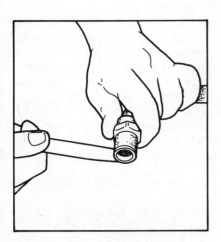

Step 7: Install the new valve. Mount it on the chassis and reconnect the plumbing. If there are threaded connections, it's a good idea to put fresh thread tape on them. Wrap the tape in a clockwise direction to keep it in place as you thread the fittings together.

Step 8: Replace the access panel. When the electricity and water are turned back on, run the machine through a cycle.

Tools and Supplies

Adjustable wrench	Pipe thread tape
Electrical circuit tester	Rags or shallow pan
Nut drivers	Replacement valve
Ohmmeter (optional)	Screwdrivers

—**Fred Matlack**

PLUMBER'S HELPER
Avoiding Common Plumbing Emergencies

In the ten years he's been a plumber in St. Paul, Minnesota, Mel Roubik has been called out to fix just about everything that could go wrong with a plumbing system. Some problems are unpreventable, but many could have been avoided.

Like the time a woman called while Mel was watching the ten o'clock news. She was hysterical. A neighbor had offered to fix a drip around the water meter in her house. But after cutting the main pipe, he admitted he had no idea what to do next—and left as the basement slowly filled with water.

Sidestepping disasters like that is largely a matter of common sense. But the woman's experience does illustrate one important point about plumbing, says Roubik: "Little problems can grow into big ones."

To keep soggy and frightening emergencies from occurring Roubik advises that you inspect your plumbing system once or twice a year. If you find little problems like drips, fix them right away, before they have a chance to get bigger and more expensive.

Suppose, for example, you have a two-handled faucet that's dripping. If you don't nip the problem in the bud, your family will probably just turn the handles down harder to stop the water. In time, the screw holding the washer will gouge a hole into the faucet seat, wrecking the whole thing. "Now, instead of a washer, you need to buy and install a complete faucet," says Roubik.

What plumbing projects are fair game for the homeowner? "I say you can do anything if you take the time to figure it out," he answers. "It gets down to what's cheapest, and the value of your time." But, he adds, if you tackle small repairs, certain approaches can help keep you out of trouble. Such as:

■ Before you break into a plumbing system, have everything you'll need to put it back together close at hand. Go over the job in your head a few times, and write down what you have to buy. Then gather all the supplies in one trip, even if you have to go to several stores. And, as you start tearing things apart, lay the new parts next to the old parts to make sure you have everything.

■ "Buy only two pipe wrenches, and make sure they're small ones, not more than 14 inchers," says Roubik. Big wrenches, he explains, make forcing things too easy. He's often called in to help a homeowner who has shut off the water service to the house, but can't get it back on. "Usually it's because they've turned the valve down so hard that when they try to open it again, the threads strip on the inside," he says.

■ If you're cutting out a section of old galvanized steel pipe, get some help. While you cut, your helper can keep that pipe from shaking. Otherwise you can break joints loose further down the line, and your minor project will turn into a big headache.

■ For leak-free threaded joints, use both Teflon tape and pipe compound. Put the tape on first, in a clockwise direction. Then apply compound over that. "The only exception I make is where small bits of tape could break loose and jam up delicate control mechanisms," adds Roubik. "I don't use the tape on gas lines, right next to a dishwasher, or directly in front of a water pump with a pressure gauge."

■ When soldering copper pipe, make sure the fittings are clean inside and out. "You can use emery cloth or sandpaper, but I also like those green Scotchbrite pads," says Roubik. "They don't shred when they get wet, like sandpaper does." And while you're soldering, watch that you don't overheat the joint. Play the torch over it

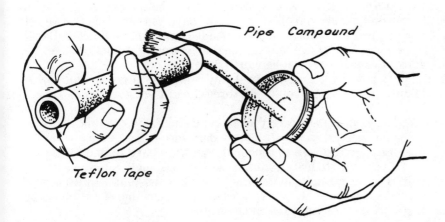

Pipe Compound

Teflon Tape

Figure 3-5. For leak-free threaded joints, apply Teflon tape in a clockwise direction, then spread pipe compound over it.

just until the solder starts to run, then take the torch away. If the joint is too hot, the flux won't stick.

■ Copper joints are harder to solder if there is moisture in them. A good trick, says Roubik, is to use pieces of bread to hold back the moisture temporarily. Roll the bread up into little balls and stuff them into the pipe. But move quickly to solder the joint, since the bread will only dam up the water for a short time before it dissolves.

■ If you have regular problems with frozen pipes, the best solution is to cut a hole on the inside of the wall near the pipe and cover the opening with a louvered register. The air from the house can keep the pipe above freezing. "There are lots of different ways to thaw pipes, but I use a small hair dryer," Roubik says.

■ To clear plugged drains, try using a small snake. If that doesn't work, call a professional. "Liquid drain cleaners can be hard on pipes and traps," he says. "I try not to use them."

Roubik says most of his work is replacing appliances, jobs that the homeowner could usually do. But what you need to know is when to replace and when to repair. Here are some of the plumber's thoughts on the subject:

Water Heaters: "My rule of thumb is to replace a water heater if it's ten years old or older, especially if there's carpeting in the basement. When a water heater goes out, 90 percent of the time it's because the tank is leaking. The rest of the time, it's the controls that go out."

Roubik says it's hard to tell how old a heater is by looking at it. But if it starts rumbling, beware. That's a sign there are deposits on the bottom that could pop the glass in the tank within a year.

Faucets: If a faucet goes bad after about five years, Roubik will usually replace it. The reason, he says, is that often the faucet has dripped for months and the inside is probably damaged. But if it's a quality cartridge faucet, like those made by Kohler or Moen, he adds, it could very well be worth fixing.

"If you need a new faucet, my motto is to go for quality. A higher-priced faucet could last three times as long as a cheap one."

Toilets: Toilets rarely need replacing, says Roubik. Most of those he does replace are older models with a flush elbow connecting a tank on the wall to the bowl. Parts are hard to find for these.

If you have to install a toilet, he cautions, make sure you get the wax ring set straight under the base. Otherwise, it will leak. And don't forget that the parts in a new toilet are loose and must be tightened before you turn on the water.

Supply Pipes: If the pipes in your house are 30 or so years old, corrosion can build up so the flow is only about half of what it could be. "Sometimes, I'll open up a pipe and I can't get a pencil through it," says Roubik.

You can't tell if a pipe is corroded by looking at the outside. A simple test is to open up the faucet on your laundry tub, then turn on the faucet that's farthest away from the service line. If you don't get a stream the size of a pencil, consider having the pipes replaced. (Roubik recommends *that* job only for do-it-yourselfers with lots of tools and plumbing experience.)

So what about those times when you do need to hire a professional? Try to get a written estimate for big projects. For small jobs, you may have to settle for an estimate over the phone. If it's an emergency and water is flying everywhere, you won't have much time for comparison shopping. But keep in mind that many independent plumbers (such as Roubik) can charge lower rates because their overhead isn't very high.—**Gene Schnaser**

KEEPING YOUR COOL
A Tune-up for Your Air Conditioner

C hances are your air conditioner's not ready for the hot muggy days coming up. Fortunately, you won't have to invest a lot of time and money to get it in shape.

The most important thing you can do to increase the efficiency and longevity of your air conditioner is to clean it regularly. Clean or replace its filters every month or two of use, and give the unit a complete cleaning and oiling once or twice a year.

Many homeowners are afraid to fool with their central air conditioners because they seem big and complicated. But gaining access to the inner workings of a central air conditioner isn't difficult. In most cases, you'll only have to remove a sheet-metal panel or two.

If your whole-house cooling system has a condensing unit mounted outdoors, make sure the air intake isn't blocked by bushes or debris. You'll need to clean the inside of the condensor, too. Air conditioners combined with heat pumps have more valves and tubing inside than conventional units do, but they're no more difficult to clean.

Room air conditioners are the easiest to deal with—everything you need is found under one housing. In some instances, you can slide the unit out of its case without even needing a screwdriver.

In the illustrated step-by-step instructions that follow, we'll show you how to tune up both central and room air conditioners. Maintenance is similar for both.

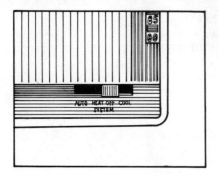

Step 1: Turn the power and the thermostat off. If your thermostat doesn't have an OFF or STANDBY position, turn the temperature to the highest setting, so that the compressor won't try to run when power is restored.

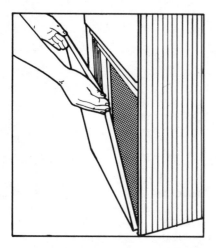

Step 2: Locate the filter. Check your owner's manual, or call the manufacturer of the air conditioner if you have trouble finding the filter. A foam filter is mounted right in the removable front of most room units. In central units, the filter is usually just upwind of the fan or blower in the air-handling unit (where all of the ducts originate). Access to the filter is almost always through a snap-out panel or easily accessible door.

Some larger units may have several filters surrounding the blower. Take a good look around before you assume that your first find is the only filter. Carefully note how the filter is installed so you can put it back in correctly after cleaning. Some filters are designed for one-way operation and won't work if they're put in backward.

Step 3: Clean the old filter, or replace it with a new one. Wash and squeeze out plastic foam filters as you would a sponge. Use a hose to spray dirt off filters made of aluminum or plastic. Direct a gentle spray at the downwind side of the filter to push the dirt back out the way it came in. Shake or blow out excess water, and allow the filter to dry.

The most common type of filter found in central systems is a disposable fiberglass panel with a cardboard frame. You can clean these filters once or twice by gently vacuuming with a soft furniture brush attachment. These filters won't stand up to rigorous cleaning; if the dirt doesn't come off easily, buy a replacement filter.

Step 4: Clean the coils in the condensing unit. Some room units can be slid out of their cases to expose the coils; with others, you may have to remove part of the housing that hangs outside the house. Pull small window units completely out of the window—they'll be easier to work on that way.

In central systems, the condensing unit is a separate fixture outside the house. Unscrew the screws that hold the grilles or louvered panels covering the unit; the covers should be easy to lift off. Put the panels aside carefully, and note where each belongs on the unit so that you'll be able to reassemble them correctly.

In any type of air conditioning unit, the coils have some type of surface treatment that increases their cooling ability. One common treatment is a series of plate fins very similar to those in an automotive radiator. These are fairly sturdy, and, with a reasonable amount of care and a soft vacuum brush, you can vacuum them from the outside (upwind) surface or hose them down from the inside (downwind) surface. Move the dirt back out the way it came in.

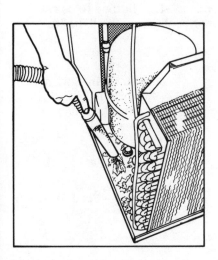

Spines or slit fins are another common surface material that look like strips of aluminum Christmas garland. Spines are a bit more flexible than plate fins, but with a light touch, they can be cleaned with the vacuum.

Use the crevice tool and work up and down over the tips of the spines. To wash spines, hose them down gently, working from the top down on the outside of the unit. Spray down at a steep angle to flush the dirt down and out. Avoid scraping or poking with any sharp instrument, since you could do permanent damage.

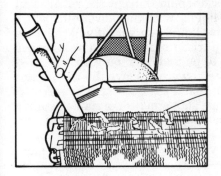

Step 5: Clean the interior of the unit by picking up any loose debris lying around inside and anything outside the air conditioner that's likely to be sucked in. For central units outside of the house, make sure that nothing obstructs the air intake, such as the bushes overgrowing the unit. Vacuum the blades of the blower and any other places you find dirt. Collections of dirt not only inhibit airflow, but they hold moisture and foster corrosion.

Step 6: Oil the motors. Look carefully at both ends of each motor. Motors not permanently lubricated should have a little cup on top of each end. (Check your owner's manual to find out if your unit is permanently oiled.) Put four to six drops of medium-weight (SAE-20) oil in each cup. Don't overoil; excess oil gathers dirt, which can shorten the life of the motor. Oiling once or twice a year should be enough.

Step 7: Reassemble the unit. Stick a label in a prominent spot on the inside of the unit, and date it so you can keep track of the time between cleanings. Replace the filters and any panels you've removed.

Step 8: Turn on the power after making sure the thermostat is still turned off. With air-conditioning equipment, you must go through a special procedure to turn the unit on after it has been off for a while. A small heater in the compressor (pump) keeps the refrigerant from condensing to a liquid. With the power off, there's a good chance that some liquid refrigerant will collect in the pump. If the pump tries to run, it could be damaged because it isn't made to pump liquid, only air.

After you turn the power on, leave the thermostat off long enough for the heater to evaporate any refrigerant that is in the pump. This process normally requires the same length of time that the power has been off—up to three hours.

If you find that your air conditioner needs more than a good cleaning—if drive belts are worn or refrigerant is leaking, for example—contact the local authorized dealer for your brand of air conditioner.

Whirlpool operates a toll-free hotline to assist you with your air-conditioner problems: 800-253-1301.

Tools and Supplies

Garden hose

Oil can

SAE 20-weight oil

Screwdriver or wrench

Vacuum cleaner with a soft-bristled furniture brush attachment and a crevice tool

—Fred Matlack

HOME WIRING INSPECTION
Knowledge Equals Power

You're getting ready to do some ironing. The air conditioner in your laundry room is running, and the lights are bright. You turn on the color television for a little diversion. Then you plug in the steam iron. Suddenly, everything stops. The room is dark, the TV screen blank, the air conditioner silent. You've blown a fuse.

Such scenes will be played out in many American homes this summer, as we overload the circuits of our homes' aging electrical systems. Only a few decades ago, when the electric bill was often—accurately—referred to as the "light bill," 120-volt, 30-ampere systems were considered normal and adequate.

But then we started plugging in more and more electrical conveniences. Today, a well-wired house may be outfitted with electrical service of 200 to 300 amps or more. And almost every home has at least one 220-volt circuit to handle such big users as ranges, clothes dryers, water heaters, and air conditioners.

Still, we blow fuses and trip circuit breakers. (A fuse panel is shown in figure 3-6 and a breaker box in figure 3-7.) And, 46,000 times a year in the United States, we start fires by asking too much of our homes' electrical systems. To help you avoid such problems in your house, we're going to take you behind your switchplates and inside your breaker boxes. We'll help you make a thorough inspection of your home's entire electrical system.

But first, a warning: Electricity can be dangerous. Before you get involved with your home's wiring, take these precautions.

■ Don't inspect any part of your electrical system until you've made sure the power is turned off. Use a voltage tester to check each circuit or electrical component you plan to work on or near. A voltage tester consists of two "leads" (insulated wires) attached to a neon bulb. When you touch one lead to a "live" wire (one that has current) and the other to a neutral wire, the bulb lights up. Test the tester: Try it out on a live circuit each time you use the voltage tester, to make sure it's working.

■ Never touch metal plumbing or gas-system pipes while you're working with electricity. If you accidentally touch a live wire while in contact with your plumbing or gas system, you'll be in for a real shock.

■ For the same reason, never stand on a damp floor or on the ground when working with electricity. Stand on a dry board, preferably one covered with a rubber mat.

■ Never assume anything, especially about someone else's work. Always use your voltage tester to check for live wires.

The Service Entrance

With safety foremost in your mind, you can proceed to examine your electrical system. Our inspection starts outdoors with a group of components known collectively as the service entrance (see figure 3-8), which bridges the gap between the power company's lines and your home's electrical system. Exposed to the elements year after year, your service entrance may well have lapsed out of mint condition.

Make sure all overhead cables hang clear of your house and nearby trees. These wires, called service-entrance conductors, typically enter a house via a weathertight service head and a length of

Figure 3-6. In a typical fuse panel, the electric service cable enters the panel box at the top. The two power leads of the cable feed power to the main power lugs, which are linked to the fuse receptacles. The fuses conduct current to the branch circuits. To turn off all the power, you can remove the main pullout. The smaller pullout beneath the main pullout protects a 120/240-volt branch circuit that feeds a large appliance (an electric range, in this case).

Fuse Panel

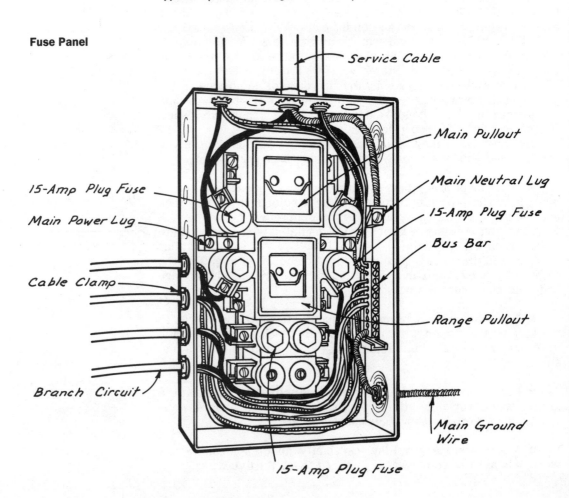

conduit known as a mast. At a point just before they pass through the house wall, the conductors are joined to the power company's electric meter. The service head, mast, and meter all should be in good shape and fastened securely to your house. Where the mast penetrates the wall, the hole should be caulked to keep out rain and rodents.

The Service Panel

If your service entrance seems shipshape, move inside, and check the service panel (also known as a breaker box or fuse box). First, carefully remove its cover; there's no telling what you will

Figure 3-7. If your service panel looks like this, your electrical system is protected by circuit breakers. The service cable enters through the top of the panel and terminates in the main breaker. The main breaker's two switches can shut off power to the entire house. Power buses at the bottom of the box pass current through the circuit breakers to the branch circuits.

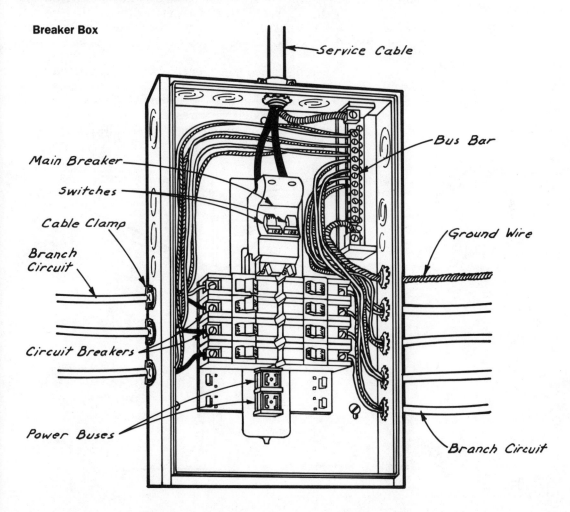

Breaker Box

Service Cable

Bus Bar

Main Breaker

Switches

Cable Clamp

Branch Circuit

Circuit Breakers

Ground Wire

Power Buses

Branch Circuit

find inside. Professional installations will look neat and well organized. If your service-panel wiring seems untidy, an amateur may have been at work. Proceed with caution.

With the panel cover off, you can see what type of wiring you're dealing with. Your wiring is either copper or aluminum and sheathed in plastic or armored (sheathed with a spiral steel jacket).

If you look closely at the cable sheath, you'll see a series of numbers and letters. For example, the cable might read: "12/2 with ground type NM 600V (UL)." These numbers and letters identify the voltage, gauge of wire, and cable type. The "12/2 with ground" means that there are two insulated conductors (one black and one white) of no. 12 AWG (American wire gauge) and one bare ground conductor. "Type NM" means that the cable is covered with a non-metallic sheath; "600V" means that it should not be used in circuits that handle more than 600 volts; and "(UL)" indicates that the cable has met the standards of Underwriters Laboratory. (Note: All of your electrical equipment should be listed by Underwriters Laboratory and have the UL seal.) If the cable sheath is marked "10/3 with ground," it means that there are three insulated conductors (one black, one white, and one that's usually red) and one bare ground conductor.

In a well-wired service panel, each circuit is protected by its own fuse or circuit breaker. Fuses and circuit breakers ensure the safety of your circuits by limiting the amount of current, measured in amps, that can flow through the wires. If you overload a circuit—plugging in, say, both an iron and a toaster oven—the fuse will blow

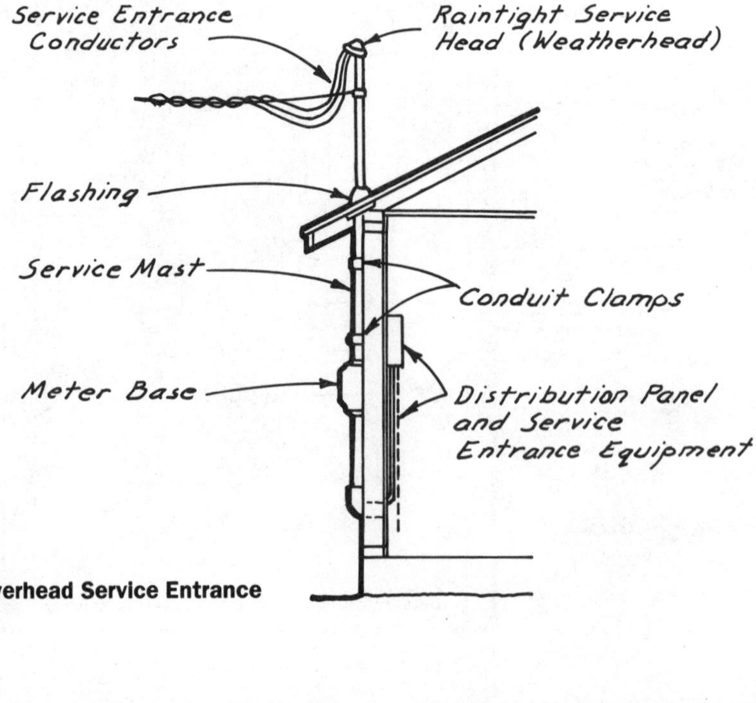

Figure 3-8. A typical overhead service entrance includes a service entrance conductor, a mast, a meter, and cables.

Service Entrance Conductors

Raintight Service Head (Weatherhead)

Flashing

Service Mast

Conduit Clamps

Meter Base

Distribution Panel and Service Entrance Equipment

Overhead Service Entrance

Table 3-2—CIRCUIT PROTECTION

Copper AWG Wire Size	Aluminum AWG Wire Size	Amperage
no. 14	no. 12	15
no. 12	no. 10	20
no. 10	no. 8	30
no. 8	no. 6	40
no. 6	no. 4	55
no. 4	no. 2	70

Note: To keep your circuits from overheating, you need a fuse or circuit breaker of the proper size. In this chart, the amperage for each wire size is the maximum for a breaker or fuse to protect that circuit.

or the breaker will trip before the circuit's wires can get dangerously hot. For this safeguard to work, your fuses or breakers must be sized to fit the gauge of each circuit's wire. Check table 3-2 for the correct fuse or breaker ratings for the wires of your branch circuits. You'll find the amperage of fuses printed on their faces or sides; circuit-breaker sizes are stamped on the switch ends.

This is an essential part of your inspection. Oversized fuses and circuit breakers are a very common—and very dangerous—home wiring hazard. When bothered by frequent circuit overloads, many homeowners take a perilous shortcut. Rather than spend the time to find out why a fuse keeps blowing, they simply pop in a bigger fuse. If someone has made this mistake at your house, correct the situation immediately.

While you have the cover off your service panel, make sure that your electrical system is grounded. Older systems weren't grounded, but today's codes require grounding, which protects you from short circuits and other possible defects in your electrical appliances. A properly grounded service panel will include a bare metal wire that's connected to a metal bar called a bus.

You should already have turned off the electrical power to the service panel and checked it with a voltage tester. Now see if the terminal screws for a few of the branch circuits are tight—particularly if your wiring is aluminum. Unlike copper wire, aluminum wire is coated with aluminum oxide, a compound that acts as an insulator and resists the flow of electricity. Aluminum wiring expands when it warms up and may tend to squeeze out from under terminal screws. Take special care that aluminum-wire terminals are tight.

The last step in inspecting your service panel is to make sure it's secured tightly to the wall and that each branch circuit cable is protected with a cable clamp where the cable enters the service panel.

Individual Circuits

Branching out from the service panel, your home's circuits may run along basement wall studs and ceiling or floor joists on their way to the outlet boxes. Your cables should be stapled every few feet; left hanging, they could pull against connections and loosen them. In exposed locations, where wires may be knocked or bumped, they should be protected by metal or PVC conduit.

If your house is old, you might discover that—instead of stapled, or plastic- or steel-sheathed cable—your wiring consists of individual wires held in place by porcelain knobs and run through porcelain tubes installed in joists. This is called knob-and-tube wiring. It is often found in old electrical systems that are sized to handle basic lighting needs but not the larger electrical appliances (electric ranges and air conditioners, for example) of today.

If you have such a system, it's important to double-check to make sure a previous homeowner hasn't overfused the system. If you need a greater capacity, the safe thing to do is replace the knob-and-tube wiring altogether. The same goes for any jobs where Type NM (plastic-sheathed) cable is openly spliced onto knob-and-tube wiring, or where telephone or Type SPT (common lamp wiring) has been used for any of your branch circuits.

Any spliced wire should be protected by a junction box. If you find a wire splice that has been made outside of a junction box, de-energize the circuit, test it with a voltage tester to make certain it's dead, then break the splice, install a junction box, and remake the splice inside the box.

To get a good idea of the condition of your outlet boxes, remove the cover plates from a few switch and receptacle boxes, and inspect their wiring. At least one of the receptacles you check should be a kitchen outlet that's subject to heavy loads—from toaster or electric frying pan, for example. To make sure a receptacle is dead, insert the voltage-tester leads into the receptacle slots.

If you're working with a switch, touch one of the voltage-tester leads to a wiring terminal screw and the other to the metal outlet box. If the receptacle or switch is dead, the neon bulb won't light. Repeat the test with the other wiring terminal screws. If the tester bulb still doesn't light, put the switch through one final test, just to be safe. Make sure the switch is turned off, then touch the leads to the terminal screws on either side of the switch. The bulb should not light. If it does, it means you have an ungrounded outlet box and a live circuit.

Look at the data stamped on the switch or receptacle and its yoke or harness (the metal strip on the switch or receptacle that allows it to be mounted on the outlet box). If it says "CU" or "CU Clad Only," it should be used only with copper or copper-clad wiring (for example, aluminum wire clad with copper). If it says "CO-ALR" (for 15- and 20-ampere devices) or "CU-AL" (for higher-amperage devices), the switch or receptacle may be used with either copper or aluminum wiring.

If your devices don't have those markings, they mustn't be used with aluminum wiring. Only such special switches and receptacles have the larger terminal heads and serrations required to cut effectively through the aluminum oxide coating and provide a good electrical connection when tightened. Again, the Underwriters Laboratory symbol should be there.

Another marking you should notice will say something like "15A 125V." This means the device can carry up to 15 amperes at voltages of up to 125 volts. Sometimes these markings are on the back of the device.

Switches and Receptacles

Once you're certain the wires leading to the switch or receptacle are dead, remove the screws that connect the yoke to the outlet box, and gently pull the device out of the box. You should find a clamp to protect and secure the cable where it enters the outlet box.

Standard wall duplex receptacles and wall switches are usually wired on the side with terminal screws or through the back with special spring clamps. (Typical wiring for a wall switch is shown in figure 3-9 and that for a duplex receptacle in figure 3-10.) The ground wire is held by either a screw at the back of the outlet box or a clip on the edge of the box (if it's metal). Check that all of the connections between wires and clamps or screws are tight, and that there are no signs of overheating, such as discolored terminal screws or melted or burned wire insulation.

Wiring ID

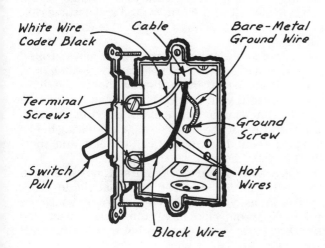

Figure 3-9. Where a cable terminates in a single pull switch, normally the black wire in a cable is the "hot" (i.e., current-carrying) wire, the white wire is the neutral, and the bare metal wire is the ground. But in certain applications, as in the switch shown here, the white wire is also hot. In such cases, it is usually (but not always) coded black at the tip.

Figure 3-10. This is what a typical grounded receptacle looks like. The one shown here is called a duplex, because it has room for two plugs.

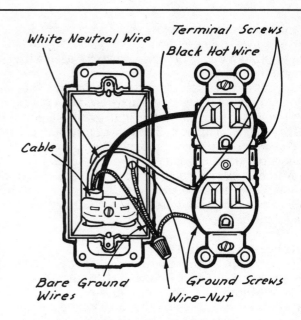

Grounded Duplex Receptacle

Your ceiling- and wall-mounted light fixtures should be equipped with integral junction boxes or properly mounted on outlet boxes, not screwed directly to ceiling joists or wall studs. If any of your light fixtures aren't properly enclosed in a junction box, you'll have to correct the situation.

By shutting off the power to the light circuit and lowering the fixture, you'll be able to see if there is an outlet box behind it and, at the same time, examine the condition of the wiring. But don't touch the wires without first checking them with your voltage tester. Also, don't just turn the light off at the wall switch and assume that the fixture is de-energized. It is always safer to de-energize the circuit at the service panel.

If the fixture has a metal outlet box, make sure it has a ground screw and that the ground wires from the cables are connected to it. Again, all wiring connections to the terminal screws should be tight.

After you have completed your inspection, you should have a good idea of the overall condition of your home's electrical system. From there you can study any of the several electrical wiring books available to learn more about home electrical systems and their repairs (a few titles are listed below).

If you plan to do any substantial work yourself, however, you must call your electrical inspector and find out what the local requirements are. In most areas, you're allowed to work on your own system but will probably be required to have your work inspected to make sure it's safe. Of course, your other option is to hire a local electrician to correct your system for you.

For Further Information

The Editors of Time-Life Books. *Advanced Wiring*. Alexandria, Va.: Time-Life Books, Inc., 1978

The Editors of Time-Life Books. *Basic Wiring*. Alexandria, Va.: Time-Life Books, Inc., 1976

National Electrical Code 1984. Batterymarch Park, Mass.: National Fire Protection Association, 1983

Richter, H. P., and W. Creighton Schwan. *Wiring Simplified*. St. Paul, Minn.: Park Publishing Co., 1983

—Roswell W. Ard

CHAPTER 4

INDOOR DO-IT-YOURSELF PROJECTS

We Americans are, on the whole, a practical lot. We like to tinker with our cars, grow at least some of the vegetables found on our dinner tables, and do our own lawn maintenance. Judging by the tremendous proliferation of home centers that cater to the enterprising do-it-yourselfer, large numbers of us are also attempting to serve as our own electricians, plumbers, carpenters, and painters.

Some statistics bear this out. In 1985, *Practical Homeowner* magazine mailed some 3,000 questionnaires to subscribers. Of the more than 2,300 respondents, 2,022 had remodeled their kitchens. And of that number, 85 percent did a substantial part of the work themselves. Similarly, of the 1,988 respondents who had remodeled a bathroom, 89 percent did much of the work themselves.

As we noted in the general introduction to this book, the amount of home remodeling activity going on nationwide has been increasing steadily over the past decade. If the respondents to our reader survey are at all representative of the country as a whole, we must conclude that a large amount of this work is being done by homeowners themselves. How do we account for such behavior?

Maybe it has something to do with the pioneer spirit or lingering memories of the Great Depression. Probably, it is in part an expression of the American tradition of rugged individualism, a dislike of being totally dependent upon others.

Whatever the explanation, it is clear that Americans in large numbers have become dedicated do-it-yourselfers. Woodworking is a popular hobby and the well-equipped home workshop is high on many people's wish list. Moreover, despite the specialization of modern professional life, an amazing number of Americans still build their own houses, while many more do a large part of the

127

Photo by Carl Doney

finish work on houses whose basic structure has been completed by professional contractors.

This chapter is made to order for the homeowner who enjoys embarking on the adventure of do-it-yourself projects. It offers step-by-step instructions for paneling basement walls, installing prehung doors, and carpeting stairs. It shows and tells how to lay tile on kitchen counters, replace a toilet, and install a home security system. Finally, it covers the basics on how to sand and refinish wood floors as well as tear out a load-bearing wall and install new ceiling beams.—**the editors**

TOP-NOTCH PANELING
Turning a Basement into New Living Space

Basements are often the most under-utilized spaces in the house. With their unfinished cement block or masonry walls, most basements have about as much appeal as the county jail. Bringing a basement out of the pits and turning it into pleasant living space is a job that requires only a modicum of do-it-yourself skills and a few basic tools.

Moisture problems are generally the biggest obstacle to enjoying basement rooms. If your basement is only slightly damp, paint the walls with a sealer, keep a dehumidifier running, or both. More serious moisture problems indicate a need for the repair of outside drainage (gutters, downspouts, and drainage tiles) to direct water away from the house. Be sure to take care of those problems before proceeding with the interior finish of the space.

Now check the condition of your walls and decide what type of insulation, if any, you wish to install, since both these factors will influence your decision on how to fur out the walls. If your walls are clean, dry, and straight, and space is at a premium, you will probably want to use ¾-inch-thick rigid foam insulation inserted between 1×2 or 1×3 furring strips run flat along the walls. This type of insulation can be fastened directly to the wall with construction adhesive, which comes in tubes made to fit a caulking gun. On the other hand, if you wish to use fiberglass batting, or if your walls are quite uneven, you will need to install a framework of conventional 2×4 studs. The latter approach will also allow room for the placement of plumbing pipes and electrical outlets behind the walls.

Once these basic decisions have been made, you are ready to begin finishing your basement walls. If you intend to use furring strips and rigid foam insulation, follow steps 1 through 3, then proceed to steps 7 through 9 for instructions on cutting and installing the paneling. On the other hand, if you plan to stud out your wall with 2×4s, begin with step 4 and proceed through step 9.

Step 1: If you elect to use furring strips, run a horizontal strip across the top and another across the bottom along the entire length of each wall. Then space vertical strips on 16-inch centers along the walls. Also, fur around all windows and doorways. Fasten the furring strips to the walls using either construction adhesive or masonry nails aimed at the mortar joints between the cement blocks.

Step 2: To install rigid foam insulation, measure and trim the pieces as needed to fit the spaces between furring strips, then use construction adhesive to fasten the insulation to the masonry walls. Now cover the insulation with 6-mil polyethylene sheeting to create a vapor barrier. Start at one end of the wall and staple the plastic to the furring strips. Insert a staple every few inches and pull the plastic taut as you go to create a smooth surface. It is best to cover an entire wall, including windows and doorways, with a single sheet of plastic, then go back later and cut out the needed openings.

Step 3: Since rigid foam insulation gives off toxic fumes when exposed to fire, it must be protected by a fire retardant material. Most panelings don't qualify as fire retardants, so a layer of drywall should be installed over the insulation before putting up the paneling. Drywall can be purchased in sheets as thin as ⅜ inch, but most building codes specify a minimum ½-inch thickness for residential construction. Fasten the drywall to the furring strips using 1-inch drywall nails or screws.

Step 4: To create a 2 × 4 wall framework, begin by nailing a top plate to the basement ceiling joists and fastening a bottom plate to the concrete floor. For the latter you will need either concrete screws or a combination of lead shields and lag screws as fasteners. Also, since your basement floor may not be completely level or regular, you may need to use shims to make the bottom plate level and parallel to the top plate.

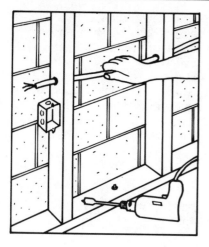

Step 5: Once the two plates are properly installed, cut 2 × 4 studs to fit the space in between them. Since these walls will not be bearing heavy loads, you can space the studs on 24-inch rather than 16-inch centers to save lumber. If you plan to use board paneling and intend to run the boards vertically, install horizontal pieces of 2 × 4 approximately ⅓ of the way down from the top and ⅓ of the way up from the bottom of the wall between the studs to provide additional nailing surfaces. After the wall framework is in place, run any desired plumbing pipes and wiring, and install any needed electrical switch and outlet boxes.

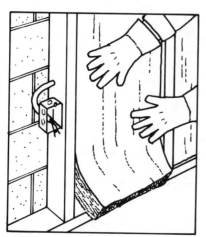

Step 6: Now pack the wall cavities with batt or blanket insulation. If the insulation has a built-in vapor barrier, turn it inside toward the living space. If it has no vapor barrier, after you have finished installing it, cover the entire wall with polyethylene sheeting in the manner previously described.

Step 7: If you have built a stud wall and are finishing your basement with board paneling, you can nail it directly to the 2 × 4 framework. However, if you have opted for prefinished 4 × 8-foot plywood sheets, you should first install a layer of drywall to provide a rigid backing for the panels. Fasten the plywood panels to the drywall using construction adhesive applied with a caulking gun. In addition, use paneling nails to anchor the panels to the wood framework behind the drywall.

If you are installing board paneling over drywall and furring strips, use construction adhesive and nails sturdy enough to penetrate the boards, but not so long that they will hit the masonry wall.

When cutting prefinished wood panels with a circular saw, mark the layout on the back side of the panel. Take care to provide the necessary support for the panel and adequate clearance for the saw blade. A careful cut made on the back of the panel will result in minimal splintering on the front.

Step 8: Begin your installation of panels at a corner. Scribe and trim one edge to fit the corner so the other edge will be perfectly plumb. Leave about ¼ inch of clearance at both the top and the bottom of each panel.

Step 9: When all panels are in place, cut and install moldings to cover all exposed edges at the top and bottom of the wall, and around windows and doorways.

Tools and Supplies

Caulking gun	Level
Construction adhesive	Measuring tools
Construction grade lumber	Nails
Drywall	Paneling
Insulation	Saw

—**Fred Matlack and Larry McClung**

A NEW OPENING FOR YOUR HOME
How to Install a Prehung Door

First impressions are important. And the first thing you see on a house is its front door. A creaky, shabby door isn't going to convey a great image.

But looks aren't everything: Your front door should also keep heat or cool air in, and drafts and intruders out. If yours doesn't stand up to those tasks, it's time for a replacement. Prehung doors are a smart choice, since they fit tight and square. They're time-savers, too, because you won't have to fit hinges, latches, or stops.

Before buying a new door, measure your old one and add about 2 inches to the width and 1 inch to the height. Now you have the approximate measurements of the rough opening that remains after you've torn out the old door jambs (the top and side boards of the door frame). The frame of your new door should match those dimensions, but with at least ½-inch clearance all around to allow you to shim the door to make it level and plumb.

Measure the thickness of your wall as well. Most prehung doors are manufactured to fit standard 2 × 4 construction, but the dealer can add extensions to the jambs if your walls are thicker. All of these measurements are critical to a proper fit.

Think about which way you want the door to swing, then make sure the door you order fills that bill. You wouldn't want the door delivered with the hinges on the wrong side.

Most manufacturers offer a choice of latch and lock packages. You'll get the best results if you have your dealer precut the holes for the hardware you choose.

Decisions made and materials at hand, you are now ready to replace your old door with the new, prehung model. Here's how to proceed:

Step 1: Pull the pins out of the hinges on the old door. Use a screwdriver to get them started, then pull them out by hand. If the pins don't come out easily, remove the screws from the jamb or from the edge of the door. The door will fall free; be prepared with blocks or a helper to catch it.

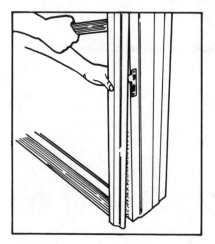

Step 2: With a small, thin pry-bar, remove the trim or facings from around the inside and outside of the door. Lift the threshold. There may be screws to remove, and in many cases, caulking or some other kind of adhesive will be holding the threshold to the flooring. Brute force is often the only way to break the threshold loose.

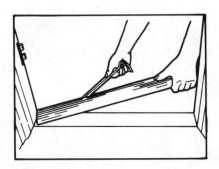

With the threshold and facings out of the way, you can get your pry-bar behind the jambs to loosen them from the framing. Pull out the jambs and shims, leaving only the rough opening.

Step 3: If necessary, adjust the size of the opening. It should be approximately ½ inch bigger than the assembled jambs of the new door. If you've ordered a door of the correct size, you shouldn't need to enlarge the opening—a tricky job, since it could mean dealing with structural framing members. But you might want to make the opening slightly smaller by nailing in layers of wood to fill any unwanted space.

Step 4: Set the new door and jamb assembly into the rough opening. Leave the shipping braces in place to hold the door and jambs square. Block the assembly temporarily into position with shims to make sure it will fit when the jambs are plumb and square. A handful of wooden shim shingles is a blessing at this point; use them as wedges to level the door and hold it securely in place.

Step 5: Lay the assembly down, and apply a heavy bead of caulking to the bottom of the threshold. Stand the unit back up, and shim it so the jambs are plumb and the threshold is level. Fasten the jambs to the framing by nailing through them and the shims into the framing.

Step 6: Remove the shipping braces from the door. Open it; be sure there's enough clearance to close it without hitting the jambs. Check that the door seals evenly all the way around.

If there are any adjustments to be made, you should be able to move the door slightly with a well-placed wedge. If your door came without the latch and lock, now is the time to install them. Some doors come with long screws that reach through the jambs and into the studs to increase security. If your door has these screws, install them at this point.

Step 7: Seal around the jambs with aerosol urethane foam. It will fill the gaps completely, and once it cures, it will practically glue the jambs to the studs. If there are spots that are too tight for the foam dispenser, use regular caulking.

Step 8: Install both the exterior and interior moldings. If the urethane foam has expanded to the point that it's protruding from the walls, either scrape it off before it cures, or wait until it dries and cut it off. Be forewarned that before curing, the foam will be a tremendously sticky mass.

Replace your interior and exterior moldings and you're finished, ready for many new, much grander entrances into your home.

Tools and Supplies

Aerosol urethane foam	Saw
Bundle of shim shingles	Scrap lumber (for filler)
Caulking	Screwdrivers
Hammer	Small pry-bar
New door	
New moldings (for the interior facing)	

—**Fred Matlack**

STEP SOFTLY
Installing Carpet on Stairs

Gleaming surfaces of polished wood look beautiful on dining room or living room floors, but bare wood on stairways looks like an accident waiting to happen. A covering of carpet adds traction to the stairs, making them safer. Carpet makes stairs quieter, too, by muffling creaky boards and heavy footsteps. Stairways and carpeting just seem to go together. Badly installed carpet, on the other hand, can look worse and be more hazardous than no covering at all, so it is important to do the job well.

Your first step is choosing the right carpet. In general, a carpeting with a fairly short nap will provide the safest, firmest footing and longest wear. You'll need just enough nap to hide the staples. If the fibers are ¼-inch or shorter, the staples will probably show.

Padding can make your carpet feel thicker and increase its longevity. You can buy carpeting with padding already attached, or buy the padding in a separate roll. We suggest buying the two separately, since you'll need padding only on the treads and not the risers. Also, attached padding will make the carpet harder to bend. Thus, if you want to turn under the edges of the carpet, you'll have to first trim off 2 inches of padding.

Professional installers work with a long roll of carpet and do six or seven steps at a time. This saves cutting time as well as carpet. Novices, however, will reduce their chances of ending up with crooked carpet if they cut the rug one step at a time.

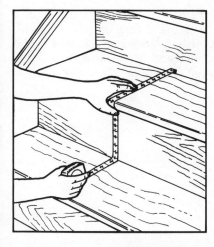

Step 1: Measure the steps. Start at the crouch (the place where the back of the tread meets the bottom of the riser), pull the measuring tape around the nose (the round part of the tread that extends over the top of the riser), and down the riser to the next crouch. Add 1 inch to this measurement just to be safe. Add up the length measurements for all the stairs, then measure the widths.

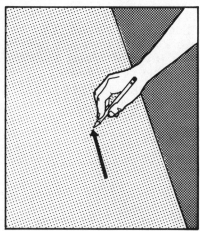

Step 2: Take your measurements to a carpet store. You may be able to save money by buying a remnant, if you can find one you like. For most sets of stairs, you'll need two 12-foot lengths. Mark the grain direction on each piece so the two will match after installation.

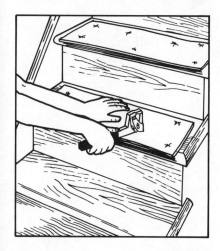

Step 3: Cut padding for the stair treads. If the carpet won't be covering the stairs' entire width, cut the padding an inch short on each side. This will leave space for turning the carpet edges under for a finished look. Lay the padding an inch from the crouch and staple it along the back and sides. The pad should hang an inch over the nose of the step so it can be pulled around and fastened later.

Step 4: Mark each piece of carpet and cut it with a utility knife. If you're planning to turn under the edges, add an extra inch. Butt the back edge of the carpet to the crouch and staple it to the tread. Make sure the staples will be embedded between the fibers of the nap.

Step 5: Pull the carpet taut and staple it to the underside of the nose. Put your first staple near the middle of the step and work toward the edges to keep the carpet smooth and tight. If you're turning under the edges, be sure to make the fold before you staple too close to the ends. Use ⅝-inch carpet tacks or small nails to fasten through the doubled edges.

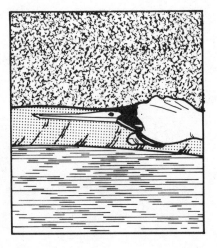

Step 6: Smooth the carpet over the riser and trim it at the crouch with your utility knife or scissors.

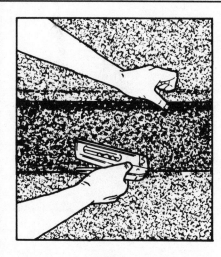

Step 7: Staple the carpet to the bottom of the riser. These staples are often the most visible, since they're facing you as you climb the stairs. If the nap on your carpet isn't long enough to hide them, try using brads.

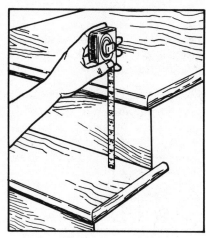

Step 8: Repeat steps 4 through 7 until you've reached the bottom of the stairway. Then measure and cut a piece of carpet to fit the top riser from the crouch to the bottom of the nose. Don't run the carpet over the nose of the top step unless the carpet will continue down the hall.

Tools and Supplies

Carpet	Padding
Carpet tacks (⅝″)	Ruler or straightedge
Chalkline	Stapler
Hammer	Staples (⅜″ or ½″)
Large scissors	Utility knife
Measuring tape	

—Fred Matlack

KITCHEN-COUNTER FACELIFT
How to Lay Ceramic Tile over Plastic Laminate

Want to give your old kitchen a facelift without tearing it all apart? Replacing old laminated countertops with ceramic tile can do the trick. Just follow the illustrated step-by-step instructions found below (which we compiled with advice from American Olean Tile). You don't even have to rip up the old countertop (as long as it's solid); you can lay the tile right on top of the laminate. Tile countertops not only look good, but can handle high heat and other extreme conditions that plastic can't.

And while you're giving your countertops a new look, you might consider adding a new kitchen sink. You'll be pulling the old one out and disconnecting the plumbing for the tile job—a lot of the work is already done.

Before You Start

Measure the area of your countertop, along with the backsplash and wall if those areas are to be included in the tiling job. With these figures on paper, start comparison-shopping for tile—there are many varieties and price ranges.

You may want to include bullnose and cove-base tiles in your purchase. These are preshaped tiles for corner and edge areas of the counter. Bullnose tiles are rounded outward to fit along counter edges, while cove-base tiles are curved inward to conform to the intersection of counter and backsplash. Measure the length of those areas to determine how many special tiles you'll need.

As a general rule, buy more tile than you'll need. You can always use the extra to replace broken ones, and down the road you may not be able to match your chosen color.

To minimize inconvenience to your family, start this job early in the day. You'll be tying up your kitchen counters and sink for at least 24 hours. Even if you enlist some help to make the tile laying go faster, you'll still have to wait overnight for the tile to set before grouting it.

Step 1: Take off the backsplash. It will be caulked to the counter and glued to the wall. Pry it off those two surfaces by gently tapping a broad-surfaced chisel with a hammer along the top and bottom of the backsplash.

Step 2: Remove the sink. How hard it is to remove depends on how it's mounted to the counter and hooked to the plumbing. Under the sink, unfasten the clamps or other hardware that hold the sink to the counter. Turn the water-supply valve off, and undo the nuts connecting the water-supply lines to the faucet assembly. Disconnect the garbage disposal according to manufacturer's instructions, and put it aside on blocks.

Before pulling the sink entirely out of the counter cabinet, raise it up to compensate for the thickness of the tile and cement you are about to add—estimate about ½ inch, total. Next, see if the plumbing connections will reach the raised sink. Normally there's enough slack for them to reach, but if there isn't, you may have to get an extension tube for the drain and add new inlet lines.

Step 3: Plan the layout of the tile. Measure to make sure all counter areas are square. If some areas aren't square, you'll have to figure how the tile can be cut to fit. To make sure the tile will fit all around, do a "dry run"—set the tile as it will be installed on the counter, but without the adhesive. Use a pencil to mark tile that you'll have to cut.

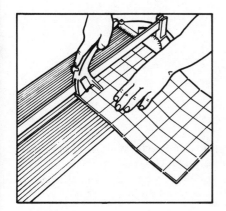

Step 4: Cut the tile to fit. You'll need the straight tile cutter for trimming long strips of tile, and the nippers for single tiles that need shaping for difficult spots. Once the tile is cut and you know how it will be installed, lay it out on your kitchen table so you can transfer it easily to the counter.

Step 5: Prepare the laminate counter by cleaning and roughing the surface with a wood block covered with 50- or 80-grit sandpaper. Roughing up the laminate is important if you are to get a good bond between the tile and adhesive. Use a household detergent to scrub the wall surface where your tile backsplash will go. The surface must be free of glue and grease.

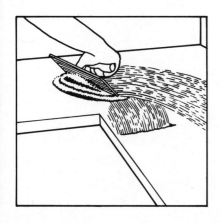

Step 6: Ventilate the room to prevent buildup of noxious fumes from the adhesive. Then, following manufacturer's instructions, spread an even coating of epoxy adhesive with the notched trowel. Spread only the area you're ready to tile.

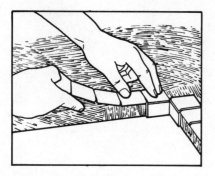

Step 7: Start laying the tile at the toughest spots: the corners. For your countertop, begin with an inside corner of the counter's front edge. Work out from the corner, installing the bullnose trim on this edge.

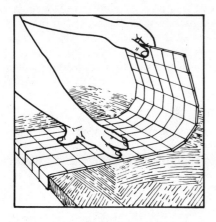

Step 8: Lay sheets of tile so the joints between the sheets are the same width as the joints on the sheets. After each section is set down, tap it with a wood block so it is correctly seated into adhesive.

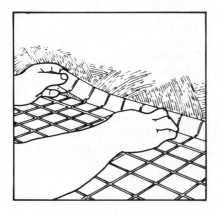

Step 9: Spread adhesive on the wall, and lay cove-base tile at the corner between the wall and counter. Lay tile on the wall surface. When you have the last tile in place, leave it undisturbed overnight.

Step 10: The next day, mix the grout according to the directions, and use the grouting float to spread grout evenly over the tile. Make sure all joints are filled.

Step 11: Sprinkle some dry grout over the tile surface to absorb excess moisture, then rub the tile with dry burlap so that joints are evenly packed with grout.

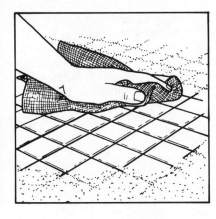

Step 12: To clean the excess grout off the newly tiled surface, dampen some sawdust with an acid solution—9 parts water to 1 part muriatic acid—and rub it over the tile with a piece of burlap.

Tools and Supplies

Broad-surfaced chisel	Putty knife
Burlap	Sandpaper
Epoxy adhesive	Sawdust
Grout	Tape measure
Grouting float	Tile cutter (can be rented for $10 or less)
Hammer	
Muriatic acid	Tile nippers
Notched trowel	Wood block
Plumbing wrenches	

For Further Information

Tile Council of America
P.O. Box 326
Princeton, NJ 08542

—Catherine M. Poole and Fred Matlack

REPLACING A TOILET
It Won't Take as Long as You Think

Toilets need to be replaced for a variety of reasons: cracked bowls, permanent discolorations, nonfunctioning mechanisms. Some toilets just need replacing because they simply don't fit in with your remodeling plans.

Whatever your reason, replacing an old toilet with a new one is an easy job that can be completed in just a few hours. In the steps that follow, we'll show how to replace a freestanding, floor-mounted toilet.

Accessories that usually come with the new fixture include all the inner workings of the toilet (ballcock, etc.) and spud washers.

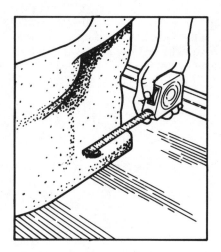

Step 1: Measure the length of the base of the new toilet to make sure it will fit in the same space as the old one. On the old toilet, measure along the floor from the center of the hold-down bolts (the bolts that attach the toilet bowl to the floor) to the wall. In order for the new toilet to fit without rerouting the waste stack, it must be the same length.

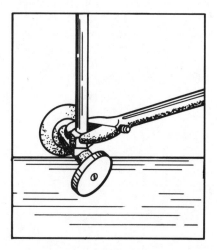

Step 2: Turn off the water supply to the tank by turning the shutoff valve on the supply line between the toilet and the wall. Flush the toilet, and bail out any remaining water. Disconnect the supply pipe by loosening the nut next to the shutoff valve with an adjustable wrench. Set the supply line aside for reuse.

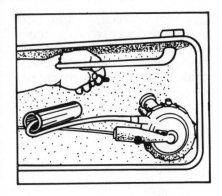

Step 3: If you want to avoid heavy lifting, separate and remove the toilet in two parts, first the tank and then the bowl. Separate the tank from the bowl by using the adjustable wrench to remove the two hold-down bolts in the bottom of the tank. Lift the tank off the bowl.

To remove the bowl, use a putty knife to pry the porcelain or plastic caps off of the hold-down bolts. Remove the nuts from the hold-down bolts with the adjustable wrench.

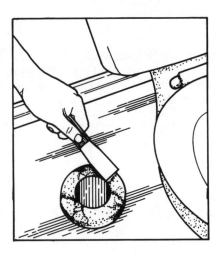

Step 4: Gently rock the bowl back and forth to break the wax seal between the toilet bowl and the floor. Then lift the bowl off the floor. Stuff a rag into the drainpipe opening to prevent sewer gas from escaping into the bathroom and to keep tools from falling down the pipe. With the putty knife, scrape what's left of the old wax seal off the drainpipe opening.

Step 5: Turn the new toilet bowl upside down, and put the new wax seal around the water outlet. Place the bowl right side up over the drainpipe opening so that the hold-down bolts are coming up through the holes in the base of the toilet.

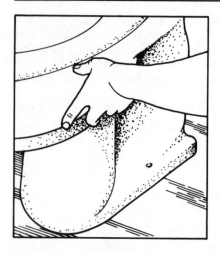

Step 6: To form a tight seal between the drainpipe opening and the toilet, press down and twist the toilet bowl. Put a level across the bowl to make sure the toilet is sitting evenly. If it isn't, you can put small metal shims under the base to make it level. Test-fit the shims, then coat them with an adhesive that is compatible with the flooring, and put them in place.

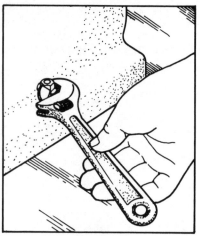

Step 7: Place nuts on the hold-down bolts coming up through the base of the toilet bowl, and tighten them carefully. Tightening these bolts too much can crack the toilet bowl. Put the porcelain or plastic caps over the hold-down bolts.

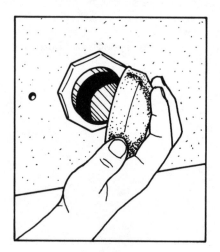

Step 8: To install the tank, turn the tank upside down. On the bottom of the tank there are two openings: The smaller one is for the supply line, and the large one is the flush valve. Place the large rubber spud washer on the end of the flush valve. Place the tank on the bowl.

Step 9: Put the hold-down bolts and washers through the bottom of the tank, and tighten them. If the tank is wobbly, you may have to readjust the spud washer.

Connect the flexible water supply line to the end of the fill tube on the bottom of the tank. Attach the other end of this line to the shutoff valve. Tighten the nuts on both ends.

Attach the toilet seat and cover according to the manufacturer's instructions.

Tools and Supplies

Adjustable wrench	Tape measure
Hold-down bolts (if necessary)	Toilet seat
	Wax seal
Level	
Putty knife	

—Fred Matlack

D-I-Y HOME SECURITY
Sophisticated Alarm Systems You Can Install Yourself

One out of every 11 homes in the United States now has a burglar-alarm system in it. Unfortunately, crime statistics tell us that 1 out of every 3 homes will be hit by crime this year.

Why don't more people own a security system? The reason is probably that the threat of a depleted bank account seems more real than the possibility of a break-in: A professionally installed alarm usually costs a minimum of $1,500.

While that's not exactly robbery itself, you'd be paying dearly for the expertise and labor of the installer. The equipment for such a setup may account for only a fraction of the cost, perhaps as little as $400.

If you're intrigued by the idea of installing an ultra-high-tech system, there are lots available, from audio sensors that pick up the sound of a break-in to infrared detectors that are activated by a burglar's body heat.

On the other end of the price scale are cheap, self-contained units sold at department stores. They're simple to install but wouldn't stop any self-respecting criminal.

Where to Start

Because most burglars start by trying to get in through a door or window, anyone thinking about installing an alarm system should secure the "perimeter" of the house first. Install entry sensors on doors and windows (see figure 4-1). Taking care of these points of entry accounts for about 75 percent of the work of installing an alarm system and the lion's share of the investment. Later, you can add higher levels of security or remote-control features.

To secure a door or window, your best option is to install small, preferably concealed, magnetic switches. These devices have two parts: the switch itself and a mating magnet. When the window is closed, the two halves are in contact and the switch is closed. But if

Protect the Perimeter

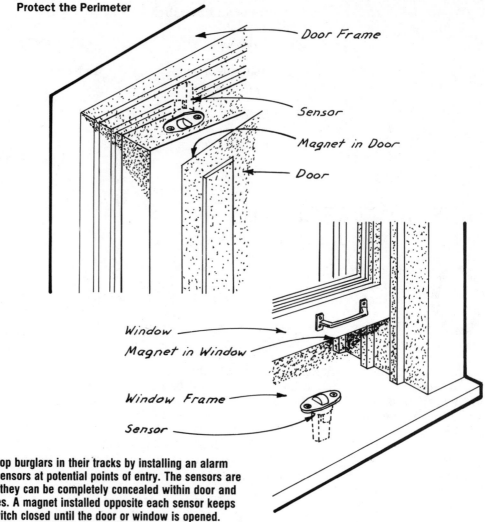

Figure 4-1. Stop burglars in their tracks by installing an alarm system with sensors at potential points of entry. The sensors are so small that they can be completely concealed within door and window frames. A magnet installed opposite each sensor keeps the sensor switch closed until the door or window is opened. Then the switch opens and the alarm is sounded.

the system is activated and a window is opened, the switch will be opened too, sounding the alarm.

For large windows through which a burglar could climb by cutting a hole in the glass, glass-breakage detectors are available. Such devices, which detect the frequency of breaking glass with an internal tuning fork, are virtually impossible to defeat.

To Wire or Not to Wire?

Intrusion sensors are only part of a complete security system. They pick up the message that someone's trying to get into your house, but a more complex piece of equipment, a receiver or control panel, is needed to read that message and activate the alarm bell or siren outside. To get that message from sensors to receiver or panel you have two options: a hard-wired system or a wireless one.

If you're looking to save money and don't mind undertaking a fairly time-consuming installation job, hard-wiring makes sense. But be aware that hard-wiring can be a hard job. You'll probably have to drill holes through walls and floors and do a lot of fishing around for wires you can't see.

A good, basic hard-wired system costs $300 to $400; a minimum of 20 hours is required to install one in the average house. If you have the skills and don't mind investing the time, by all means try hard-wiring.

About 70 percent less time is required to install a wireless system, but at least twice as much money. With a wireless system, you don't have to wire each sensor to a central control panel; the components of wireless types use radio frequencies to communicate with each other. You install the battery-powered sensors in doors and windows exactly as you would for a hard-wired system, but once that's done, all you've got to do is set up the receiver in an accessible spot (see figure 4-2).

There are a number of wireless systems available, and more hit the market each month. Keeping track of new features to find the best system for your needs requires some checking around. But in general, for a wireless system to compare favorably with a hard-wired version, it should have the following capabilities.

Immunity from Radio Interference

The average home is bombarded with many types of radio signals: commercial radio and television broadcasts, microwave trans-

Figure 4-2. The receiver in a wireless system indicates whether each sensor is open or closed and lets you know if a sensor needs maintenance (a new battery, for instance). The receiver should be no farther than 200 feet from any sensor and should be easily accessible.

A Wireless Setup

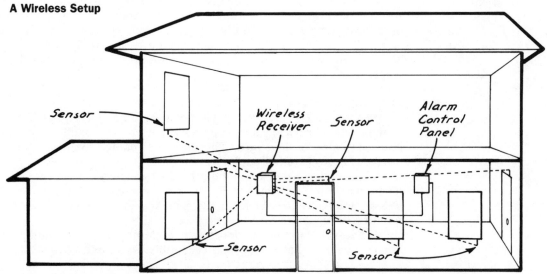

missions, garage-door openers, mobile and cordless telephone frequencies. If your system can't keep its wits in the midst of this onslaught, you'll have to put up with false alarms—a decided nuisance. The most stable systems send a computerized "data word" consisting of 8 to 20 bits of information to signal alarms. The receiver will respond only if it receives the *exact* signal it expects.

Supervision

A supervision feature requires individual transmitting sensors to "check in" with the receiver from time to time. That way, the receiver knows the status of each sensor. It can tell if a battery is low and will let you know with a maintenance signal. There's also an added benefit to supervision: If you're home when the alarm sounds, you'll be able to look at your control panel and know exactly which transmitter activated it.

Concealment

Statistics on security-system performance are very clear on one point: Concealment of sensors and any associated wires is essential. Until recently, all wireless systems used an outboard transmitter— a little box the size of a cigarette pack that was fitted to a door or window frame or nearby wall. The wiring from magnetic switches was connected to the transmitter, and since the transmitters were usually clearly visible, they could tell a burglar which doors and windows were protected and which were not.

Nowadays you can buy sensors that contain their own transmitters and are small enough to fit in the door frame. These sensors are less than 5 inches long and about an inch wide, including the built-in magnetic switch.

Wireless alarms are available with 4 to 32 channels. Because one channel is needed for each sensor, most people find they want a system with around 16 channels. Such a system should be enough for first-floor doors and windows with a channel or two left over to operate an emergency hand-held "panic" transmitter, if one is desired. A "panic" transmitter enables you to manually sound the alarm from anywhere in the house in case of a break-in or medical emergency.

Making a Big Noise

Sensors and receivers may be the heart of an alarm system, but they're not what will alert your neighbors or the police that the house is being broken into. The only real choice for a sounding device is between a bell and a siren.

If you live in a densely populated area you may want to go with a bell, which will be cheaper. But bells have a limited range and are less directional than sirens. And bells make a lot less noise. So if you live in a suburban or rural setting, buy a siren.

Whatever you choose, locate the sounding device outside the house in a place that's not easily accessible. As an extra precaution, you should enclose it in a protective, tamperproof case. A good bell or siren cabinet has a tamper switch that automatically sounds the alarm if the enclosure is pried away from the wall.

But while you're protecting your sounding device, don't hide or disguise it. The very presence of it on your house tells would-be burglars: "This house is protected."—**David Petraglia**

NEW LIFE FOR OLD WOOD FLOORS
Refinishing for Added Luster and Value

Few floor treatments can match the beauty of a newly laid wood floor. But in an older home, a restored wood floor has a special charm of its own—and it can add thousands of dollars to the value of the house. Complete professional refinishing can cost from 75¢ to $1 or more per square foot, depending on the floor's condition. But by putting in your own time and effort, you can get professional results for less than a third of that cost.

Sometimes the best option is simply to clean the floor and add a new finish over the old one, without the labor and expense of a complete sanding. Besides saving work, you'll save the old floor's patina—that mellow look of age so many try to duplicate. To test the condition of your existing floor finish, press hard against the wood with a quarter and scrape a small strip. If the finish flakes off, appears brittle, and raw wood is revealed, complete removal will be needed. There's no reason to put a new finish on something that won't last.

But if the quarter doesn't scratch the wood easily, the surface can be spruced up without resorting to a full sanding. The first step is to apply a *deglosser*, which is available at paint stores. A deglosser is a mild version of paint remover, and will remove the years of dirt, wax, and films that have darkened your finish. Mop it liberally on the floor, then rub it into the surface with a medium-grade steel wool.

The effect of the deglosser will vary depending on the existing finish, but it should remove some of the old finish, and leave the surface ready for refinishing. A good paint store will be able to recommend a coating that's compatible with the original surface.

Completely removing the finish from older floors may require a stronger solvent such as a paint or varnish remover. These chemical removers can be cost-effective for stripping a small area, but they're probably not a good idea for a large area. Paint and varnish removers must be applied thickly, and in small areas, scraped up immediately.

If the results of chemical removal aren't satisfactory—or if the area to finish is too large—your last resort is to remove the surface of the floor with professional sanding equipment.

The tools you'll need are available at reasonable rates from any good tool-rental center. You'll need a commercial drum sander, an edger, a large shop vacuum, safety goggles, a dust-mask, a hammer, a nail-set, a small pry-bar, and a common orbital sander.

The dealer who rents you the drum sander and edger will normally provide a supply of belts and disks. Typically, belts (for the drum sander) and disks (for the edger) are supplied in three "grits": Coarse (20-3½), Medium (36-2), and Fine (80-0).

Before you begin, remove all furniture, floor vents, and door-stops from the rooms you are sanding. Countersink any exposed nail heads with your hammer and nail-set. Even though the sanding machines are normally equipped with built-in dust bags, you'll be glad later if you block off stairways and/or doorways with plastic or cloth sheets.

If the surface of the floor is flat, with no warpage and few visible ridges or heavily damaged areas, start sanding with the medium-grade paper. Don't let the term "medium" fool you. The drum sander is a powerful machine, and one pass with medium grit will remove $\frac{1}{32}$ to $\frac{1}{16}$ inch of wood.

It will take a few passes over a patch of test floor to get the feel of operating the drum sander. Test your technique in an area that will be covered with a piece of large furniture, such as a bed. The most important thing to remember is to *keep the machine moving.* But don't go too fast or it won't cut properly. A good pace is about one yard per minute, sanding with the grain. At this rate, you'll use up about one belt per average-sized room. (See figures 4-3 and 4-4 for instructions on proper sanding methods.)

Going forward, the machine will pull itself along. Once you reach the wall, tilt the machine to lift the drum, and position yourself for the next pass. You'll sand about 10 inches of floor with each pass, and should lap each pass by 3 or 4 inches. With a little practice, you'll quickly find the technique that's best for you.

A few important tips: Never shut the sander off when the drum is sanding; always tip the machine back, then switch the machine off. This will help you avoid unnecessary ruts. And don't try to remove a low spot by sanding continually with the grain. The sander will take more and more material from the good areas as well, and you'll produce ruts.

The drum sander will let you get within a few inches of the walls; use the edger to sand the borders. If you don't have to remove baseboard moldings, don't. It's extra work to replace them later, and older moldings can be easily broken in removal. Try the edger to see how close you can get. Often, the edger will sand right up to the molding.

Keep the edger moving constantly in a rapid, semicircular motion from left to right. Only edge as much as you need to bring the new floor surface even with that left by the drum sander. Start with medium-grit paper, and use one disk per average-sized room.

Sanding a Lightly Worn Floor

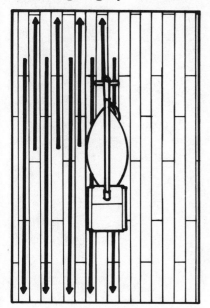

Figure 4-3. A typical slightly worn floor should be sanded *with* the grain, starting with a medium-grit (36-2) sandpaper. Sand two-thirds of the length (or width) of the room from one direction, then turn the machine around to sand the remaining third.

Sanding a Heavily Worn Floor

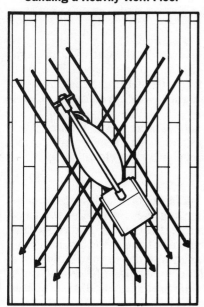

Figure 4-4. For heavily worn, uneven, or damaged floors, use a coarser sandpaper (20-3½) and sand *diagonally*, first to one side, then to the other. This method works well for removing gouges, ridges, and low spots. Keep the machine moving or you'll produce ruts.

Photo 4-1. The oak and mahogany floor in this foyer was successfully rejuvenated through sanding and the application of a tough varnish finish. (Photo by Mitch Mandel)

Once the heavy sanding is done, go over the entire area again with both machines, this time using fine-grade paper. The finer paper will smooth out the marks left by the medium paper, and will remove most gouges and digs you might have caused as you developed your heavy-sanding technique.

After fine-sanding, let the dust settle for at least 24 hours. Then vacuum the rooms thoroughly. It's a good idea to remove any lingering dust with a damp (not wet) sponge or a tack cloth.

Choosing the Right Finish

Once you've either cleaned or sanded your floors, it's time to choose a finish. There are two basic categories of finishes for wood floors: those that *build* a surface on top of the wood, and those that *penetrate*, strengthening the upper layer of the wood itself.

Shellacs and varnishes are among the finishes that build a surface. The original floor finish in older homes usually consists of a few coats of shellac followed by a natural resin and an oil-based varnish.

Shellacs continue to be a good option for floors. They apply thinly and build easily, and each coat dries and can be recoated in just a few hours (a light sanding between coats is recommended).

Shellacs are available in clear or yellow, and can enhance the wood's natural color. However, a shellac finish does not resist water well; periodic waxing is necessary to make it more watertight.

Varnishes are oil-based finishes that contain resins, which provide hardness upon drying. Varnishes containing either phenolic, alkyd, or urethane resins are the most common. Alkyds and phenolics will add a yellow cast to the wood; most urethanes will not color the wood at all.

Of all the varnishes, urethanes provide the toughest finish. This would seem to make them ideal for high-traffic areas, but not necessarily: A urethane finish can be *too* hard for heavy traffic. Alkyd and phenolic-based varnishes are a better choice, since they produce a more elastic, flexible finish. And any traffic patterns worn into these finishes can be patched or refinished later; urethanes, by contrast, do not patch easily.

Penetrating sealers, also called "Swedish" or "Danish" finishes, contain resins similar to varnishes but do not build on the upper surface of the wood. Instead, the resins harden within the pores of the wood, becoming part of it. Although they will darken different woods to varying degrees, penetrating sealers (such as polymerized tung oil) will leave the texture of the wood's grain visible. Unless waxed, these finishes won't add much luster to the surface. But they are among the most durable of finishes around, and are ideal for floors that will be exposed to water, chemicals, and abrasion.

Applying penetrating finishes is a cinch: Simply mop on each coat and wipe up the excess. They need only a few hours of drying time between coats. Penetrating finishes are nearly indestructible, and will last as long as the floor itself with normal use, yet they can easily be patched.

Don't apply any floor finishing product without making absolutely sure the room is adequately ventilated. Wherever possible, shut off all exposed gas pilot lights in the house when you are working, and do not relight them until the rooms have been allowed to ventilate.

When choosing a finish for your wood floors, consider the *entire* space, not just the floor itself. If you are refinishing an upstairs hallway and bedrooms in a home that doesn't have a lot of natural light, the shiny finish of a varnish may help brighten the space. And since the hallway will get a fair amount of traffic, alkyd or phenolic varnishes would be good candidates.

Or perhaps you're refinishing the floor of an occasionally used dining room where you intend to place an area rug. You may want a glossy surface with moderately good wear characteristics, but little coloring of the wood. Urethane varnish is a candidate here.

Maybe your wood floor is in a sky-lit kitchen, and you're concerned that your small children or the family dog will leave lasting impressions on a varnished surface. This is a case for a penetrating finish, which will also stand up to accidental spills.

Paint stores, hardware stores, and home centers are full of products for preparing and finishing wood floors. A little planning, experimentation, and advice from a good paint store will ensure that your floor refinishing project yields beautiful and lasting results.—**David Petraglia**

TEARING OUT AND BEAMING UP
How to Find, Remove, and Support Load-Bearing Walls

Sooner or later in your life as a homeowner, the urge to tear out a wall will probably strike. The "demolition syndrome" often creeps up on its victims when they realize that removing part or all of a certain wall would transform two small rooms into a more expansive and enjoyable living space.

If the offending wall is a nonstructural partition, the job may be simple, though somewhat messy. But if the wall bears some of the home's structural weight, tearing it out is a more formidable challenge. Before you proceed with such a project, you'll need to know the basics of tearing out and beaming up.

Your first step is to find out whether or not the wall in question is load-bearing. If it is, you must replace it with a beam or header, properly sized and installed to carry its structural burden.

First, study the skeleton of your home to determine in which direction the floor and ceiling joists run. If the wall you'd like to remove is *parallel* to the joists above and below it, it probably isn't load-bearing. On the other hand, if the wall is *perpendicular* to the joists, it very likely *is* holding up part of the house.

The best places to check to determine direction of joists and rafters are the basement and attic, where the framing is exposed. Or, in older houses that haven't been repainted or papered in a while, "ghosting" of the framing is often obvious on ceilings. Irregularities in the ceiling or flooring surfaces may also give clues to framing directions.

Before you remove a wall, it's important to understand how much of a load it's supporting. Most easily estimated are *dead loads*, or the fixed weight of the structure. The dead load comprises everything that is supported by the wall and all of the weight above it, including the roof or additional stories.

Added to this weight are *live loads*, which consist mainly of furnishings, but may also include gatherings of people. Normal live-load weights are calculated at 40 pounds per square foot (psf). If a roof section is included in the weight to be supported by the new beam, wind and snow are also significant parts of the potential live load. Snow can add up to 30 or 40 psf, and wind gusts can add 50 psf or more.

Calculating the total load is a fairly straightforward procedure, once you've identified all the components of the dead and live loads. But selecting the right beam to carry that load is more complex, requiring choices between various design options and possible costs.

Unfortunately, there are no safe, general rules of thumb for header sizing, because so much depends on the type and quality of the wood you use (or the strength of a metal beam)—not to mention the vagaries of dead and live loads. But the options to consider include steel (wide-flange beams, channels, angles); wood (either a solid beam or, even stronger, three or four boards nailed together); or combinations, called flitch beams, in which a plate of steel is sandwiched between layers of wood.

A Typical Beaming-Up Scenario

Let's assume you want to remove 16 feet of load-bearing wall between two rooms to create a space that will be 16 × 20 feet, or a total of 320 square feet. The new beam will have to support the ceiling above that space, or 160 square feet (the other half of the load is supported by the walls at either end of the new room).

Let's assume that each of those 160 square feet has a dead weight of 22 psf. This means that the new beam will have to bear a total dead load of 3,520 pounds. A standard live load of 40 psf adds another 6,400 pounds, for a total load of 9,920 pounds.

Dividing the total load by 16 (the length in feet of the span) reveals that the new beam will have to support 620 pounds per linear foot.

Next, it's time to select a beam. If we choose a sandwich of wood boards to bear the 620-pound-per-foot burden, we might decide to use four 2 × 10s or three 2 × 12s made from kiln-dried Douglas fir. (A thicker or deeper beam may be required, depending on the species and grade of the wood selected.)

The way the boards are fastened together is also important. Perhaps the most common way is to glue the layers together and then pound nails at 8- to 10-inch intervals on both sides of the sandwich, using a regular nailing pattern. For longer spans, a flitch beam may be the best solution (though sizing composite beams is more complicated than sizing beams made from a single material).

An adequate steel beam for the load in our example would have a designation of W8 × 13, which indicates a height of 8 inches and a weight of 13 pounds per linear foot. A W10 × 11.5 steel beam would also do the trick. Because steel is sold by weight, it would be cheaper than the W8 × 13 beam; but it would also be 2 inches deeper from top to bottom—less than ideal in a room with low ceilings.

The simplest place to put the beam is under the joists that it will support. With this placement, the full dimensions of the beam (or header) will be revealed under the ceiling, lending itself to an "exposed beam" look. But you might prefer to conceal the beam by cutting openings in each joist so you can fit the header flush with the ceiling line. The joists (and their loads) can be connected to the beam with metal joist hangers (see figure 4-5).

Another important thing to remember is that by "heading off" an overhead load, you create two concentrated loads, one at each end of the beam. This load, too, must be adequately supported. Masonry walls are good candidates for providing the needed beam support; steel or wood posts will also work. And don't forget that the load must be carried all the way down to the foundation (you may have to add posts in the basement directly beneath the load-bearing points).

If the span you intend to create is more than a few feet long, you'll have to erect temporary supports (shoring) before tearing out the load-bearing wall. You should, of course, know just how large a load must be "caught" and how you're going to add the new beam,

Figure 4-5. A new beam can be placed underneath the joists it supports or (as shown here) installed flush with the ceiling. Cut openings in the joists and attach them to the beam with metal joist hangers. Place the 2 × 4 "kickers" for the temporary shoring system 2 to 4 feet apart (the closer they are, the stronger the support will be). A diagonal brace will help ensure that they don't bend under the load. (Illustration by John Kline)

Supporting a Load

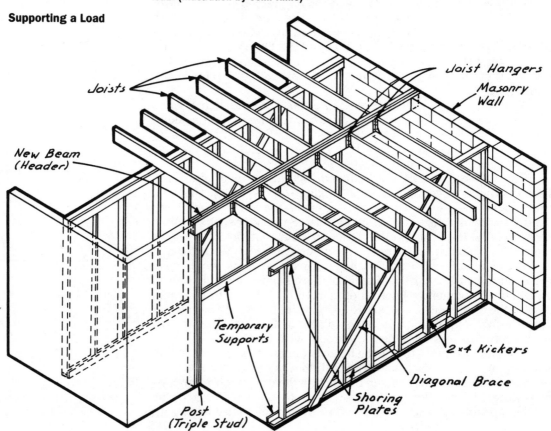

before you put up the temporary supports. (Figure 4-5 illustrates the proper method of supporting a load while a new beam is being installed.)

One safe method of shoring up a span of moderate length is to nail together two 2 × 4s perpendicularly. Make four of these L-shaped "plates": Two of them should run the entire length of the wall to be torn out (one on either side), and two should go on the ceiling, supported directly above the floor plates by several 2 × 4 "kickers" placed at intervals of 4 feet or so. You might also nail a diagonal brace to each of the vertical 2 × 4s to keep them from bowing under the weight.

Then it's time to do the actual tearing out and beaming up. To make sure you're on solid ground each step of the way, consult the books on our list. It would also be a good idea to consult a master carpenter, whose experience will head off any disasters.

For Further Information

Manual for House Framing. Washington, D.C.: National Forest Products Association, 1961

Ramsey, Charles G., and Harold R. Sleeper. *Architectural Graphic Standards*. New York: John Wiley and Sons, 1981

—Charles Klein

CHAPTER 5

Outdoor Do-It-Yourself Projects

Many of the projects we undertake to beautify and improve our homes take place indoors. However, dedicated home remodelers do not confine

themselves to the insides of their dwellings; they also seek to improve the quality and appearance of their homes' exteriors. Most basically, this means paying attention to the condition of exterior walls, foundation, and roof. It may occasionally involve recaulking around windows, repainting trim, and possibly the kind of wall washing or addition of exterior insulation described in chapter 3.

But taking care of the exterior of our homes leads us beyond the confines of the structures themselves into an interaction with the landscapes within which they sit. It means planting trees and shrubs, building walkways and patios, erecting fences, and installing exterior faucets and lights. Thus, the design ideas and projects described in this chapter are quite broad in scope.

The chapter opens with step-by-step instructions on how to accomplish a very basic and useful task: pouring a concrete slab. This is a skill that can have many applications. You can use it to create a walkway, a patio, or a floor for a garage, porch, or cellar. Once you have gained experience working with concrete, you can employ your skill in other ways: for example, building durable steps, or legs for lawn benches.

Other step-by-step projects found in this chapter include the installation of ridge and soffit vents, automatic garage door openers, outdoor faucets, and landscape lighting. We also show you how to replace the screening material in the groove-and-spline type of metal-encased door and window screens. Finally, we offer you some practical tips on landscaping and creating interesting pathways through your yard or garden.—**the editors**

159

Photo by Mitch Mandel

A CONCRETE ACCOMPLISHMENT
How to Pour a Concrete Slab

Having a contractor pour a 4-inch concrete slab (floor) for you will cost about $2.60 per square foot. You can do it yourself for about half that—and you'll learn a valuable skill in the process. With it, you can turn a dirt-floored cellar into a basement, convert a shed into a garage, repair a sidewalk, or transform an unused patch of ground into a walkway, car park, or patio.

Pouring a concrete slab is not difficult with the right tools and conditions. But concrete is a lot easier to put in than to take out, so it's wise to prepare well and proceed carefully. If you take the extra time to build precise and sturdy forms, you'll avoid leaks, bulges, and other last-minute problems. Use good, straight lumber for your forms and screed board (used to scrape the concrete so it's level with the tops of the forms), and double-check to see that everything is level and square.

Most professionals order their concrete well in advance, then set the forms, and grade and tamp the base, just before they pour the "mud." If you haven't worked with concrete before, take the easy route and build the forms first. Then you can measure them before ordering the concrete to avoid finding yourself with too much or too little.

All the specialty tools you'll need can be rented (see "Tools and Supplies" below). Try to keep your tools clean as you work. They'll be easy to wash when the concrete is fresh, but are very hard to clean once the cement has set.

You'll also want to find some helpers. Six arms should be able to handle a couple of yards of concrete very nicely. You'll need two fairly strong people to operate the screed and one more to direct the concrete from the truck's chute.

Step 1: Build the forms. For a 3½-inch slab, lay straight 2 × 4s along the perimeter. Drive support stakes into the ground every 3 or 4 feet along the outside of the 2 × 4s. Raise or lower the form of 2 × 4s until the top edge of the board is where you want the top of the slab to be. Then nail the stakes to the form with duplex nails (double-headed nails that can be easily pulled when you want to remove the forms). Add some more stakes diagonally to keep the form from being pushed outward by the pressure of the concrete.

Step 2: Prepare the base by removing all topsoil, loose dirt, and any organic matter that could decay and cause the slab to settle. In dry, frost-free areas, undisturbed subsoil is usually an adequate base. If you'll have either frost or moisture under the slab, put down several inches of tamped gravel to prevent water from accumulating. Install a layer of 6-mil polyethylene over the gravel (to keep moisture out of the concrete), and lay some 6 × 6-inch wire mesh over the plastic. The mesh will reinforce the concrete and hold it in place if it cracks.

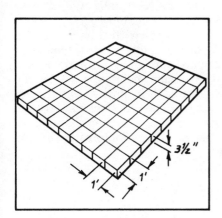

Step 3: Measure the forms and order the concrete. If you're using 2 × 4 forms, the slab will be 3½ inches thick. Round that number off to 4 inches so you'll have some extra concrete for insurance. Calculate the volume of the forms (length × width × depth) to the nearest cubic foot, then divide by 27 to find how many cubic yards of concrete you need. For most jobs, you'll probably want "3,000" mix, which means that after curing for 28 days the concrete will withstand 3,000 pounds of pressure per square inch.

Step 4: Pour the concrete (making sure the wire mesh is off the ground slightly) and immediately use the screed to scrape it level with the top edge of the form. The two operations should be done simultaneously, if possible. Start pouring in the hardest-to-reach corner and work your way to the other end. Move the screed board across the forms as you pour, scraping the bottom edge of the board along the top edges of the forms with a side-to-side motion. If you can pour and screed together, less concrete will build up behind the screed board, making it easier to push around.

Step 5: "Float" the slab to further smooth the surface. To do this, place a bull float (a long-handled, trowellike tool about 3 feet wide) on the surface of the wet concrete, lower the handle to raise the front edge of the tool slightly, and push it slowly across the slab. Then raise the handle and pull the float back toward you. Overlap your strokes, working from one side of the slab to the other.

Step 6: Wide or long, narrow slabs will tend to crack if they're not divided into smaller sections. Use a seamer (a 4 × 5-inch metal plate with a handle and a ridge down the middle of the underside) to make the divisions. Place a long board across the form to use as a straightedge, and run the seamer up and down it. Divide long slabs into short, sidewalk-style blocks; section odd-shaped slabs into rectangles. Then, if stresses develop, the slab will crack along the seams rather than across the flat surface. Next, use an edger tool to round off the sharp edges and corners of the slab.

Step 7: As the surface of the slab starts to dry, you'll notice its sheen begin to fade and dull. Now use a fresno polisher (a large, long-handled steel trowel) to do a last smoothing of the surface. If the tool you rent doesn't have extension handles, wait until the concrete sets enough to support you, then kneel on two 18-inch-square pieces of plywood placed on the surface (these kneeboards spread your weight over the surface of the concrete so you don't sink in). Start troweling at the farthest corner and work toward yourself so you can finish by rubbing out the kneeboard marks.

Step 8: Cover the slab with a plastic sheet for two weeks. This slows the evaporation of moisture, allowing the concrete to cure properly. Left uncovered, the concrete will dry too quickly, producing a weak, brittle slab. Remove the forms a day or two after the pour. Pulling them too soon could damage the soft concrete.

Tools and Supplies

Bull float

Concrete

Edger

Forming lumber
   and stakes

Fresno polishing trowel

General carpentry tools

Gloves

Gravel

Hand float

Hand trowel

Knee boards

Plastic sheet

Rubber boots

Screed board

Seamer

Shovels and rakes

Wheelbarrow (if the
   truck's chute won't
   reach the slab)

Wire mesh

For Further Information
Portland Cement Association
5420 Old Orchard Rd.
Skokie, IL 60077

—Fred Matlack

NO SWEAT

Eliminate Condensation with Roof and Soffit Vents

The roofs on many houses are rotting away from the inside out. Water is the culprit, but it's coming from indoors, not outside. The problem is condensation, and the remedy is simple: Get the warm, humid air out of the attic before it soaks your roof sheathing. With illustrations and step-by-step instructions, we'll show you how to rid your attic of moisture-laden air by installing soffit and ridge vents.

Condensation occurs when warm, moist air comes in contact with a cool surface. In your attic, that cool surface is usually the underside of the roof. Any air infiltration from living spaces into the attic will allow warm air to migrate to the roof sheathing. If the moist air stays there, condensation will build up, soak in, and cause rot. Just a little air movement can prevent that buildup.

A fairly reliable rule of thumb says you need at least 1 square foot of vent for each 150 square feet of attic space. In most cases, the 1 to 150 ratio will protect you from serious problems, but the placement of those vents is as important as their total area. The vents should be divided about equally between the soffit (the underside of the roof overhang) and the upper half of the roof. A good combination of ridge and soffit venting will leave the least amount of dead space in your attic.

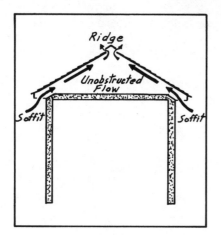

Step 1: Measure the length of the roof ridge. Ridge vents are usually sold in 10-foot lengths, but they can be cut. Get enough to cover the entire length of the ridge, along with end caps and connectors.

Soffit vents come in various sizes and shapes, including long perforated strips that replace the entire soffit. If you use individual 8 × 16-inch vents, place one every 4 feet. Space smaller vents closer together.

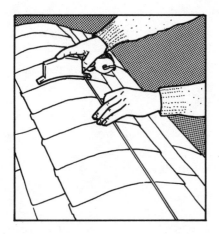

Step 2: Check the installation instructions for your ridge vents. Most call for an opening at least 2 inches wide. Use a chalk line to mark the shingles, then cut them with a hook knife or a flooring chisel. Stop the opening 6 inches short of the end of the vent. Inspect the exposed sheathing and remove any nails on the cut line.

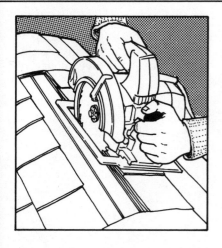

Step 3: Cut and remove the sheathing from the ridge area of the roof. Set the blade of the saw so that it just penetrates the sheathing. Avoid cutting into any framing members. If you find one running down the ridge and obstructing the opening, cut the sheathing back as far as possible to make up for the loss of vent area. Avoid hitting the shingles with the saw blade; the sticky asphalt and mineral coating on the shingles will ruin the blade.

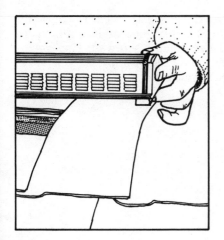

Step 4: Mount the ridge vent, following the manufacturer's instructions. Caulk the end caps and joints and lay the vent in a bed of caulking on the roof. Nail through the flanges and shingles into the sheathing. You'll probably need roofing nails at least 1½ inches long to reach the sheathing through four or five thicknesses of shingle.

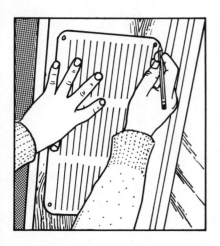

Step 5: Choose the locations for soffit vents. It's easier to cut the holes if you locate the vents between framing members, but don't hesitate to place a vent across a rafter if that's the way your spacing falls. Try to space vents so there's one in each rafter cavity.

Step 6: Cut holes to accept the vents. Drill a hole at each corner and saw from hole to hole with a saber saw. Check for obstructions to airflow, and move any insulation out of the way. It's important to have plenty of open space to encourage airflow.

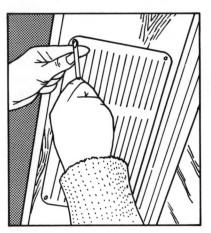

Step 7: Fasten the flanges of the vent to the soffit. If the soffit is made of thin plywood and is difficult to nail into, use small sheet metal screws. (The use of screws has the added advantage of allowing you to remove the vents easily for cleaning.)

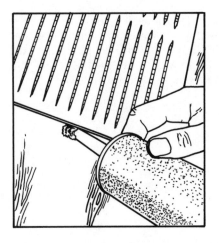

Step 8: Seal any cracks and crevices that could admit wasps. They are unpleasant tenants and can plug vents with their nests.

Tools and Supplies

Caulking gun and caulk

Chalkline

Drill

Hammer and nails

Hand-held circular saw

Hook knife or flooring chisel

Nail puller

Ridge and soffit vents

Saber saw

—Fred Matlack

MAKE YOUR GARAGE DOOR AUTOMATIC
The Ups and Downs of Installing an Electric Opener

Automatic garage-door openers are one of the all-time great conveniences. They may seem like a luxury—until the first time you arrive home in a downpour with six bags of groceries in the trunk and a baby in the carseat. Then, with a press of the remote-control button, the door goes up, and you're in. That's when this "luxury" begins to seem more like a necessity.

Automatic openers provide a measure of extra security along with convenience. When the door is shut, it is, in effect, locked; it can't be opened by hand from outside.

What follows is a series of illustrated steps for installing an automatic opener and some tips you won't find in most instruction manuals.

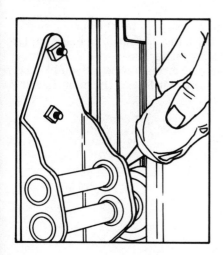

Step 1: First, manually check the operation of your garage door. An automatic opener won't work if the door sticks. If you can't get the door to work smoothly after some lubrication and minor adjustments, consider having it professionally adjusted. Garage doors are heavy, and the springs that balance them pack a dangerous punch, so don't take chances if you're not familiar with their repair.

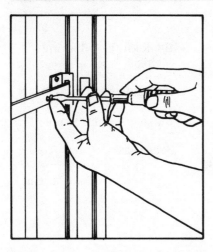

Step 2: Remove the old door lock. The new opener will have its own built-in lock. If you don't want to remove the mechanism, you can block it by driving a screw through the locking bar into the door to prevent accidental locking.

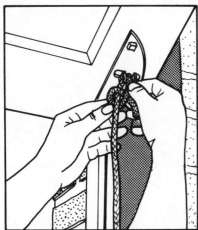

Step 3: Remove any ropes, chains, or rods that aren't necessary for the operation of the door. The rope you had tied to the door to pull it shut won't be needed any longer, and it could tangle and prevent the opener from working properly.

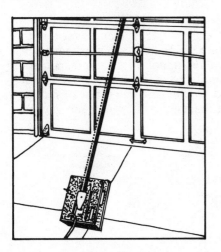

Step 4: Locate a power supply for the opener. Some large units require hard wiring, but most models simply plug into a receptacle. In either case, you'll probably want to use an unswitched circuit. Next, assemble the hardware for your opener according to the manufacturer's instructions.

Step 5: With the door fully open, make sure there's enough clearance between the ceiling and the door to accommodate the opener's track and hardware. Temporarily hang the unit and manually open and close the door to check the clearance again. Be sure the track is mounted so that it remains over the center of the door through the entire cycle. If everything works smoothly, finish mounting the unit.

Step 6: Install the manual opener switch. Wherever you mount it, make sure it's out of reach of small children. Run the wires to the opener, and staple them in place.

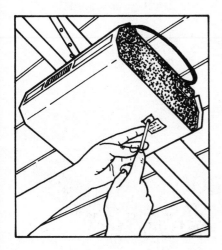

Step 7: Adjust the limits and force of the opener, following the manufacturer's guidelines. Now give the door a trial run. It should open and close completely. If it doesn't, reset the travel limits. If the door stops and reverses in mid-cycle, check for obstructions or binding. Then try increasing the force setting. But don't set it too high; you should be able to stop the moving door manually with only gentle pressure to the bottom edge.

Step 8: Test the closing limit. Lay a 1-inch-thick piece of wood on the floor where the middle of the door will close on it. The door should stop and reverse when it hits the wood. If it only stops, you have a potentially dangerous toe trap. Increase the downward travel of the door (or lengthen the arm between the door and the opener) until it reverses when it hits the board.

Tools and Supplies

Garage-door opener
  manual

Hammer

Pliers

Screwdriver

Wrench

Manufacturers

Chamberlain Consumer
  Products Group
Duchossois Industries, Inc.
845 Larch Ave.
Elmhurst, IL 60126

Frantz Manufacturing Co.
301 W. 3rd St.
Sterling IL 61081

Genie Home Products, Inc.
22790 Lake Park Blvd.
Alliance, OH 44601

Dallas Corporation
6750 LBJ Freeway
Dallas, TX 75240

Stanley Automatic
  Openers Division
The Stanley Works
5738 E. Nevada
Detroit, MI 48234

—Fred Matlack

ADDING AN OUTDOOR FAUCET
A Second Spigot Makes Chores Twice as Easy

I t's not something you think much about until warm weather
arrives, and there hasn't been any rain for days. But then you
remember what a hassle it is to water plants all around your
house when you have only one outdoor faucet. In the illustrated
steps that follow, we'll show you how to make life easier on you
and your garden hose by adding a second outdoor spigot.

The first point to consider is the type of faucet to buy. If you
live in an area that never sees frost, get a sillcock. Otherwise, buy a
frost-free faucet. Both types are readily available at home centers.

To determine the amount of pipe and the number of elbows
you'll need, measure the distance from the supply to your installation site, and count the number of bends the pipe will have to make.
Get a tee for tapping into the supply line and an in-line valve, which
allows you to shut off the water to the faucet without shutting off
the house supply.

Once you have all the necessary tools and supplies at hand, you
are ready to begin the installation process.

Step 1: Choose a location. First, decide how the additional faucet will be used: for washing the car, watering the garden, filling the pool? Next, consider the feasibility of the installation. Figure out the best way to do it keeping in mind the distance you'll have to go to tap into the water supply and the number of walls you'll have to rip open to do the work.

Think about what will be going on inside the wall. In cold climates, the valve end of the faucet should extend at least several inches into heated or frost-free space: If this is not the case, it's likely to freeze.

If possible, run the pipe into a utility room or some other place where it won't be an eyesore. Figure out how thick the wall is at that point, and add a few inches to determine the proper length for the frost-free faucet.

Step 2: Drill the hole for the faucet installation. A 1-inch drill bit will work for most ½-inch frost-free faucets (be sure to choose one long enough to go all the way through the wall). Use a spade bit on wood, drywall, or plaster walls; you may need a hole saw to get through metal siding. You'll need a masonry bit to get through brick, block, or stone walls; or you can rent a hammer drill (about $35 a day) to make the job easier.

Whatever kind of wall you have, drill the hole at a slight angle so that the faucet will drain to the outside. If you don't have someone to hold a level and guide you tape a small pocket level to the top of the drill so you can keep track of what you're doing. A ¼-inch tilt per foot should do the trick.

Step 3: Turn the water off at the nearest valve, and drain the pipe. Cut the pipe, making sure you can move the loose ends enough to get the tee into the line. You may need to cut about ½ inch off one of the ends to make space for the tee.

Step 4: Install the tee, valve, and branch line. Any branch line, especially one to the outside of the house, should be run through a valve. The extra valve costs a little more but makes repairs easier.

If you're working with copper pipe, take the "guts" out of the valves to avoid damaging them when you solder the joints. Make sure the faucet is in the proper position before you make the final connection to the line. If you've never soldered or glued plumbing pipes before, read up on the subject in a good book, such as the Time-Life series book, *Plumbing* (Alexandria, Va.: Time-Life Books, 1976).

Step 5: Seal around the faucet. Make sure that the body of the frost-free faucet is tilted so it will drain completely after each use, then fill and caulk around the pipe where it comes out through the wall. If possible, do your caulking behind the flange, then press it tight against the caulking. Next, go back inside, and caulk around the pipe where it penetrates the inside surface of the wall.

Step 6: Turn the water supply on, and check for leaks. It's always a good idea to turn the water on slowly while watching and listening. Even the best plumber occasionally leaves a pinhole or an incompletely soldered joint. Run enough water through the pipes to be sure the air is purged, then do a thorough inspection for wet spots.

Step 7: Hook up the hose. Don't forget to disconnect the hose at the first sign of cold weather. Otherwise, the faucet won't be able to drain, and any water trapped in it will freeze and break the faucet.

Tools and Supplies

Adjustable wrench (10″)	Pipe fittings
Drill and bits	Pipe wrench (12″)
Faucet	Tubing cutter and soldering supplies (for copper plumbing)
Handsaw and pipe cement (for plastic plumbing)	

—Fred Matlack

KEEPING BUGS WHERE THEY BELONG
How to Replace Window and Door Screens

Screens in doors and windows are all that stand between you and voracious mosquitoes on warm, muggy, summer nights. But, like everything else, screens age. They become so blocked with dust and corrosion that light and air can't get through. They also develop holes from wear and rust—holes that become highways for annoying insects.

You can wash, brush, or vacuum dirt off your screens and brush off mild corrosion. If a screen is still in good shape but mottled by mildew or corrosion, a light spray of black paint will restore it. But if there are holes or the screen can't be cleaned easily, it's time to rescreen.

Replacements

Aluminum and fiberglass are the most common screening materials. Home centers carry fiberglass screen in long rolls of various widths—the salespeople will cut exactly the length you request. Aluminum screen also comes in various widths, but it's frequently sold in prepackaged rolls; you may have to buy more than you need. Fiberglass, which is easy to work with, is probably the better material for rescreening, since it doesn't corrode as quickly as aluminum and costs half as much. Aluminum screening is stronger than fiberglass, though, and is the better choice where kids and pets put a lot of wear and tear on screened doors and windows.

In the steps that follow, we'll show you how to rescreen a groove-and-spline frame—the most common kind of metal frame—using either fiberglass or aluminum screening. (The spline in this type of screen consists of a metal, vinyl, or rubber strip used to hold the screening material in a groove found around the perimeter of the frame.)

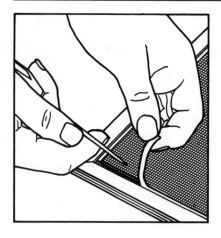

Step 1: Measure the width and length of the screen frame. The screening material should overlap each edge by ½ inch when you install it—so be sure to figure the overlap into your calculations.

With a screwdriver or an awl, pick up one end of the spline at a corner and pull it out of the frame. If the spline is intact and flexible, reuse it; if it's broken or brittle, you'll have to replace it. Take a piece of the old spline and the dimensions of the screen frame with you when you shop for materials.

Step 2: With the spline out of the groove, pull the screen out of the frame. Remove all bits of screen from the spline groove. Wash, brush, or scrub the frame to remove dirt and corrosion (aluminum cleaner will get it really clean). If you plan to paint the frame, this is the time to do it. Be careful not to let paint collect in the spline channel.

Step 3: Cut the screening to size, leaving the ½-inch overlap at each edge of the frame. If you're using aluminum screening, trim each corner diagonally, using a utility knife. The diagonal trim helps the edges of the screen lie flat across the corners where the spline grooves meet. Because fiberglass is more flexible than aluminum, you won't need to trim the corners of fiberglass screening.

Step 4: Line up the screen. If you're using fiberglass, simply make sure the weave lies parallel to the frame edges. To line up aluminum screen, lay it on the frame so that the trimmed corners match the corners of the frame. The weave should be parallel to the frame. Put a weight on each corner to hold the screen in position. With the convex wheel of the screen roller, roll the screen into the grooves. Use long gentle strokes when you roll it, being careful that the screen doesn't shift.

Step 5: Spline the edges. Hold the screen in place and pull the spline taut. With the wheel of the screen roller, push the spline into the groove. You'll be pushing fiberglass screening into the groove along with the spline. Tilt the roller to push gently against the outside edge of the channel as you squeeze the spline into the groove.

You crimped the aluminum screen into the groove in step 4. Now tilt the roller to the inside edge of the spline groove as you push the spline into the frame channel to seat the screen.

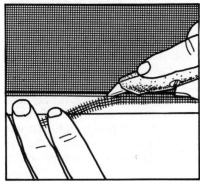

Step 6: Trim off the excess screen. To cut either fiberglass or aluminum screen, hold the excess screening tight and close to the spline. Angle the point of the utility knife into the groove, and slide the blade along the top of the spline. Avoid using an angle where the knife could cut into the spline.

Step 7: Install your new screen in the window or door.

Tools and Supplies

Protective gloves	Spline
Screen roller or screen installation tool	Tape measure
	Utility knife
Small screwdriver or awl	

—Fred Matlack

LIGHT UP YOUR LANDSCAPE
Safe and Simple Outdoor Lighting Installation

Want to turn your yard into an exciting nightspot? Or maybe you'd just like to make it a safer place to be after dark? We'll show you how to install underground electrical cable and a light fixture in your yard. And you won't have to tear up your landscape or become an electrical expert to do it. But be sure to check your local electrical code before starting work. The code may require you to

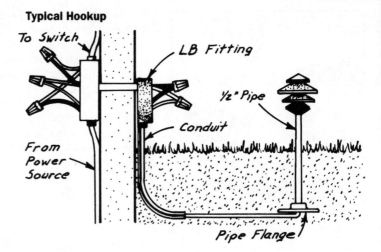

Typical Hookup

To Switch

LB Fitting

½" Pipe

Conduit

From Power Source

Pipe Flange

Figure 5-1. It's not particularly hard to install an outdoor light. Just be sure to protect any aboveground portions of cable with conduit.

hire a registered electrician to connect your new cable to your home's indoor electrical system.

Before you start, think about what you want from your new light fixture. Where do you need illumination? To light a specific area without spilling unnecessary glare across the rest of the yard, choose a low fixture that directs light downward.

You'll also need to choose a location for the power supply and switch. If you don't want to install a separate switch for the fixture, you can tap into the fixture box of an existing porch light. Otherwise, you'll have to tie into a power source (at a receptacle, junction box, or distribution panel) and run new wires to the switch you're adding (see figure 5-1).

The fixture's position and the place where you connect the underground cable into your home's electrical system will determine where the cable will run; make sure it won't interfere with sewer connections, water lines, or other electrical or telephone cables. And don't run underground wiring through an area where drainage is poor.

You can anchor your new light fixture in concrete or simply tamp earth around it. The permanence of concrete can cause problems; fixtures mounted in tamped earth are much easier to repair or replace.

Once you have chosen the location for the light and assembled the necessary supplies, you are ready to begin the installation:

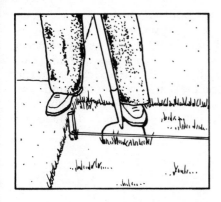

Step 1: Use stakes and string to mark where you plan to dig the trench for the electrical cable and the hole for the light fixture. Make the trench the width of your shovel blade and the hole for the fixture wide enough to leave you room to dig down a foot or more. Cut the sod along your string lines with a lawn edger or an axe.

Step 2: Lift out the sod one small piece at a time. Lay the pieces in order on a drop cloth. Keep the sod moist and shaded until you're ready to replant it.

Step 3: With the sod out of the way, dig the trench and the hole for the light fixture. The trench for your underground feeder (UF) cable should be 12 inches deep. For the fixture, the taller it is, the deeper you should dig. Even for a short fixture, you'll need to go down at least 12 inches. For a 4- or 5-foot post, you'll need a hole 2 feet deep.

Step 4: Drill a hole through your house wall to gain access to the junction box where you'll tap into your home's power supply. Make the hole just big enough to accommodate a piece of conduit.

Step 5: Cut one piece of conduit long enough to span the distance between the junction box on the inside and an LB conduit fitting (a 90-degree elbow with a removable panel for wire splicing) on the outside. Cut and bend a second length of conduit to extend from the LB fitting down into the trench. Any aboveground portion of your cable should be protected inside conduit. File the cut ends of the conduit so it won't damage the insulation on the wire.

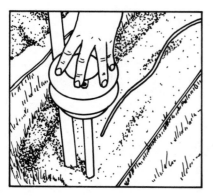

Step 6: Connect one end of the cable to the lighting fixture, then set the fixture into the hole you've dug for it. Tamp just enough earth around the base of the fixture to hold it in place.

Step 7: Run the cable through the trench and conduit into the junction box. With the power turned off at your service panel, wire the cable into the box. Then reactivate the circuit and check the operation of the light.

Step 8: When you're sure the light has been properly wired, fill the trench and the hole around the fixture. Tamp the dirt firmly; if you don't pack it down well, the ground may sink later. Lay the sod back on top, and roll it smooth. Water the sod regularly until it's thriving again.

Tools and Supplies

Conduit	Lighting fixture
Drill	Soil tamper
Drop cloth	Spade
Edger or axe	String and stakes
LB conduit fitting	UF direct-burial cable

—Fred Matlack

GRASS-ROOTS RENOVATION
How to Give a New Look to a Landscape

Very few people can shape an outdoor vista with the Midas touch of Capability Brown, the great 18th-century English garden designer, or André Le Nôtre, who laid out Versailles. But anyone with a patch of earth to call his own can turn it into the envy of the neighborhood. Like a home remodeling, a yard-and-garden renovation can significantly boost a property's enjoyment value—and its market value, too.

Sometimes renovating a landscape means cleaning up the mess that time and nature have left behind—the gardener's equivalent of finding a buried treasure. Jody and Nan Powell's experience is a case in point. Soon after they came to Washington to work with President Jimmy Carter's administration, they acquired a house that had been unoccupied for some time. The weeds in the yard were waist high. But the Powells soon discovered that the tangled growth was hiding scores of rosebushes.

Neighbors told the Powells that the garden had been the pride of its previous owner, a Naval captain named Diehl. Every year for 45 years, Diehl had planted a rosebush in honor of his wife's birthday. Since they had never tended a rose garden, the Powells called the Potomac Rose Society—a local club of expert rose growers, part of a national network—to ask for assistance.

One fine Saturday morning, three rosarians (which is what rose growers call themselves) appeared at the Powells' door. They were able to identify more than half of the 60-odd rosebushes, but disagreed vociferously about the rest. Most of the roses were old-fashioned varieties, many of them scented. This pleased the Powells, who recalled that in their native Georgia, many people wear scented rosebuds to church on Mother's Day.

Photo 5-1. Decks and arbors can be effectively utilized as part of a complete landscape design. (Photo by Carl Doney)

The rosarians gave the Powells detailed instructions on how to take care of their roses—a free public service that many rose societies offer. Taking care of Captain Diehl's legacy would be demanding, but the Powells resolved to make their garden bloom.

Nearly nine years after they took possession of the house, the Powells have a tidy, exhibition-quality garden in the nation's capital. They added a few new rosebushes—one of them is named after Rosalynn Carter—as well as a deck with a luxuriant grape arbor. Always meticulous, they use garden timbers to separate the beds of azaleas, ferns, vegetables, and herbs from the lawn.

"We wouldn't have put in 60 rosebushes ourselves," says Jody Powell. "We have them now because they were here. But if he could look at the roses now, Captain Diehl would be proud of us."

The Powells found themselves on top of a botanical gold mine; but equally dramatic results can be created from scratch. Whether you're restoring an old garden or creating a new one, it's best to begin by planning the landscape's *structure*—its shape and contour, along with any pathways, retaining walls, raised beds, and outbuildings you'd like to include. Make yourself a usage map as well as a sketch of the garden you wish to create (see figure 5-2).

What you use your yard space for will have an effect on your landscape plan. Staking out areas for volleyball and barbecues, or vegetable and flower gardening, will suggest principal traffic patterns. These can be delineated by pathways—such as continuous pavement or stepping stones (brick is the cheapest walkway material, but flagstones and pebbles have a special aesthetic appeal).

Stones are a staple material in many gardens, finding uses in pathways, raised beds, and retaining walls. The least expensive sources of stones in most areas are countryside quarries. Such quarries usually have a good selection of stones in various shapes, colors, and sizes. If you are planning to build a stone wall, choose and fit the stones with extra care. Such a wall can last decades, if not centuries, and it is the pride of any garden.

Railroad ties are another material often used in building retaining walls and steps. But they should be used with caution; they're saturated with poisonous creosote. Ties discarded by railroads often have much of the poison leached out. Even so, don't place any food-producing plants next to them. On the positive side, railroad ties are relatively easy to handle, and each tie builds a lot of wall. They can be cut with a circular saw when the plan calls for short sections. It's best to anchor the ties every 2 feet or so with an old cast-iron pipe hammered into the ground 2 or 3 feet deep.

While you're considering the structure of your renovated landscape, you'll also want to think about its overall aesthetic character. One broad category of gardens approximates nature, favoring drifts of wildflowers, cultivated flowers that look like wildflowers, alpine plants strewn around rocks, or smooth transitions between bushes and trees, flowers and grass.

Yard Strategies

Figure 5-2. Your first step in planning a lawn renovation should be to draw up a usage map that shows traffic patterns and areas designated for particular activities. Then you can decide whether you want an informal garden with a natural look or a more formal yard emphasizing geometric arrangements and clipped hedges.

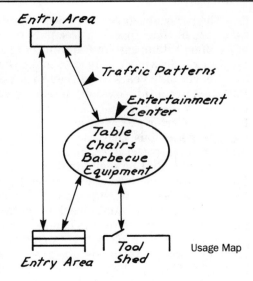

Usage Map

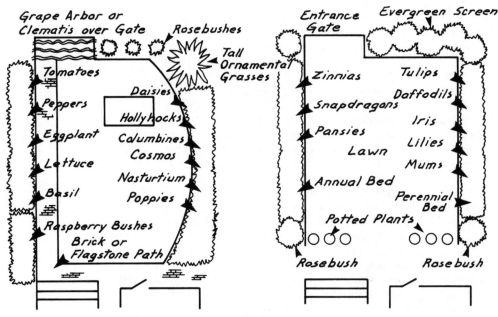

Informal Garden

Formal Garden

The opposing category is formal design, which emphasizes geometric arrangements such as rectangular flower beds, precisely clipped hedges, or an *allée* of Bradford pear trees.

In deciding which way to go, novice gardeners will find it useful to visit other gardens and look through lavishly illustrated garden

Photo 5-2. Stone and brick pathways can function to delineate different types of space usage in a yard. (Photo by J. Michael Kanouff)

books. Paging through seed catalogs can also lead to good ideas. Joining a local garden club could be the biggest help of all. Since gardeners are a gregarious and helpful lot, the chances are excellent that you'll find people in the club who not only offer good advice, but who also give away plants and seeds. Moreover, many garden clubs place bulk orders with seed companies, receiving discounts of up to 40 percent.

You might also consider hiring a landscape architect to take a walk with you through your garden. Take good notes on his or her observations and suggestions, then implement the ones you like as you can afford them. Buying a few hours of a landscape architect's time will yield professional advice you won't find anywhere else.

After the structural elements and design of your garden are defined, consider what kinds of plants give you the most satisfaction: flowers for color, or a lawn for a barefoot stroll, or both; a vegetable patch or a wildflower meadow. Shrubs and trees are critical centerpieces for some gardeners; others plant them last, almost as an afterthought, for shade or privacy.

A lawn is among the most easily maintained elements of a planned landscape. But renovating a scraggly lawn still requires plenty of effort. Patches of dead grass and weeds must be dug up, and the soil raked and reseeded. If half of the lawn is dead or weed-infested, it's best to rip out the old sod and start anew. Late fall (about six weeks before the first frost) or early spring (a month before the last possible frost) are the best times to sow grass seed.

Photo 5-3. Large stones can often be effectively incorporated into an attractive landscape design. (Photo by Mitch Mandel)

A prerequisite for good turf is soil that allows the grass to form a strong root system. Grass roots grow best in cool weather, and in soil that is loose and free of stones or roots. When reseeding a lawn, it pays to dig up or till the soil to a depth of 8 inches. Another smart

idea is to send a soil sample to your local Department of Agriculture extension agent for analysis. Your soil may need organic matter or lime, which you should add before sowing seed.

The cardinal rule of yard renovation is never to despair. Do not give up—not even if your property looks as lively as a parking lot, or your progress seems small compared with the large weedy field that still has to be cleared. Remember: No plot of soil must remain a disaster area for long. Renewal is a law of nature. With a little knowledge and some persistent effort, you can put nature's renovating powers to work in *your* yard.—**Charles Fenyvesi**

A WALK ON THE WILD SIDE
The Pathway is the Key to Successful Landscape Design

No element of garden design is more important than pathways. They outline and divide the garden's space, controlling human activity within this "outdoor room." Paths can either guide the garden stroller gently among the visual delights, or else push him through abruptly like a box on a conveyor belt.

If you intend to design, lay out, and construct your own garden paths, some thinking and stalking through the garden space with squinted eyes is necessary before you start sketching with paper and pencil. Look at the beautiful pictures in books on garden design and remind yourself that most of them are in California. Certain materials, designs, and many plants, will not be suitable for your area. Think about the limitations of your climate. In northern New England, fountains and swimming pools are not practical; in Arizona and New Mexico, lush green lawns are inappropriate.

Next, consider what you plan to do in your garden. This will help determine the shape and number of paths. If you have young children, a wide path with a good, hard surface will offer them years of tricycle-riding pleasure, while a narrow wood-chip path would not be as fun nor as inviting.

If you think of your garden as a place to daydream and read or sketch, you may want to design a spur path leading away from the main garden to a shady grove of trees with a screened summer house or hidden patio. The path can twist and turn to give the illusion of a journey. But if your pleasure is garden entertaining, outdoor night parties made dramatic with lighting concealed at the base of a crooked tree, then paths must be broad, comfortable, and safe.

If you have a fine view at the end of the garden, or a teak bench or good piece of garden sculpture, the path should be sly, concealing the treasure until the last minute, while coaxing the visitor along with interesting plant groups. Do not make a bowling-alley path that lets the visitor see the teak bench from the back door. Very boring.

In any case, make paths wide enough to allow for plants to bend and hang over them. As a rule of thumb, 4 feet is a minimum width. Of course, like other such rules, this one is frequently broken with success.

The Front Door Path

The most important garden path—even if your "garden" is little more than a few tubs of geraniums and ferns—is that which leads to the front door of your house. It is the transition zone between the public world of the street and your private place. The first impression a visitor gets of you is through this approach to the house.

Photo 5-4. An entrance path should follow a fairly direct line between the driveway or street and the front door to prevent visitors from carving out their own paths across the yard. (Photo by Mitch Mandel)

Paths to front doors differ from pleasure-garden paths in a very important way: They usually define the shortest distance between two points. Don't build an entrance path with fanciful curves and meanders, or the delivery boy and the mailman will tread their own beeline to the door.

Paths can be pebbles, cobblestones, cut stone, old brick. They can be stepping stones across earth as well as water, or unglazed tiles, or butted railroad ties that make a continuous, rough-textured walkway (do not use railroad ties around edible plants; ties are saturated with poisonous creosote). Macadam or asphalt walks suit large gardens with vast distances, and make a nice bicycle surface. Asphalt paths can also make the garden accessible to family or friends who are in wheelchairs or use walkers.

Wildflower meadows, striking and beautiful, are increasingly seen in all parts of the country. One of the most attractive pathways through such a garden is the simple, broad swath of velvety, well-mown grass. The contrast between the shorn, brilliantly green turf

Photo 5-5. Large stones can be used for walls or steps, as well as pathways. (Photo by John Neubauer)

Path Patterns

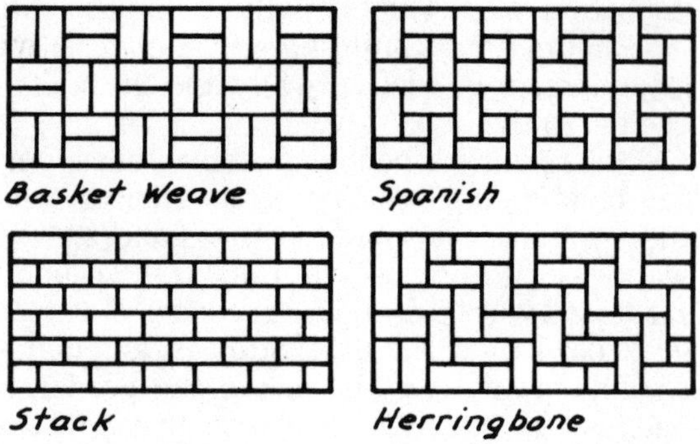

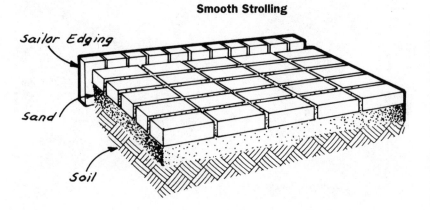

Figure 5-3. There are many attractive patterns from which to choose when building a garden or lawn path out of bricks. (Illustration by Sally Onopa)

Basket Weave

Spanish

Stack

Herringbone

and the hazy, fox-colored grasses and starry wildflowers is exceptionally pleasing.

The woodland garden has also become important, with the shade-loving wildflowers and ferns growing under the trees. The pathway in a woodland garden must be made of a natural material: Wood chips or shredded bark are attractive and springy underfoot—and far easier to maintain than gravel, which needs constant maintenance and attention.

Gravel is a controversial material for garden paths. Certainly washed pea-gravel, that loose stuff that crunches and rolls beneath your feet, is one of the worst path materials in the world. But bank-run gravel, which contains some clay, packs down into a hard, firm surface and looks good in many gardens. Weeds will grow in it, however, and low places blossom into mud puddles.

Old brick, with its mottled earth tones, is the favorite material for garden paths, but new brick pavers are now made that simulate the color and appearance of old, worn brick. In some places, these may be cheaper and stronger than the real thing. For diehards, though, nothing can equal the mellow old brick path. (Some common

Figure 5-4. A level bed of damp sand 2 inches deep makes a firm but flexible cushion for a brick path. Bricks set on end can make a distinctive edging. (Illustration by Sally Onopa)

Smooth Strolling

Sailor Edging

Sand

Soil

patterns for brick paths are shown in figure 5-3, and advice on building a smooth brick path is offered in figure 5-4.)

Safety Considerations

Consider safety as well as aesthetic factors when choosing path materials. I like the look of stone paths and steps, and cut granite is available in my area very cheaply. Alas, nothing on earth is more slippery than granite in rain and ice, and the long transitional spring and fall periods in northern Vermont provide plenty of both. Stone garden paths are too dangerous for me.

Whether you're building an entry path or one for the garden, don't get carried away by mixing too many eye-catching textures together. The effect of mixing brick, gravel, stone, and tiles is rather like wearing a pair of plaid slacks with a striped seersucker jacket, a Hawaiian shirt, and an electrified bow tie—simply too much. The number one rule to observe when selecting materials and a design for a garden path is: *Keep it simple.*—**Annie Proulx**

CHAPTER 6

THE HOME WORKSHOP

There is nothing quite so frustrating for the avid do-it-yourselfer than to begin a project, suddenly need a particular tool, but have no idea where in the house to look for it. Almost as frustrating is to lack an appropriate place to work—a place blessed with both adequate light and space. Clearly, every practical homeowner needs a workshop, a place to organize tools and store them ready for use when they are needed.

Unfortunately, few homes are constructed with a specific space allocated for a workshop. The enterprising home remodeler, woodworker, and repairman has to carve out a work place from space originally intended for some other purpose. The home workshop usually ends up in a basement or garage, places that may have to be accommodated to other uses as well.

Even if you are fortunate enough to be able to take over an entire basement or garage for your workshop, you still need to make an effort to use the space in an orderly and efficient way. Therefore, we open this chapter with an account of numerous ingenious ways in which professional woodworkers have learned to make effective use of limited shop space.

As you move on through this chapter you will read some practical tips on effectively using the tools you already own and some good advice on investing in new tools. You will also read about some valuable tools too expensive to purchase, but generally available for rent. Finally, we will let you in on the trade secrets of a number of craftsmen concerning such matters as nailing for strength, minimizing messes when painting, avoiding common mistakes when edge-gluing boards, putting the ultimate edge on a knife, and making effective use of measuring and leveling tools. We think you will

191

Photo by Mitch Mandel

learn some novel tricks from these experienced craftsmen, and have a good time while doing so.—**the editors**

BIG SHOPS IN SMALL SPACES
Tips on Making Your Work Space Work Harder

In their shops, do-it-yourselfers are the masters of all they survey—which usually amounts to a dark, cramped corner of a garage or basement. Table saws and wood scraps share this humble realm with old bicycles and spare tires, occasionally trying the patience and limiting the productivity of even the most dedicated shop owner.

But it doesn't take a warehouse-sized space to make a great shop. In fact, some of the best shops we've seen are some of the smallest. The key to a better work space isn't necessarily in finding *more* room; it's in making the smartest use of the room you already have. Here are some tips to get you started:

Make Mobile Work Surfaces: Movable work surfaces are handy in shops of any size. Ed Jackson, a Minnesota woodworker, converted a heavy metal table to a portable workbench by adding casters. He wheels it to wherever he needs extra space or support for large jobs. California woodworker Marlyn Rodi has an old but sturdy kitchen table that he moves around in his shop. Commercial folding workbenches, like Black & Decker's Workmate, offer portability plus clamping power. Even sawhorses and a sheet of plywood can provide portable, temporary work space.

Make Work Surfaces a Uniform Height: Work benches are generally built about 4 inches below waist level. But Robert Tupper, a veteran South Dakota woodworker, built his portable workbench to match the height of his table saw. That way he can use the bench for extra support when he saws oversized material.

Don't Be Caught in the Dark: Poor lighting limits shop efficiency. But you can easily correct that problem with hanging fluorescent fixtures, shaded incandescent lamps, or small portable task lights. Joe Veracka, a wood-carver who lives in Chicago, lined the entire perimeter of his shop with fluorescent fixtures. His goal was to eliminate all shadows, especially those over workbench areas. One way to find out where you need better lighting is to walk around your shop holding a pencil vertically and noting where it casts shadows.

Cut Down on Cords: Don't make life difficult by snaking extension cords all over the shop. If you group power tools in the

Photo 6-1. The large workbench in the center of Jacqueline Reinauer's Atlanta shop serves not only as her favorite work place, but also provides needed support for long pieces of lumber being ripped on the adjacent table saw. (Photo by Mitch Mandel)

center of a work area, consider installing overhead outlets. They'll eliminate cords in your walkways. Install plenty of outlets over workbenches, too. You'll probably find that one outlet every 3 feet is ideal.

"File" Your Equipment: Cyril Bruzek, a Minnesota craftsman, has put several two-drawer file cabinets under his workbench. He uses some for manuals, plans, and drawings. Others hold hand and power tools. Robert Tupper uses what he calls "tool boards" to organize his tools. They're sections of Peg-Board that slide into slots under his workbench. One board holds metalworking tools, one is devoted to upholstery tools, and another stores measuring tools. When he needs something, Tupper pulls the proper board out just far enough to get the tool, then pushes the board back in.

Make Big Tools Portable: All efficient workshops have one thing in common: plenty of casters to keep things moving. All power tools in Marlyn Rodi's small shop are on casters. Tools on wheels are easy to rearrange, he says, and can be dollied over to the workshop door for special operations, such as ripping extra-long lumber.

Keep Materials in an Out-of-the-Way Place: Stored materials shouldn't take up precious floor space. Rather, they should

Photo 6-2. Jacqueline Reinauer's shop is not only well organized, it is also well lit, thanks to several sets of overhead fluorescent fixtures. (Photo by Mitch Mandel)

be stowed in a place that's inconspicuous, yet easily accessible. Robert Tupper's solution is a rack on casters, which he has divided into sections for lumber of various sizes. Arizona woodworker Paul McClure stores materials in overhead racks made of metal pipe. The racks consist of ¾-inch pipe sections screwed to T-joints and elbows. They're held in place with floor flanges, which are screwed to the ceiling joists.

Borrow from Unused Space: Look for unused space in unconventional places. Marlyn Rodi doesn't let space over a washer and dryer in his garage shop go to waste. His workbench extends over the top of the appliances to provide another 70 square feet of working surface. Other places to scrounge for space: between open studs, behind doors, and under stationary benches.

Be Generous with Peg-Board: Equipped with a full complement of hangers, brackets, and accessories, Peg-Board is one of the best shop organizers. Joe Veracka covered the walls of his entire shop with it. He suggests making Peg-Board racks that hang on the wall like pages in a book (look at the swinging panel displays at lumber yards and home centers for ideas). Instead of buying hooks,

Photo 6-3. Peg-Board fitted with a generous supply of hangers can be a most effective tool organizer in the home workshop. (Photo by Mitch Mandel)

Paul McClure suggests using short sections of ¼-inch dowel pounded into the Peg-Board.

Don't Hide Small Parts: Cut rummaging time by storing small parts and fasteners in cabinets with clear plastic doors. Mount the cabinets at eye level so you don't have to shuffle through all the drawers to find what you need.

Consider Multi-Use Tools: If you are short on space but want to undertake some fairly ambitious projects, take a look at some of the multi-function power tools, such as those made by Shopsmith. One or two machines can take the place of a shopful of big power tools: table saw, drill press, horizontal boring machine, lathe, and disk sander.

Accessory manufacturers are also coming to the rescue of shop owners who are short on space. Compact work centers let you clamp portable tools onto one table for light-duty work in small spaces. The Sears Work Center, for example, turns your drill into a drill press, your circular saw into a table saw, and your router into a shaper—all on a compact bench complete with a woodworking vise and power switch.

Double Up on Hand Tools: Small hand tools such as pliers, screwdrivers, and open-end wrenches have a habit of disappearing

Photo 6-4. Atlanta woodworker Mike McNally makes efficient use of space by hanging jigs and templates from the rafters in his small shop. (Photo by Mitch Mandel)

just when you need them. Ed Jackson solved that problem by expanding his arsenal of hand tools. He now owns three sets of small, frequently used tools: one in the kitchen, one in the garage, and the third in his shop. He claims that the time he saves by not having to search for the right tool has more than paid for the extras.

Don't Be a Pack Rat: This may be the toughest tip of all to follow. But whether your shop is large or compact, collecting junk will make it smaller. Get in the habit of throwing things away; if you haven't used it in a year or more, you're probably not going to.

Manufacturers

Black & Decker, Inc.
10 N. Park Dr.
Hunt Valley, MD 21030

Shopsmith, Inc.
6640 Poe Ave.
Dayton, OH 45377

Sears Roebuck & Company
Sears Tower
Chicago, IL 60684

—Gene Schnaser

BOOST YOUR TOOL POWER

Simple Tips for a Safer, More Efficient Shop

E ven seasoned do-it-yourselfers often assume that you can't improve on a new tool. But not Marlyn Rodi, a woodworker from Los Angeles, California. If there's a way to make a tool simpler to use, easier to store, or better at its job, Rodi doesn't hesitate to do a few alterations or adjustments. As a result, his shop is full of tools that are better than new.

Rodi owns what may be the world's smallest complete woodworking shop, built into a 13 × 17-foot garage. Crammed into such a small area, his large array of hand and power tools puts bench and storage space at a premium. He selects his tools not only for what they do, but also for how *much* they do compared to the storage space they require.

We recently talked with Rodi about how he stretches his tools' power by customizing them. His tricks might provide an idea or two on how to make your own tools work better:

Hammers, Sledges, and Axes: To make large tools, such as sledgehammers and axes, easier to store, Rodi drills holes in the handles so he can hang them up and out of the way. The hole should be perpendicular to the head, so the tool will hang flat against the wall. To avoid weakening the handle, drill the hole an inch or so from the end of the handle. "Before I started doing this," says Rodi, "my big tools were always laying in a pile; I wasted time rummaging around for the one I wanted."

When Rodi buys a new sledge or axe, the first thing he does is to reinforce the handle by slipping a 4- to 6-inch section of pipe over the handle and welding beneath the head. "If I swing and miss my target," he says, "the protective pipe takes the blow, and usually keeps the handle from snapping" (see figure 6-1).

Sometimes a tool in mint condition *looks* nice, but its very newness can be a problem. For example, when the striking face of a hammer is smooth and slippery, it can slide right off nail heads, causing the nails to bend. Rodi uses a piece of emery cloth to

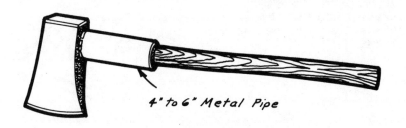

4" to 6" Metal Pipe

Figure 6-1. Reinforce the handle of your sledge, axe, or maul by slipping a section of metal pipe over it and welding the pipe to the head. It will prevent the handle from cracking if you swing and miss your target.

roughen up a new hammer's face; or he simply rubs it against a concrete floor or cement block.

On claw hammers, Rodi checks the inside edges of the V-slot. If they're not sharp, he touches them up with a file. This makes the hammer better at gripping nails.

Drills: One hassle with power drills is the chuck key. Some new drills come with a clip that attaches the key to the power cord, but many of these clips allow the key to slide out of arm's reach. Rodi tapes the key directly to the cord a few feet from the drill.

"One addition I made to my drill falls into the category of luxury," he adds. "I bought a small, stick-on level vial and attached it to the top of the drill. It helps me keep the hole straight when I'm drilling into a vertical piece of lumber. It's much easier than holding up a square as a guide."

Saws and Cutting Tools: As soon as he got his bandsaw, table saw, and mitersaw, Rodi put a good coating of paste floor wax on top of the work tables. The wax protects the metal surfaces from rust, and helps keep lumber from sticking and binding. Every few months he adds a coat, and his saws still look like new. He also gives his handsaws the wax treatment.

Another of Rodi's tricks helps him make precision cuts with his circular saw. With a sharp awl, he scribes lines on the saw's base, straight out in front of both sides of the blade (see figure 6-2). Using these marks as guides, he always knows where the saw kerf will be.

Screwdrivers, Socket Sets, and Files: Rodi never throws away an old screwdriver. When he needs a special type that isn't in his tool drawer, he fashions his own from one of the castoffs. He

Figure 6-2. To get precision cuts with a circular saw, scribe lines in the saw's base, straight out in front on both sides, to delineate the area of the saw kerf.

Scribed Lines

cuts the end off, then uses a file to make the end he needs. One type he's made is a tack-puller, by heating up the end of a screwdriver, bending it about 35 degrees, then filing a V-slot into the blade.

Socket sets often come in boxes that seem designed to mix up their contents. Usually, the problem is too much space above the sockets when the lid is closed. Rodi fixes that with a little foam rubber. Using a razor knife, he cuts a section to fit inside the lid, thick enough to keep the sockets in position when the box is closed.

Another tool that usually needs help is the file or rasp. Though wood handles are available, most files come with bare tangs, which are dangerous and difficult to use. Rodi makes his own handles by drilling out a section of wood dowel to slip over the tang. "Metal doorknobs also make good handles," he says.

Ladders, Sawhorses, and Workbenches: Rodi has found it helpful to mark the balance point on both legs of his ladders (see figure 6-3). When he needs to carry one, he grabs it near the marks, and it always balances. Another good idea (common among painters) is to pad the leg-ends of extension ladders with foam rubber, old socks, or towels to protect your house from scratches and ladder marks.

To keep sawhorses from getting cut and nicked, Rodi suggests adding a replaceable 2 × 4 across the top to protect the sawhorse from abuse. He has two sawhorses; one is a little larger than the other so they'll stack neatly.

When a job calls for an extension cord or two, Rodi recommends this trick: Tie the ends together with half of an overhand knot before plugging them to each other. The knot keeps the cords from coming apart. But his shop is wired to keep the need for extra cords at a minimum.

"One thing that has worked great for me," he says, "is the ceiling outlet in the middle of my shop. It lets me cluster my stationary tools in the center and plug them in without extension cords snaking through my work area." The result of such simple modifications: a shop that's both efficient and safe.—**Gene Schnaser**

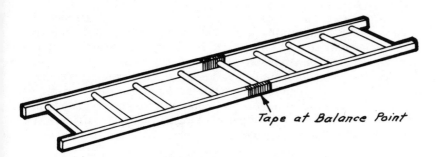

Tape at Balance Point

Figure 6-3. Mark the balance point on both legs of your ladder so you will know just where to grab when you have to carry it.

INVESTING IN TOOLS
When Professional Quality Is Worth the Expense

One of your neighbors who builds furniture in his spare time buys the most expensive tools around. The woman next door does some weekend remodeling and repair work and picks up bargain tools wherever she can find them. Who's doing the right thing?

"They both may be," explains Don Peschke, editor and founder of *Woodsmith*, a newsletter published in Des Moines, Iowa, and read by more than 235,000 woodworkers. "It's just that they have different needs and different points of view. It's likely neither would dispute that higher-priced tools offer more features, more power, and longer life. But not everyone is looking for a tool that will last forever.

"Cheaper tools work fine if you're just setting up a shop or planning simple projects. A $9 drill can last for years if it's used only occasionally. But the same drill in the hands of a professional remodeler might be burned up in a day. If you buy tools off the bargain table and expect them to do heavy, professional work day after day, there's no question you'll be disappointed.

"Generally, I would advise buying the best tools you can afford. But go slowly if you're just starting in remodeling or woodworking. I know of several people who got excited about woodworking and bought $1,500 worth of equipment, only to discover that they didn't really have time to pursue lots of projects.

"Many features can account for higher tool quality," notes Peschke. "With a hand tool, it's a matter of size, weight, balance, material used, and the way it's processed, assembled, and finished.

"Take hammers, for example. A good one has a head of drop-forged steel instead of cast iron; it's ground and polished instead of painted. And the face will be beveled and rim-tempered to avoid chipping or breaking.

"High-quality hammers can have steel, fiberglass, or wood handles. Plastics and fiberglass don't necessarily indicate low quality. In many cases, manufacturers have used better grades of those materials to produce superior tools (see figure 6-4).

"Sometimes you have to look hard to see the differences between professional-quality and consumer-quality power tools. But in today's competitive tool market, you are pretty safe in assuming that higher cost translates into longer-lasting tools.

"As the price goes up," says Peschke, "you can expect longer and better cords, heavier-duty switches, and housings of super-tough nylon instead of lower-grade plastics. Inside, you can expect more use of ball bearings, copper windings, brass brush holders, and hardened wrought steel gears.

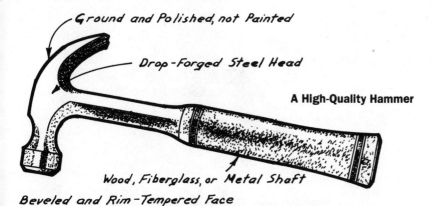

Ground and Polished, not Painted

Drop-Forged Steel Head

A High-Quality Hammer

Wood, Fiberglass, or Metal Shaft

Beveled and Rim-Tempered Face

Figure 6-4. What grade of tool should you buy when you go tool shopping? In the case of a hammer, a tool you are likely to use often, it pays to go for professional quality.

"Look for a higher power-to-weight ratio and special features like case-hardened drill chucks, variable speed, use of microprocessors, and digital displays for blade and bit position.

"I like to stay away from low-end stationary tools and put out the extra money for professional models. I've found that the lower-priced benchtop tools simply don't have the features of more expensive stationary tools. If you use them hard, they wear out much faster. And they're harder to sell when you want to trade up to higher-quality tools.

"Three tools I would spend more money on for general woodworking are a good table saw, a drill press, and a router. Most of the projects we run in *Woodsmith* can be built with these three power tools alone. With them in your shop, along with some hand tools, you can build just about anything. As for hand tools, I'd spend the money to get a good plane and a high-quality set of chisels.

"For new tools, I try to decide what I need, then wait for that tool to go on sale. Usually, the first part of the year is a good time to watch the ads.

"With used tools, I like to stick to classified ads or garage sales. But you can get some good bargains at auctions, especially on heavy, specialized tools that other bidders aren't familiar with. Just don't get so caught up in the bidding that you wind up paying more for the tools than they're worth.

"If I'm buying secondhand tools, I try to stick to the industrial-quality models. The service life of a low-priced tool can be quite short. And you can't predict its useful life by looking at it. When a cheap drill or sander dies, there's not much to do but toss it in the garbage. Repairs on cheap power tools often run as much as or more than the original price. But repairs may be worthwhile on a higher-priced tool, and service is usually more available.

"The depreciation factor also favors buying more expensive tools. You may be able to resell a higher-quality tool for 60 percent

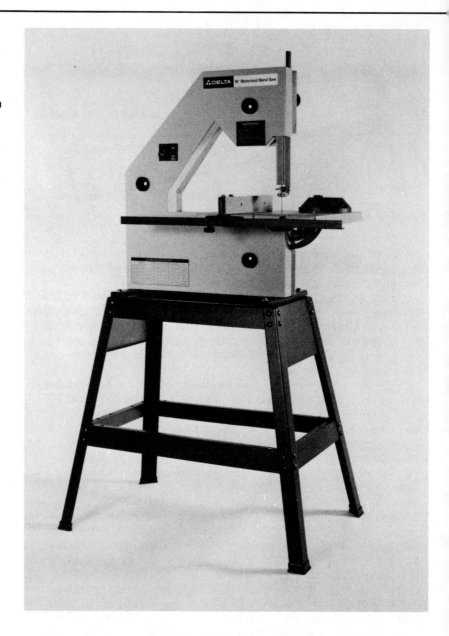

Photo 6-5. It often pays to spend more money and go for quality when purchasing stationary tools such as this band saw. (Photo by Candi Billman)

or more of its cost, while a cheaper tool might sell for 30 percent or less of what you paid for it. A good-quality tool can be a decent investment.

"Accessories and attachments are critical to tool performance. You can have problems with industrial-quality tools if you use them with inexpensive blades or bits. If you try to get by with a cheap

Photo 6-6. This profile-copying gauge is one inexpensive tool that can be quite useful to the resourceful do-it-yourselfer. (Photo by Carl Doney)

saw blade, a table saw won't perform well, no matter what you paid for it.

"I recommend carbide-tipped blades and bits. They're expensive—a set of eight for a router can cost $150—but they're well worth it, if you're serious about doing good work."—**Gene Schnaser**

MAKE THE MOST OF YOUR ROUTER
Maximizing the Usefulness of This Versatile Tool

The router is a johnny-come-lately to the power tool scene. It wasn't until World War I that patternmaker R. L. Carter, of Syracuse, New York, fashioned a primitive router by attaching a bit from a hair clipper to an electric motor. Today, routers are the third most popular power tool in America, just behind electric drills and circular saws. (See figure 6-5 for a sketch of the working parts of a high-quality, electronic router.)

We can't think of anyone more qualified to give advice on buying and using a router than Patrick Spielman. He taught high school woodworking for 28 years; now he spends up to 30 hours a week using his routers (he owns five) to make wood projects for his craft business in Fish Creek, Wisconsin. He has also written six books on woodworking, including a 224-page guide called *The Router Handbook* (New York: Sterling Publishing Co., 1983).

Spielman says one of the reasons routers are so popular is their versatility. Once you learn what the tool is capable of doing, you can use it to help you make furniture, cabinets, signs, custom moldings, and hundreds of other projects.

Patrick Spielman has done a lot of thinking and experimenting on how best to buy and use routers. He has many helpful bits of advice to offer.

Buying a Router and Accessories

Don't pinch pennies. Spielman likes models that have at least 1 horsepower and prefers to have the cord coming out the side so he can lay the router on its top to change bits. He says that the pressure switch should be on the router's handle, and likes threading-type controls for depth adjustment.

Choose bits carefully. He advises buying a few, high quality bits rather than collecting a drawerful of cheap ones. Inexpensive bits dull fast, and getting them sharpened usually costs more than they're worth. Carbide-tipped bits cost two or three times as much as speed-steel ones, but stay sharp longer and aren't as easily dulled by plywood or particle board.

Inside a High-Speed Router

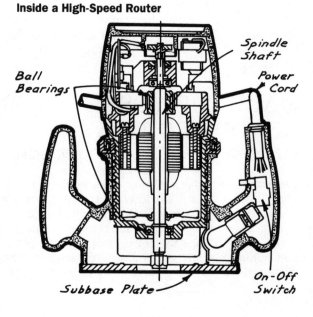

Figure 6-5. This cutaway drawing of an electronic router shows the working parts, including ball bearings at the top and bottom of the spindle shaft that permit speeds up to 25,000 RPM.

Be fully equipped. For accessories, Spielman suggests buying a router table, a template guide, eye and ear protecters, and a shop vacuum to clean up dust and chips. "You can buy edge guides for your router," he says. "I've got them, but I'd rather use the router table. For joints, such as dadoes, I just clamp a straightedge to the work and run the router against it."

Router Techniques

Use glue as a clamp. To hold a piece of wood that's too small for clamps, Spielman fastens it to a larger piece with hot-melt glue. The trick, he says, is to use short beads, which hold the pieces together, but don't penetrate the wood. Later you can pull the pieces apart and clean up the excess glue with a chisel.

Work on your freehand technique. You won't have to rely on templates and patterns any longer if you develop your freehand. Spielman recommends practicing on scrap lumber. Make sure you can see the bit and the area around the cut. Either remove the subbase of the router to open up the viewing area, or buy a clear plastic subbase. Proper position is important in freehanding. "Clamp the work well in from the edge of the workbench so you have to reach for it," he says. "That will force you to put your arms on the bench or on the work, which gives you better control."

Use extra care with laminates. When trimming the edges of plastic laminates, Spielman uses a straight bit, then rounds the laminate edge lightly with a fine mill file. If you use piloted bits that bear against the laminate during trimming, Spielman advises lubricating the laminate with wax or petroleum jelly to prevent damage. And if you use ball-bearing trim bits, apply enough pressure to keep the bearings from spinning freely and marring your work.

Save time on signs. Wood signs are popular router projects. After engraving a sign, Spielman paints the entire board with fast-drying spray paint. Then he uses a rasp to clean off the top surface, leaving the letters perfectly painted. "You can leave some paint

Router Feed Direction

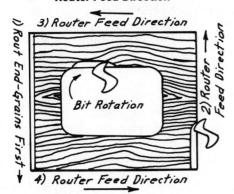

Figure 6-6. If end-grain is to be routed, do it first to avoid tear-out. Follow the proper feed direction (indicated here by arrows) for both outside and inside routing.

randomly over the board's surface if you want a more rustic effect,'' he says.

Avoid splitting. To prevent splitting on edge work, do the end (across-the-grain) edges first, then the sides (see figure 6-6). Experiment on scrap pieces to find the right feed rate. The feed rate on end grain will be slower than going with the grain. Feed the work against the rotation of the cutting blade and let the router stop by itself, up and away from the work.

Router Maintenance

Clean it thoroughly. Keeping the base of your router waxed and free of pitch and gum will make it easier to use, says Spielman. You should also use lacquer thinner on a small cloth to clean your bits. "One fellow I know likes to keep his bits stored in a jar of Fantastic," he says. "The cleaner *does* help dissolve the pitch and grime on the bits, but personally I don't like fishing for them in a jar. I prefer to keep my bits in a drawer, all standing on end."

Router Safety

Unplug it first. Always unplug the router before making adjustments or changing bits, Spielman advises. After you've made the adjustment and plugged the router back in, trigger it for a quick rev-up. If anything is wrong, you'll find out before starting any work.

Cover up. One final word of advice: Wear goggles or a full face shield, along with hearing protectors, whenever you use a router.— **Gene Schnaser**

GREAT TOOLS FOR RENT
When You Need a Special Tool Just for the Day

Using the right equipment can help you do faster, better, and often safer jobs. Thousands of labor-saving devices are available in most areas for rent by the house, day, week, or month. The fear that rental equipment may not be as good as what you can buy at the hardware store or a home center is a myth. Rental equipment must be extra-sturdy to bear up. But before taking a rental tool home, make sure it works properly and that parts aren't missing.

Why Rent?

"There are a raft of reasons to consider renting tools or equipment, rather than buying, and some of them aren't that obvious," explains C. A. Siegfried, of the American Rental Association. Here are a few of the most important ones.

Preserve your "working capital." While there are some tools almost no one would rent—a $12, ¼-inch drill, for example—the most obvious advantage of renting is that you don't have to buy tools or equipment you might need only occasionally.

Tackle otherwise impossible jobs. Often, with rented equipment, you can handle jobs yourself that would ordinarily have to be contracted out.

Get jobs done faster. A large, specialized tool, like a floor sander, more than justifies its rental cost by the amount of time it saves.

Minimize maintenance problems. While most stores expect you to bring tools back in good shape, you generally don't have to worry about maintaining rental equipment—greasing, changing oil, sharpening blades, and so forth.

Avoid the "packed-garage" syndrome. If you buy a gas welder for a welding project, you have to store it when you're finished using it. Most of us have too little storage space to start out with. By renting, you gain storage space.

Gain advice and access. Rental-store operators will usually make certain you know how to use a piece of equipment before you leave the store. It's in their own interest to do so, and their advice can be worth money to you.

Double-check buying plans. Even if you think you might want to buy a tool or piece of equipment, renting can make sense. By renting, you can gain experience with an item you plan to buy.

Remarkable Rentables

If there is a tough job to do, chances are good there is a tool made to do it and that it's for rent. For example, you can rent a drywall-lifter that eliminates the back-breaking struggle of hanging drywall. It elevates a full sheet of drywall and holds it until you can fasten it securely.

"There are literally dozens of specialty tools for rent that people don't often know about," says Siegfried. Such tools include log splitters, brush chipper/shredders, floor nailers, tile cutters, posthole diggers, engine hoists, power drain augers, concrete mixers, power sprayers (including ceiling texture sprayers), floor sanders, fence stretchers, lead-melting pots, pipe cutter/threaders, hydrostatic testers, welders, water pumps, forklifts.

Here's an annotated sampling of commonly discovered "wonder machines."

Sandblasters. Smaller sandblasters resemble a hand-held garden sprayer and hold up to 40 pounds of sand. Hooked to an air compressor with a capacity of at least 2 horsepower, these machines blast away at just about anything that needs cleaning. You can clean up brick, remove rust from metal, strip away paint and spills from concrete, even get a grained effect on wood or etched effect on glass. Usually the sand, which can be recycled, will be available where you rent the sandblaster. These tools can be rented for about $15 a half-day or $25 for a full day.

Concrete saws. Picture what a miserable job removing a section of concrete could be without a concrete saw, which is designed to make straight cuts on wall surfaces or floors. Hand-held models are available with gas and electric power. They can be rented for about $5 an hour or $25 a day.

Sod cutters. If you want to remove old sod or cut your own new sod, a sod cutter can save the day. These machines are self-propelled; you guide them as you would a rotary tiller. The depth of cut is generally adjustable from just under the surface to as deep as 2 ½ inches. Sod cutters can be rented for about $45 a day.

Impact hammers. Not all jack hammers require big air compressors; electric hammers are available to help you avoid back-breaking sledgehammer work. Breaker hammers let you dig, demolish, and break, using only regular household current. Rotary hammer drills are great for drilling round holes in concrete. These tools can be rented for about $5 per hour or $30 a day.

Trenchers. Digging a 2-foot trench in loose sand is one thing; digging through compacted clay can spell misery. Power trenchers let you quickly and easily dig trenches for electrical, telephone, gas, or water lines. Other uses include digging trenches for small footings or underground sprinkler lines. The compact, gas-powered machines work well for snaking through areas where bigger machines can't go or would ruin landscaping. Power trenchers can be rented for about $12 an hour or $50 a day.

Photo 6-7. A concrete saw is a tool you probably will not often need. When you do, you can rent the saw and buy the appropriate blade for cutting concrete, metal, or asphalt. (Photo by Angelo Caggiano)

Power compactors. A power compactor can make the job of compacting surfaces before pouring concrete a one-person operation. Often called "vibra plate" compactors, these machines can be used to work around foundation walls, footings, curbs, gutters, and streets. Relatives of this machine include the concrete vibrator (used to eliminate air bubbles and achieve uniform density in concrete) and the power tamper. Power compactors can be rented for about $10 an hour or $55 a day.

Stump removers. Stump removal is a tough problem, but luckily, there's a machine you can rent to do the job. A stump remover doesn't actually remove the entire stump, but it does chip a stump down to about ½ foot below ground level. Rotating teeth do the work, while you make the adjustments with a hand crank. Chips can be thrown away or saved for mulching. These tools can be rented for about $56 for a half-day or $95 for a full day.

Pressure washers. If you want to clean up house siding or muddy equipment, or if you have other tough cleaning jobs, pressure washers work wonders. The portable units deliver pressures

Photo 6-8. A power compactor makes short work of the gravel tamping that should precede the pouring of a concrete slab. You can rent this tool by the day. (Photo by Angelo Caggiano)

from 1,000 to 3,000 pounds per square inch (psi). If the job involves grease and oil or other chemicals, you might want to rent a steam cleaner to blast away grime. You can rent a pressure washer for about $8 an hour or $50 a day.

Wallpaper steamers. Need to strip old wallpaper off your living room walls? Throw the scrapers away and do it the easy way. Typical wallpaper steamers hold 2½ gallons of water and deliver steam at 14 psi to loosen layers of old wallpaper of any kind. You hold a pan-shaped steam plate, which is connected to a boiler, against the wall; the steam escaping loosens the paper in about five seconds. Steamers operate with household current and have both low-water and high-pressure safety shut-offs. They can be rented for about $7 for eight hours.

Rental rates vary from store to store and city to city. For rates in your area, check in your yellow pages under Rental Service Stores and Yards.—**Gene Schnaser**

NAILING FOR STRENGTH
Making Every Swing Count

Duane Clarke got a lesson in nailing his first day on the job. After lunch, he came back to find half of the handle on his brand-new hammer sawed off. He told the foreman, who smiled and explained that, since the end of the hammer wasn't being used anyway, he had taken the liberty of removing it.

Duane tells the story to students in seminars he gives for a major home center in Burnsville, Minnesota. The foreman, he explains, was making a point: A hammer works better if you grab it by the end of the handle. Eight years on home construction crews and several years of teaching others to build homes, decks, and garages have kept Duane thinking about proper nailing procedures.

"The holding power of a nail depends basically on how big a nail you use, the kind of nail you use, where you position it, and what wood you're nailing into," he explains.

"Nail suppliers have big charts on what nail to use where. But in rough construction, only a few nails get used in a majority of the work: 16d cement-coated sinkers for rough framing, 8d cement-coated sinkers for flooring and roof sheathing, 16d galvanized casing nails for hanging windows and doors, and 4d, 6d, or 8d finishing nails for interior trim.

"I like to use cement-coated nails rather than common nails, because the coating makes them easy to drive in, and the resin helps seal the holes. "Once you start driving a cement-coated nail," he advises, "keep driving it until it's in. If you stop, it grabs and is easily bent.

"When selecting nails for length, keep in mind the thickness of the lumber. Generally, nails are driven first through a thinner board into a thicker one. The nail should penetrate two-thirds of the way into the second board (see figure 6-7), unless you're nailing hardwood, in which case, you don't want the nail to go much farther than half-way into the second board.

The Right Angle

"If you ever get into a situation where nails penetrate all the way through the second board, you can increase their strength by clinching. Use two hammers, one held against the head of the driven nail and the other to bend over the point of the nail with the grain.

"If you watch professional carpenters closely, you'll see that they position each nail to match the arc of the hammer. In other words, they angle the nail away from them slightly so that, when the hammer strikes, it hits the nail squarely on the head. In rough framing, nails are usually driven at an angle toward the center of the board to increase the nails' holding power.

"Beginners sometimes have trouble with toenailing. Instead of big spikes, use 8d nails, two on each side. If you're nailing a stud into a plate, first position the stud next to your line. Then move it back about ⅛ or ¼ inch and tap a nail straight into the plate to hold the stud as you nail from the opposite side (see figure 6-8).

"Drive the two nails in, then come around and drive in the opposite two. Then pull out the holding nail. When you drive the nails, keep in mind that the idea is to have them come through the center of the stud into the plate.

"In most nailing, the basic idea is to position the nail so the load will fall across the nail, rather than along its length. You want the strain to be crosswise to the nail to take advantage of its shear strength. If possible, try to position nails so any weight will push them deeper (see figure 6-9).

"I use a 22-ounce framing hammer for rough carpentry. It's exactly 16 inches from the end of the handle to the top of the head and can be used to mark off 16-inch centers. For finish work, I use a 16-ounce hammer. On both, I prefer the straight claw to the curved claw; I don't have to reach over as far when pulling out nails.

Skewed Power

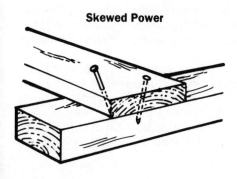

Figure 6-7. Angling nails toward the center, called *skewing*, gives them more gripping power. The nails should penetrate two-thirds of the way into the second board if you're working with soft wood.

Figure 6-8. Toenailing is easier if you first drive a holding nail to keep the stud in place. Once you've driven two nails into the opposite side, remove the holding nail and toenail that side of the stud.

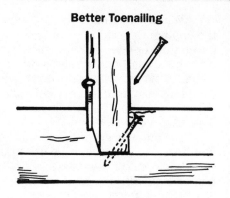

Better Toenailing

Figure 6-9. This is the best nail placement to bear a heavy load. The load force will tend to drive the nails deeper.

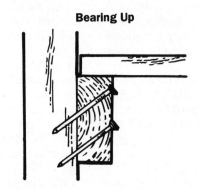

Bearing Up

"One thing that often plagues carpenters is splitting. If you find that the boards you're nailing are splitting, one trick you can use is to blunt the end of the nail before driving it. Another is to use beeswax on the nail so it will penetrate more easily.

"You can also predrill holes for the nail. Cut the head off of a nail, chuck it in your drill, and use it to make the hole."

Special Situations

"There are two kinds of nails that can be used to attach lumber to masonry: cement nails, which look like regular nails, only thicker; and cut nails, which look like the old-fashioned square-head type. Cut nails seem to hold better. I usually try to drive them only about ½ inch into concrete.

"If I'm putting up an interior wall on a basement slab, and know that the wall is going to be permanent, I'll use both cut nails and mastic under the bottom plate. Generally I put a cut nail between every other stud.

"Nailing patterns for drywall can vary. My rule of thumb is to select nails that penetrate 1 inch to 1¼ inches into the wood. I use

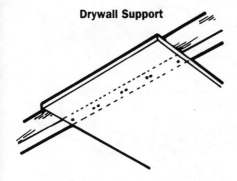

Drywall Support

Figure 6-10. The best nailing pattern for drywall on the ceiling is one nail near each end with three sets of two nails in between.

'two sets of two' for putting drywall on walls and 'three sets of two' for drywall on ceilings (see figure 6-10). This simply means using nails in pairs, spaced evenly between the edge nails. I drive the first nail of the pair in, then the second, then go back and give the first nail another tap.

What about power nailers? "Unless I'm planning a project that's quite large, I don't think they're worth the bother. It's too easy to miss the mark. In some new houses, you'll see a whole line of nails alongside a joist where the nailer missed. On a professional crew, they can be useful, but usually only when a pair of carpenters work together, one using a chalkline to mark the lumber so the nailer knows exactly where to aim."—**Gene Schnaser**

THE QUICK COVER-UP
Some Slick Tricks for Painters

For most of us, painting doesn't score very high on the enjoyment meter. It's messy, time-consuming, and more than a little boring. Yet there is something very satisfying about giving new life to drab or peeling surfaces with a fresh coat of paint.

For advice on how to take some of the time and tedium out of painting, we turned to John A. Gordon, director of the Center for Coatings Technology at Eastern Michigan University. Gordon has spent most of his career working for the country's largest paint manufacturers, and has also taught paint technology at the University of Missouri and Kent State. Here are some of the tips he's gathered over the years:

■ Lining roller trays cuts cleanup time. Plastic works great; you can even slip a plastic garbage bag over the tray (see figure 6-11). A lining also prevents the high alkalinity of latex paints from interact-

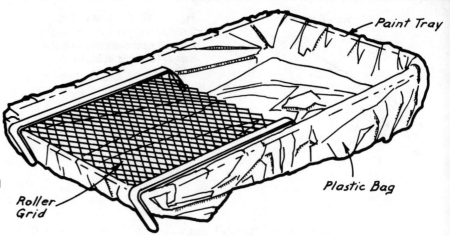

Figure 6-11. You can cut cleanup time by covering your paint tray with a plastic garbage bag. A metal or plastic roller grid will keep the plastic from wrinkling and the roller from slipping.

ing with the aluminum tray. If you use plastic lining, buy a gridlike roller screen that fits inside the tray. The screen keeps the plastic from wrinkling and the roller from slipping.

■ Putting paint tools and trays inside plastic bags will keep them from drying out for a few hours or overnight. Some people even store the bagged tools in the freezer.

■ When you paint overhead, paint drips down into the brush. To get it out, wash the brush, then comb it with a bronze wire brush—the kind often used for cleaning barbecue grills.

■ It's easier to *cover* up than clean up. When mixing paint, prevent splattering by putting the can inside a cardboard box, or a garbage or grocery bag. Any splashes will be neatly confined. If you use a coffee can as a paint reservoir, you can make a special lid that will keep paint from running down the side. Cut a circle or half-circle in the middle of the lid, leaving a 1-inch rim. Then use the inside edge to wipe your brush (see figure 6-12).

■ To clean oil-based paints, varnishes, and urethane off your hands, try using ordinary salad oil. It removes the paint without irritating your hands the way solvents do. Salad oil will also remove oil-based paint spilled on wood finishes.

■ Cut prep time by cleaning the outside of your house with a garden hose or a rented pressure washer before painting. Unless you're using latex, wait until the surface is completely dry before painting.

■ If there are patches of mildew, use a bleach solution (1 pint per gallon of water) to kill the mildew and bleach out the stains. If

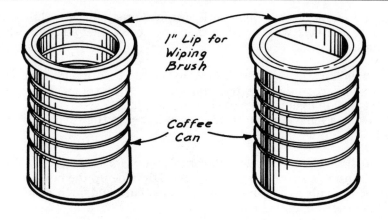

Figure 6-12. For dripless painting, use a coffee can and turn its plastic lid into a brush-wiper. Cut a circle, or half-circle, in the lid, leaving about an inch around the edge.

you don't kill mildew, it will grow under your new coat of paint and ruin it.

■ Inside the house, use shellac to seal water stains. Otherwise, the water-borne stains will bleed right through latex paint. (I once experimented to see how many coats of latex it would take to cover a water stain. I gave up after 15 coats!) Shellac dries quickly. Use alcohol, not mineral spirits, to clean it from brushes.

■ Take off electrical plates before painting, but use care when working around exposed wiring. Tie garbage bags over fixtures such as chandeliers.

■ Try attaching a carpenter's nail apron to the top of your stepladder to store small items like putty, nails, or screws that you may need while painting.

■ Quart-sized or smaller cans are hard to carry and easy to tip over. To remedy this, put each small can inside an empty gallon can. It will be easier to carry, and if it spills, you can simply pour the paint back into the smaller can.

■ The best thing I've found for speeding up interior painting is the power roller. The first time I used one, I painted a living room, dining room, hallway, and bedroom in one day.

■ There's no need to throw away solvent after one use. Pour it into a metal can and cover it. After the paint particles settle out, pour off the clear liquid for reuse. You can do this a number of times. To test, rub some between your fingers. When it feels sticky, throw it away.

■ Brushes can be expensive. If you have some that are dried out and hard, soak them overnight in water-washable paint remover.

Then clean and comb them with a bronze bristle brush. This overhaul works best with brushes that have been used with oil-based paints.

■ When storing paint, blow into the can before sealing it. This will add carbon dioxide, reducing the oxygen level (which causes paint to skin over), and making the paint last longer. You can even throw in a small chunk of dry ice to increase the carbon dioxide level.

■ If you want to keep full cans of paint for long periods, store them upside down for a month, then right side up the next month, and so on. This moves the paint's pigment back and forth, and keeps it from settling out.

■ New galvanized metal doesn't take paint well. If possible, let it weather for a year before painting. Never use solvent-based paints, such as alkyd resins, on galvanized metal. They turn soapy on contact with the metal and lose their adhesion. Use an acrylic or vinyl-acrylic paint instead.

■ When buying brushes, get nylon bristles for latex (the high pH of latex will ruin expensive hog-bristle brushes). Good nylon bristles can be used for solvent-based paints, as well.

■ How much paint should you buy? Assume that most paints will cover about 400 square feet per gallon. But latex goes on so easily that it's possible to stretch it too much. You may be able to cover up to 700 square feet per gallon—but a second coat will probably be necessary.

Most paint companies list the approximate coverage you can expect on each paint's label. Adjust these figures for the application method you're using: For brush or roller, add about 10 percent for wastage. Airless sprayers lose about 20 percent to overspray, and air spraying wastes 40 percent of the paint. Also, remember that rough, textured, or porous surfaces eat up more paint than sealed areas.—**Gene Schnaser**

STICKY PROBLEMS
Clamping Down on Common Mistakes

Gluing problems are usually expensive. Any piece of furniture can become high-priced junk if the glue joints fail, regardless of fancy design or finishing.

Whenever glue failure occurs, most of us blame the glue: wrong kind, no good, too old. But, says Dr. Robert

Snider, there are at least a dozen other reasons why a woodworking glue may fail on the job.

Snider, who has a degree in chemical engineering, is a leading glue expert at Franklin International, one of the nation's largest glue manufacturers. He has been with Franklin for 45 years. He's also a woodworker and is well aware of the glue problems that come up in home workshops.

"Gluing success boils down to using the right glue properly," he explains. "Finding the right glue is the easy part; using it correctly is a bigger challenge."

According to Snider, most home projects are done with ready-to-use adhesives that include liquid hide glues, aliphatic resins, and polyvinyl acetates. The latter two, he says, are the most commonly used. Aliphatic resins are the yellow glues, such as Elmer's Professional Carpenter's Wood Glue; polyvinyl acetates are the white glues, such as Elmer's Glue-All and Franklin Evertite.

While neither is waterproof, the yellow aliphatic resins are water-resistant and stronger than white glues. Both set in about an hour and cure to full strength in 24 hours.

Adhesives work by drying or cooling, or by chemical reaction. The yellow and white glues work by drying. After the glue is spread, parts to be joined are pressed together until the glue sets.

During this time, the glue and the water it contains penetrate the wood. As the water evaporates through the pores of the wood, the glue sticks to the wood-fiber walls. The glue gains strength as the water leaves this adhesive film.

A first step in troubleshooting glue problems is to make sure you're following the manufacturer's directions carefully. A thin glue line and a tight joint will give you a strong, not-so-noticeable bond.

Common Gluing Problems

Here is a sampling of the most common gluing problems, along with some suggestions on how to avoid them.

Low gluing temperatures. Cool temperatures slow setting time. It may take a glued joint twice as long to set up in a cold shop as in a warm one. Low temperatures cause a loss of joint strength; the glue can't form a continuous film as it dries. Don't try to use white polyvinyl acetate glue when the temperature is below 55°F. For the yellow aliphatics, the minimum gluing temperature is about 40°F.

Weak dowel joints. To create a well-glued dowel joint, the dowel should fit loosely enough in its hole to allow the glue to squish up around the sides of the dowel, which must be long enough to extend to the bottom of the hole. The dowel should be loose enough to push in with a finger, but not so loose it wobbles in the hole. The best procedure is to apply glue to both the sides of the hole and the dowel. Grooved dowels allow the glue to come up in the grooves, but don't guarantee glue will be outside the grooves.

Let It Dry

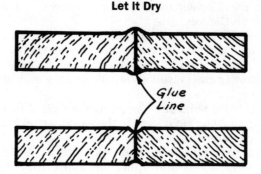

Figure 6-13. When an edge-glued panel is clamped, moisture from the glue will swell the wood next to it. If the panel is planed while the wood is swollen, sunken glue lines will form after the wood dries. To avoid the problem, let glued wood dry at room temperature for at least three days before finishing.

Starved end-grain joints. To prevent glue from soaking into the end grain and producing a weak, glue-starved joint, "size" the end grain with a mixture of glue and water. Dilute the glue just enough so that, when it's applied, glue drops don't form at the lower edges of the wood.

Sunken glue joints. If the glue joints in your finished work are sunken below the wood surface, chances are you worked the wood too soon after gluing. As wood absorbs moisture from the glue, it swells along the glue line. If you plane the wood before the glue is dry, you'll remove more wood near the glue line than elsewhere (see figure 6-13). This will result in sunken joints that will show through veneer (see figure 6-14). To avoid this problem, let the glue (and wood) dry at least three days at room temperature before finishing.

Irregular surfaces. If you are gluing lumber edge to edge, make sure each of the boards has approximately the same moisture content. If, for example, you glue a board that has 10 percent moisture to one that contains 4 percent, you'll end up with an uneven surface. The board with higher moisture content will shrink more than the other one, leaving an irregular surface at the juncture.

Uneven staining. Spots of glue on wood surfaces can fill the wood pores and prevent stain or finish from being absorbed. Light-colored spots appear. To avoid this splotchiness, remove surface glue with a damp sponge or rag immediately after it oozes out. Or, after a half-hour or so, when the glue has thickened, use a scraper or metal spatula to remove it.

No Coverup

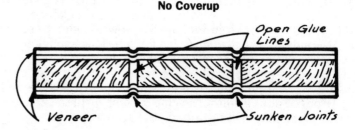

Figure 6-14. Sunken glue joints in a panel will show through veneer applied over them.

Glue softening. Sometimes applying a finish to glued lumber can cause a small ridge at the glue line, or even weaken or open the joint. Wash-off solvents can also soften glue and cause joint failure. The trouble can be corrected by changing to a solvent-resistant glue or by changing your finish or solvent. Liquid hide glues resist most solvents (except water), and aliphatic resins also perform well. Polyvinyl acetates are affected by a number of active organic solvents such as acetone or methylethyl ketone.

Improper clamping. The purpose of clamps is to bring boards close enough together to produce a thin, uniform glue line and hold them until the glue is strong enough to bond the assembly. If boards fit together perfectly, you wouldn't need clamps.

But since machining of wood is never perfect, a certain amount of clamp pressure is needed. Usually 100 to 150 pounds per square inch (psi) is enough. It's also important to apply clamp pressure uniformly along the joint. When gluing veneers, it's best to use only enough pressure to get good contact; you want to avoid show-through of imperfections from the lumber beneath.

Poor glue penetration. Glue can fail to penetrate when you're repairing previously finished projects. It's difficult, if not impossible, to reglue dirty joints or those filled with old glue.

Except in the case of some antiques, the solution is to dismantle and clean the joints. Remove all old paint, wax, dust, oil, grease, and glue from the surfaces you want to glue. Warm vinegar will generally soften the most stubborn glue. Dipping parts to be glued in warm water and letting them dry completely will help open the wood pores and allow glue to enter more freely. Warming the parts on top of a radiator or in the sun also helps open up pores.

These are a few of the gluing problems both beginning and professional woodworkers are likely to encounter. A good book on using glues is *Adhesives and Glues* by Robert S. Miller. It has an especially good section on fixing furniture with glue and includes an excellent summary of gluing techniques for the do-it-yourselfer. To get a copy, send $4.50 to Franklin International, P.O. Box 07802, Columbus, OH 43207.—**Gene Schnaser**

THE ULTIMATE EDGE
A Pro Slices through Myths about Sharpening Tools

"Let me see your jackknife," says John Juranitch. I draw out my well-worn Schrade Old-Timer and hand it over. Juranitch produces a special edge tester, an invention of his that resembles a pocket pen. He uses it to show me how desperately my knife needs sharpening and where its edge has gone wrong.

Juranitch should know. His 30-year search for the ultimate edge has culminated not only in the first complete book on sharpening, but also in a consulting and manufacturing business. He also holds the world's record for shaving his face with an axe. (No kidding. Look him up in *Guinness*.)

"The sad fact," Juranitch laments, "is that most of us are so used to dull edges that we start to believe the tools we use were *meant* to work that badly. But anyone can learn to put true shaving sharpness onto an edge. And it's a worthwhile endeavor; working with truly sharp tools is easier, less tiring, and much, much safer."

Secrets of a Sharp Blade

What are the secrets of a samurai-sharp blade? One of the most critical is what Juranitch calls "relief," the gradual tapering of the area above the cutting edge (see figure 6-15). A knife edge that appears sharp to the naked eye may actually look more like a chisel under a microscope. To make the knife truly sharp, you'll need to remove some of the blade above the edge. The ideal goal is to make it $^2/_{100}$ inch thick, $^1/_4$ inch above the cutting edge, or as thin as you can get it without chipping the blade (see figure 6-16).

Juranitch says that the mission of his book, *The Razor's Edge Book of Sharpening*, is to put to rest all the gimmickry and old wives' tales about sharpening. Here are some common myths he debunks:

New tools are as sharp as they can be. Wrong. Knives and other tools with factory-fresh cutting edges might be considered dull by a pro. Manufacturing and sharpening are really two different procedures. An experienced meat cutter, for example, would never use a new blade before sharpening it.

Sharpening stones must always be lubricated. Another myth. If you use oil in sharpening, it will cost you money, make a mess, and give you an inferior edge. When you use oil in honing, you inadvertently make a grinding compound—a mixture of oil, grit, and metal fillings. This mixture passes over the edge, dulling it. Water does the same.

Precise bevels are critical. Bunk! "Show me even a professional who can eyeball the difference between a 19- and a 22-degree bevel," says Juranitch. "Just keep the blade at less than a 25-degree

Get Relief

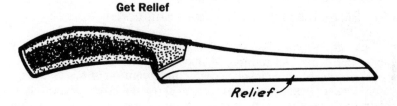

Figure 6-15. Relief, the thickness of the blade above the cutting edge, is the most important factor in making a knife sharp.

Relief

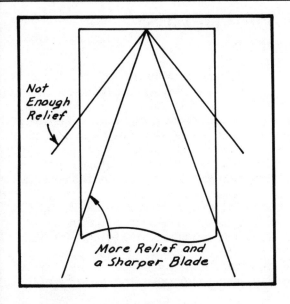

Not
Enough
Relief

More Relief and
a Sharper Blade

Figure 6-16. Before sharpening a blade, grind it down to make its relief as thin as possible.

angle when sharpening. Generally, the lower the angle, the sharper the edge."

Avoid buying stainless steel. This idea probably got started because Grandma's first stainless-steel butter knives were less than satisfactory. In testing high-carbon steel knives against stainless steel, Juranitch found that stainless steel lasts up to four times longer than high-carbon steel. And stainless won't rust.

Most sharpening tools really work. The old saying is: "If it won't sell, just call it a knife sharpener." Drawers are full of gadgets claimed to sharpen anything. Obviously, there are big differences in sharpener kits. The best kits have two hones: a rough one for coarse sharpening and a finer stone for setting edges. Look for hones that are at least $5 \times 1\frac{1}{2}$ inches; you can't get a proper stroke on anything smaller.

Only butchers need a steel. A steel is a rod-shaped tool with an abrasive surface. It's a good maintenance tool for anyone who owns cutlery. If a knife doesn't have a good edge to begin with, steeling it won't do much good. But proper steeling will make a sharp edge better.

An edge is sharp if you can shave the hair on your arm with it. That's not sharp enough. *Really* sharp is when the hairs literally pop off your arm without the blade touching your skin.

John Juranitch's book, *The Razor's Edge Book of Sharpening*, is available for $13.50 postpaid from Razor-Edge Systems, Inc., Box 150, Ely, MN 55731. Juranitch will also send information on his edge tester and sharpening kits.—**Gene Schnaser**

A MEASURE OF SUCCESS
Some Rules for Using Rules

On the wall of Kim Rasmussen's Minneapolis office hangs a motto that reads, "The faster I work, the behinder I get." To the owner of Northern Sun Construction, which specializes in energy-efficient housing, it's not a joke. It's a tribute to precision that begins with the first step of construction—measuring.

We talked with Kim recently about the basics of measuring as he worked on a new superinsulated home in St. Paul. His observations will help anyone about to tackle a home project.

"For most of our measuring we use the framing square and a 25-foot metal tape," says Rasmussen. "The square has one 16-inch leg and one 24-inch leg. These lengths make it easy to mark for studs either 16 inches on center or 2 feet on center.

"We rarely use a folding rule. But if you do use one, it's best to lay it on edge to take measurements. Otherwise, the thickness of the rule leads to inaccuracies.

"Though we still depend on our framing squares, an innovation becoming quite popular is what we call a speed square. It's triangular, and each leg is about 6 inches long. Speed squares are made by a number of manufacturers and work beautifully, especially for measuring angles."

"The 25-foot tape is a must for a serious carpenter," he continues, "not only because of the length, but because it's 1 inch wide and rigid enough to make measuring easy for one person working without any help (see figure 6-17).

"When taking inside measurements with a tape, you can read the measurement that shows and simply add on the length of the measuring tape (usually 2 or 3 inches). But another, more accurate way to do it is to also use a combination square. Position the square upside down in one corner. Then draw the steel tape to the blade of the square and add the length of the square's blade. It's fast and precise.

"Don't forget that measuring tapes can lie. Let's say you're working with a crew where one person is doing the measuring and someone else is doing the cutting. If the cuts aren't coming out right, take a minute and draw out all of the tapes you are using on a board to see that they measure the same.

Figure 6-17. A 1-inch-wide rule will stay rigid when you need to take long measurements.

"In other words, 'synchronize' your tapes. I almost got fired once working for a finishing carpenter. He called out the measurements, I did the cutting. But all my cuts were ¹⁄₁₆ inch short. After about an hour, we checked the tapes and found mine was reading short because the end was slightly bent.

"Story poles are lengths of lumber, either one piece or two pieces nailed or clamped together, that allow you to quickly transfer specific measurements (see figure 6-18). For example, you can use a story pole cut off at a desired height to fur out a ceiling to make it level. Or you can use a story pole to level out a basement floor for concrete.

"We use a version of a story pole to cut studs. If we are framing with 8-foot studs, for example, we cut off one stud to the exact length and nail a scrap of plywood on the end (see figure 6-19). Then we can use it as a master pattern, sliding it over uncut 2 × 4s to quickly mark a cutting line.

"When making duplicate, repetitious cuts, it's important to avoid what I call the 'growing-pattern syndrome.' Someone will cut one stud to length, then use that cut stud to mark the next stud, and so on. After two or three cuts, you can be off quite a bit. If each stud is off ¹⁄₁₆ inch, for example, by the time you cut four studs, you will be off ¹⁄₄ inch. It's best to use just one pattern for marking every cut.

"Sometimes it's how you do the measuring that counts. When we use a compass, it's mostly to mark out ceiling boxes when hanging wallboard or paneling. But to avoid intricate measuring for fixtures, outlets, furnace ducts, etc., we use hard carpenter's chalk.

"Instead of measuring, we simply rub chalk around the edge of the protrusion. Then we push the sheet into position and hit it

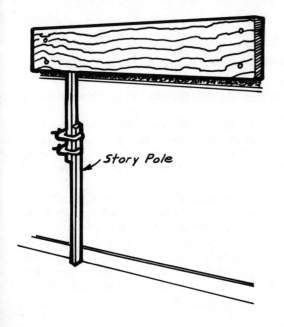

Story Pole

Figure 6-18. A story pole is useful for lots of jobs, such as installing a nailing board for cabinets. Use one to duplicate specific measurements that otherwise must be done over and over again.

Accurate Stud Cutting

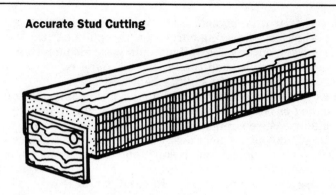

Figure 6-19. When cutting studs for framing, cut one to the exact length and nail a scrap of plywood on one end. Then use it as a guide when measuring the rest of the studs.

lightly with our hands. The chalk transfers to the back of the sheet, and we have a perfect cutting guide.

"One cardinal rule of measuring: Don't take anything for granted. It's a big mistake to assume any room in your home is square and plumb, even if it was built last summer.

"Sometimes a stud wall can be built true and square, but one or two studs may be bowed out enough to make a corner crooked once the wallboard or paneling has been installed. A careful carpenter measures the tops and bottoms of walls and all along the wall, and checks to see that all corners meet at right angles. You can use a framing square to do this, but you can also make yourself a large try square from scrap wood to do the job."—**Gene Schnaser**

ON THE LEVEL
Tips to Help You Keep Your Projects Square and Plumb

"**E**ver hear of the Norwegian level?" Brian Ringham asks with a smile.

"Back in the old days, in southern Minnesota where I grew up, the old Norwegian farmers who couldn't afford a level would use a pan of water," he explains. "When the water was the same distance from the rim all around, the board it was sitting on was level. It worked!"

A lot of things have changed since the days of pan levels. But the owner of Ringham Construction in Minneapolis advises that the importance of keeping projects square and level hasn't.

"Taking the time to make things level in the beginning stages of any project will pay off many times over. It's easy to fudge on leveling, especially if you're in a hurry," he says. "But if you take shortcuts to start out with, you'll be paying for them throughout the project in time wasted making adjustments.

"There's hardly anyone these days who can't afford a general-purpose 2-foot level; you can find them for less than $5. And if you can spend more, the choice of levels can be almost overwhelming.

"One thing to remember when using levels is that the bubble should be centered exactly within the vial. A lot of folks think it's good enough if the bubble is touching one line or the other. That will be close, but not precise.

"Another thing to remember is that a level can get out of adjustment, especially if it's been dropped or tossed around. You can check the accuracy of your level, then either adjust the vial or replace it with a new one. Here's how to check for accuracy.

"Lay the level on a flat surface on its working edge. Check the position of the bubble. Then turn the level 180 degrees (swap end for end), and recheck the bubble. It should be in the same position.

"The second test is to do the same thing, but this time turn the level over on its opposite working edge (swap top for bottom). Again the bubble should be in the same position.

"You can also check for plumb by holding the level against a flat surface perpendicular to the floor. Check the bubble in the plumb vial. Then turn the level over, so the opposite working edge is against the wall, and recheck the bubble.

"Stores that sell expensive levels often have a special jig to test the accuracy of a level before you take it home. Keep in mind that levels can only be as accurate as the amount of surface they cover. For example, the vial in a combination square is useful, but the level measures a very short distance. I use a 6-foot level when I need real precision.

"The line level is handy for long distances. The key to using it is to keep the line as taut as possible. I use nylon instead of cotton line. I pull the line as tight as I can and then try to give it an extra pull to get it super taut. Even so, over a distance of 20 feet or more, the level will still depress the line slightly. You need to adjust for this slight depression.

"Expensive transits and laser-beam devices can be used to establish level over distances. But you can also use a clear plastic hose. Hold one end vertically next to the mark you want to transfer

Long-Distance Leveling

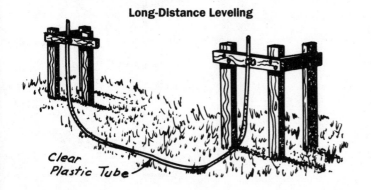

Clear Plastic Tube

Figure 6-20. When your leveling involves long distances, a water level can be both precise and economical. Hold one end of a clear plastic hose next to the mark you want to transfer, and fill the hose with liquid until the water is level with your mark. At the other end of the hose, the level of the liquid will be exactly the same height.

and fill the hose with liquid until it's level with your mark. The level of the liquid at the other end should be exactly the same height (see figure 6-20).

"This works well for leveling posts, for example, or for getting a level line around a room to help you put in a level floor or ceiling. You can buy plastic hose levels, but they're simple to make. All you need is a suitable length of transparent plastic hose, and an adequate supply of water.

"Levels can also be used to help you measure slope; some have vials indicating inches per foot. These make it simple to position plumbing pipes that need to drain.

To Find a Slope

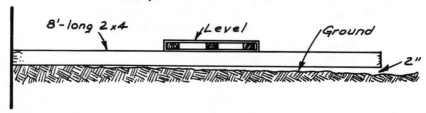

Figure 6-21. To measure the pitch of your yard as it slopes from your house, place one end of an 8-foot 2 × 4 against the base of the house wall, level the board, then measure from the other end of the board to the ground. If that end is 2 inches off the ground, the pitch of your yard is ¼-inch per foot.

Figure 6-22. If you suspect one of your walls is not plumb, check it with a level held against the base of the wall. Center the bubble in the level's plumb vial, with either the top or bottom end of the level tight against the wall. Measure the gap between the wall and the other end of the level, then extrapolate to find out how far the whole wall is off. In the case illustrated here, the wall is 1 inch out of plumb.

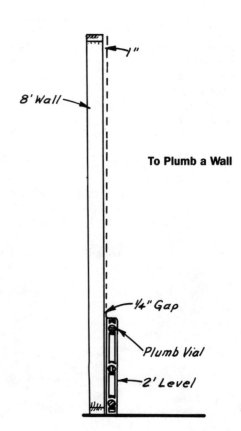

"You can also set a level on a 2 × 4 to determine slope. For example, let's say you're building a patio and need to know how steeply your backyard slopes away from your house. With one end of an 8-foot 2 × 4 against the house at the base of the wall, level the board, and measure from the ground up to the other end of the board. If it's 2 inches off the ground, the pitch of the yard is ¼ inch per foot (see figure 6-21).

"Likewise, you can use a level to estimate how far walls are out of plumb (see figure 6-22). Hold your level with one end on the floor along a wall. When you center the bubble in the plumb vial, you see that there's a ¼-inch gap between the top of the level and the wall. If you are using a 2-foot level, and the wall is 8 feet high, you'll know the top of the wall is 1 inch out of whack.

"Levels deserve good care, not only because they cost money, but because you want them to be accurate. If your level gets a nick in it, take time to smooth it out. I take my 6-foot wooden level in the house every night to avoid having it go through freeze-and-thaw cycles that could affect its accuracy."—**Gene Schnaser**

INDEX

Rodale Press, Inc., publishes
RODALE'S PRACTICAL HOMEOWNER™, the home
improvement magazine for people who want
to create a safe, efficient, and healthy home.
For information on how to order your subscription,
write to RODALE'S PRACTICAL HOMEOWNER™,
Emmaus, PA 18049.